PEOPLE POWER
An eyewitness history
The Philippine Revolution of 1986

Dedication

This book is dedicated
to Mary, the Mother of God,
in gratitude
for her reassurance
that she is truly
the patroness of the Philippines,
the mother whom we call through the Rosary
and who protects us, listens to us
and walks with us at all times—
in turmoil, in darkness, as we stumble
through our tears and conflicts,
swiftly with the drumbeat of history
or securely with the pace of day-to-day
upon this beloved earth which once she trod
and through which she moves still among us—
such sweet assurance
of the loving providence of God.

PEOPLE POWER
An eyewitness history
The Philippine Revolution of 1986

Produced under a grant
from the James B. Reuter, S.J., Foundation
Manila, Philippines

Editor
Monina Allarey Mercado

Preface and scenarios by
Francisco S. Tatad

Published by
WRITERS AND READERS PUBLISHING, INC.
in association with
TENTH AVENUE EDITIONS, INC.
New York City

Printed in Hong Kong by Toppan Printing Co.
(Hong Kong) Ltd.

ISBN 0 86316 131-6

First printing, May 1986
Second printing, June 1986
Third printing, January 1987

Contents

Dedication   2

Foreword   7

Preface   8

I   The Assassination of Benigno S. Aquino, Jr., 1983   9

II   Rallies, marches, and demonstrations, 1983 to 1985   31

III   The Election Campaign, 1986   43

IV   The Election and Ballot Watch, 1986   67

V   The People's Uprising, February 22 to 25, 1986   111

Epilogue   304

Historical Notes   309

Photo Credits   319

Acknowledgments   320

Credits

Producer	:	**BASIC/FOOTE, CONE, & BELDING, PHILIPPINES**
Creative director	:	**DOMINADOR F. GALLARDO**
Senior editors	:	**ROFEL G. BRION**
	:	**ANCILLA MARIA A. MERCADO**
Managing editors	:	**KAREN M. HERNANDEZ**
	:	**ROGELIO VICENTE A. MERCADO**
Associate editors	:	**MARIO SALCEDO NERY**
	:	**RAFAEL A.S.G. ONGPIN**
	:	**MARIA TERESA P. PATERNO**
	:	**RAUL A. RODRIGO**
Editorial staff	:	**JOHN A. CABATO ● STELLA F. CHIU ● EMMANUEL A. MERCADO**
	:	**JUDY P. PATERNO ● JOSE G. PEDROSO ● TRINA A. PINEDA**
	:	**MARLA S. SILAYAN ● ROSSANA M. ZAMORA**
Editorial consultants	:	**DOREEN G. FERNANDEZ (Oral history)**
	:	**SONIA P. NER (Philippine history)**
	:	**HENRY TOTANES (Philippine history)**
Photography	:	**JOHN K. CHUA**
	:	**MANUEL R. FERRER**
Cover design and pictorial lay-out	:	**HARRIS V. MADRIAGA**
Text lay-out	:	**ROYLINO F. BABIA**
Art assistants	:	**RICARDO L. GRIMALT II**
	:	**EDGAR R. OLIVA**
	:	**EMIGUEL M. PUOD**
	:	**ANGELITO DE LUMIN**
Production manager	:	**BERNABE A. KITANE II**
Production coordinator	:	**ALFONSO B. TOLOSA**
Typesetters	:	**VIRGILIA C. BONGCAC**
	:	**BERNARDINO S. PEREZ**
Secretarial pool	:	**MARIA LOURDES O. CABRERA**
	:	**NEONITA L. SUINAN**
	:	**BENJAMIN E. ORTIZ**
	:	**RONALD GIL F. GARCIA**
Provincial legmen	:	**MARIA FE D. GUTAY**
	:	**REYNALDO F. BORROMEO**
	:	**RAUL F.A. MANALO, JR.**

Foreword: A Brave Example to the World

The dramatic collapse of Ferdinand E. Marcos' regime in the face of an enormous nonviolent insurrection has important lessons. The events in the Philippines showed that dictators need not be accepted passively, and that effective alternatives to violent revolts exist. The principle is to withdraw the sources of power.

The Catholic bishops spoke out against Marcos and counseled nonviolent resistance. Opposition politicians planned a campaign of economic and political resistance. The general population mounted huge demonstrations to show that it would not submit to election fraud and murder. Soldiers mutinied, and officials and diplomats defected. Thousands of people turned back tanks ordered to attack nonviolent rebel troops at Camp Crame.

The Filipino people's brave example to the world may well stimulate new nonviolent freedom struggles elsewhere. Which country will be next to follow their example: Indonesia, South Korea, Chile?

The Philippines' was not the first successful nonviolent overthrow of a repressive regime. The rule of Czar Nicholas II of Russia collapsed after about a week of the mainly nonviolent February-March revolution of 1917. The regimes of General Hernandez Martinez in El Salvador and General Jorge Ubico of Guatemala were dissolved by nonviolent insurrections of about two weeks each in 1944.

Nonviolent action includes at least 198 distinct methods ranging from mild symbolic protests to potentially paralyzing forms of social, economic, and political non-cooperation, and to the disruptive forms of intervention. Nonviolent resisters have been defeated, achieved mixed results, and been victorious in the face of enormous odds as in the Philippines.

We often forget that nonviolent struggle was sometimes used successfully even against the Nazis. In Norway, the teachers' resistance kept the schools out of fascist control and prevented the establishment of a totalitarian state. Non-cooperation and underground escape networks saved many Jews' lives. A more-than-week-long public demonstration by 6,000 women, most of them non-Jewish, in Berlin in 1943 resulted in the release of at least 1,500 Jews.

Each successive case of nonviolent anti-communist struggle in Eastern Europe since 1953 has been more difficult for the Soviets to crush. Resistance in East Germany in June 1953 was crushed in two days. The improvised Czechoslovakian resistance in 1968-69 ultimately failed, but it held off Soviet control for eight months, which would have been impossible by military means. In Poland, resistance continues after five years with major achievements, including a large illegal information system that publishes papers, magazines, and books.

Nonviolent sanctions operate on an important insight into the nature of political power: the power of all rulers and governments is vulnerable, impermanent, and dependent on sources in society.

A ruler's power depends on the degree of cooperation, submission, obedience, and assistance received from the subjects, both the general population and paid helpers. Nonviolent non-cooperation and disobedience cut off the sources of the ruler's power. If the defiance continues despite repression, it will disintegrate even a dictatorship.

Contrary to the usual assumption, dictatorships are not omnipotent. They contain weaknesses; nonviolent sanctions exploit them. Given that these nonviolent sanctions exist, the question becomes to what degree they can be applied and to what degree they will be effective.

In the past, most nonviolent struggles have been improvised, without large-scale preparation or training. Thus they may be simply prototypes of what could be developed by deliberate efforts. It seems certain that a combination of scholarship and preparation could make future nonviolent struggles much more effective. It is possible that this technique could become a full substitute for violence in liberation struggles and even for national defense.

GENE SHARP
Director, Program for Nonviolent Sanctions
Center for International Affairs
Harvard University
Cambridge, Massachussetts

Preface: A Marian revolution

This is an eyewitness account of revolution. It is different from the usual such account in that it is not one, but several witnesses speaking.

It also speaks of a different sort of revolution, one that is nonviolent, fought not with arms but with what has since been called "people power."

Revolutions tend to be ugly, even when successful. This is an exception; it is a "beautiful revolution." Its "combatants" include men, women, and children who had more fun than fear during the event, and who like to think of what they went through as a religious experience. Their triumph confirms for them not the strength of an army nor a political grouping, but the power of prayer. They feel they have been part of a miracle.

The revolution took place in Manila on February 22-25, 1986. It came as a dramatic sequel to an electoral contest waged between President Ferdinand Marcos, in power for 20 years, and Mrs. Corazon Aquino, widow of the assassinated political leader Benigno Aquino, Jr. Many had predicted that Aquino would get the votes, but that Marcos would claim power, and that the Filipinos would simply accept it as they had in the past accepted corrupt elections.

It did not turn out that way at all. The Filipinos surprised themselves. For the first time in their modern history, they decided to oust a government—the most powerful one they had known since Philippine independence.

A sector of the military provided the mechanism that allowed men, women, and children to go out into the streets in support of the rebellion, but once out there, they took command of the field and protected the army from possible attack instead of the army protecting them.

Ironically, it was not hate or anger that drove the masses into the streets. They had come to hate the regime, yes; they were certainly outraged by the naked trampling of their votes, yes. But it was something better than hate that guided their steps in the end. It was Faith.

Faced with the naked fact of the regime's ruthlessness, they had in the very beginning prayed for divine intervention in their history, offered countless Masses, and sought the special intercession of the Blessed Virgin, to whom they had dedicated the year before as a Marian year. They offered more Masses as it became clear that the strongman had begun to dig in, in defiance of the popular will. And now in the middle of military revolt, they held on to their rosary beads as they faced troops and tanks. They made a Marian celebration of the revolution. It made no sense at all. And yet they won.

It is an unparalleled story in modern times whose magnitude and sweep defy anything from Cecil B. de Mille. In telling it here, we thought it appropriate to give the reader not a single observer's narration or interpretation of the events, but rather several participants' narration of what happened.

As perhaps in any undertaking of this nature, it has not been easy to choose whose personal account to include and whose to leave out. In the end we had to limit ourselves to those stories without which no complete narration of the events is possible. To recapture the drama in its original flavor, we felt it desirable to ask the participants to tell their stories in the first person.

Many have since said that the Filipinos have shown the world how to make revolution. The purpose of this book, however, is not to teach anyone how to make revolution—even a nonviolent, bloodless revolution. It is simply to tell a good story, as it really happened—the story of a people determined to live the ways of peace, justice, and freedom as a Christian nation. It is also to make a modest offering of thanks for that miracle of deliverance which most of its participants faithfully attribute to the Lord of history through the intercession of the Blessed Virgin.

FRANCISCO S. TATAD
Manila, Feast of the Annunciation, 1986

I The Assassination of Benigno S. Aquino, Jr., 1983

Scenario

FRANCISCO S. TATAD

August 21, 1983, in Manila was to be a day for a big homecoming. Benigno Aquino, Jr., arch-opponent of President Ferdinand Marcos, was coming home after three years of self-exile in Boston. The government had tried, in vain, to prevent his return by every conceivable means. Imelda Romualdez Marcos, Ferdinand's powerful and ambitious wife, had tried to dissuade him, saying it wasn't good for him. The Minister of National Defense, Juan Ponce Enrile, had asked him to postpone his return until all reported threats on his life had been removed. Philippine officials in Washington and New York had denied him a valid passport. The government had warned all foreign aircraft not to allow him to board on pain of losing their landing rights. And General Fabian Ver, Armed Forces Chief of Staff, had threatened to turn him back if he arrived in Manila without any travel papers. But nothing could stop him.

Meantime the city buzzed with the rumor (*tsismis* is the popular Filipino word for it) that Marcos had fallen into a coma, after undergoing kidney surgery. He had been seen nightly on television, and quoted daily in the newspapers. But these were obviously old film clips being rationed to the stations, while the newspapers simply quoted stories invented by his minions. The media knew, but did nothing to unmask the deception. And except for Imelda, none in the Cabinet knew where, or how, lay the strongman.

She was not talking, and for very good reason. In power since 1965, Marcos had been ruling with her, without a known successor since he declared martial law in September 1972. He had abolished the office of Vice President, and in case of death, total disability, removal, or resignation, a 14-man Executive Committee was to take over. This included his wife, who was already the First Lady, Minister of Human Settlements, Governor of Metro Manila, and Member of Parliament.

She lacked neither the influence nor the drive to succeed her husband. But it was obvious that in case he died, she would need time to consolidate her position before announcing to the world that he was gone. This meant denying everybody else any and all information about her ailing husband.

Had she, in fact, succeeded here? Why was Aquino coming home precisely at this time?

Like Marcos, Aquino had led a charmed life. He had been the youngest foreign correspondent in the Korean War, the youngest governor of his province Tarlac, the youngest adviser to President Ramon Magsaysay, the youngest member of the Philippine Senate, and had loomed as the most obvious successor to Marcos before the latter declared martial law, changed the Constitution, and cancelled the 1973 elections. Imprisoned in 1972, and sentenced to death by a military court for "murder" and "illegal possession of firearms," he ran from behind bars at the head of a 21-man ticket in the 1978 parliamentary elections, and nearly polarized the nation after Imelda's ticket robbed him of his place in the *Interim Batasang Pambansa* (Parliament).

In 1980, Marcos allowed Aquino to leave for the United States for a heart bypass operation. He decided to stay on in Harvard. But he missed no chance to reassure his supporters in Manila that he would be back — at the right time. Was this the time?

Armed with an illegal passport secured under the name Marcial Bonifacio — the first word for martial law; the second for Fort Bonifacio, where he had been detained for nearly eight years — and dressed in a white suit and a bullet-proof vest, and in the company of foreign correspondents, he boarded the China Airlines in Taipei on the final leg of his flight home.

A crowd of thousands, led by his mother Aurora, and his boyhood friend and political kindred Salvador Laurel, waited in the Manila International Airport to give him a hero's welcome. But, as his plane reached the terminal, a military boarding party appeared and led him out through a side door leading to the ground. Seconds later, a shot rang out. "Oh, my God!" Pandemonium. Shouts and screams. More shots later. When the shooting stopped, Benigno Aquino was dead, sprawled on the tarmac along with his supposed assassin.

It was this death, more than anything else, that shocked and outraged the Filipinos. Something in them died; something in them too was born. "The Filipino is worth dying for," Aquino had said. They said: *"Hindi ka nag-iisa!"* (You are not alone!)

For days, millions marched past his bier to catch a glimpse of his face and his blood-drenched suit. Four to six million joined the funeral cortege and marched for eleven hours. It was the country's biggest, and longest, funeral.

The government angered the already angry population by banning domestic TV coverage of the wake and the burial, while the rest of the world watched everything via satellite. Radio Veritas, the Catholic radio station, was the only notable station on the job. Pro-government newspapers ran some stories and pictures, but were under strict orders not to photograph or say anything about the crowds.

On the assassination itself, the government dragged its feet. Marcos' first impulse was to blame the murder on the communists, while reproaching Aquino for not heeding official requests to delay his return. The government was much quicker to suspend the landing rights of China Airlines than to investigate the crime. It took days before Marcos ordered the officers and men of the Aviation Security Command confined to quarters.

The *Batasang Pambansa* passed an opposition resolution condemning the treacherous murder and expressing the nation's grief. But one senior Cabinet minister criticized the body for eulogizing "a member of the political elite to excess." In response to an opposition demand for an independent commission to investigate the crime, Marcos formed a group composed of handpicked favorites. This incensed the public, and he was compelled to name a truly independent group. This was to be known as the Agrava Fact-Finding Board.

Voices

CORAZON C. AQUINO, widow of Benigno S. Aquino, Jr. (Ninoy)

I talked to Ninoy for the last time on August 20, 7:00 p.m., Boston time, which was August 21, 7:00 a.m., Taipei time. He told me that he would soon be leaving for the airport. I told him I was informed that General Ver had warned any airline bringing Ninoy in that Ninoy would not be allowed to disembark, and that the airline would be asked to fly Ninoy back to his original port of embarkation.

Ninoy said that they could not do that to him, because he is, was, and always will be a Filipino. And he told me that most likely he would be rearrested and brought back to Fort Bonifacio. In that case, he said he would ask General Josephus

Ramas to allow him to call me up. If, on the other hand, he was placed under house arrest, he would call me up as soon as he arrived at our home in Quezon City. Then he told me that if he were brought back to Fort Bonifacio, there would be no need for me to hurry home. Instead, he said I should take my time finishing my packing. And in the event that our children and I would be issued passports, he said that I should take our three older daughters on a side trip to Europe.

Our only son Noynoy and our youngest daughter Kris were scheduled to leave for Manila a week after Ninoy arrived.

At 2:30 a.m., Sunday, August 21, Boston time, the phone rang and my oldest daughter Ballsy, who answered it, was shocked when Kyodo agency in New York asked her if it was true that her father had been killed in the Manila International Airport. They were asking for her confirmation. UPI and AP also called asking for verification; but it wasn't until Congressman Shintaro Ishihara of Japan called me from Tokyo and verified the shooting report that my family had to accept the cruel fact that Ninoy had been shot dead.

The children and I cried when I told them of the bad news. After a few minutes, we all knelt down to pray the Rosary and ask the Blessed Mother for help.

AURORA A. AQUINO, mother of Benigno S. Aquino, Jr. (Ninoy)

Remember that Ninoy was born on a feast day of the Blessed Mother, November 27. That is the feast day of Our Lady of the Miraculous Medal. When he was a little boy, we used to take him to Mass on his birthday in San Marcelino church, the shrine of Our Lady of the Miraculous Medal. His father used to tease him: "Ninoy, look at all the people who have come to church for your birthday." I think that stuck in his mind: that a lot of people went to church with him on his birthday. That is why he always enjoyed his birthday. He always liked being with people and he enjoyed being with a lot of people on his birthday.

At a young age, Ninoy studied in the Ateneo, where he used to wear the blue ribbon of the Blessed Mother. Although young people sometimes take religion for granted, something becomes implanted in their minds. Ninoy's devotion to the Blessed Mother must have been implanted in him at this early age.

During his detention, when he was in his early

40s, he started to pray the Rosary. He prayed very many Rosaries, as many as he could, because he had all the time to pray in more than seven years of detention.

I don't know if I should say this, because he never liked to mention it to other people. He told me that one night he was really very, very despondent, really lonely, and somewhat bitter when he was kept in solitary detention in Laur. That night, he said, it was as if he saw a glimpse of the Blessed Mother.

That was why his devotion to her was so deep. When Lupita, his sister, went to claim his body a few hours after he was killed, she found his rosary beads in his pocket. They had snapped apart.

FRANCISCO RODRIGO (SOC), opposition leader

Ninoy sent an emissary here to get a consensus on whether or not he should return home. The emissary was Tony Gonzalez. Dodo Ayuyao called me and said that Tony wanted to talk to me. We met on his yacht and he told me about his mission.

I found out that the majority of his family was against his coming. His mother was against it. I think even Cardinal Sin was consulted and had said that he should not return. I said that he should return. Two years before, I had said that he should not come back, but the situation here had changed. This was around June of 1983.

I believe that he had to come back for two reasons. First, people were beginning to forget Ninoy, or, if they did speak of him, they would be derogatory. They were calling him a steak commando, who was having a good time in the States while his countrymen were suffering. Second, we needed him for the cause. The moderate democratic opposition needed someone like him. We were fast becoming irrelevant. People were falling by the wayside; they were becoming radicalized.

I told Tony to tell Ninoy that things had come to the point where I had to refuse speaking engagements. What would happen was that I would denounce the government in my speech. And then in the open forum someone would ask me "What then is our plan?" But our way is through the ballot. When I told them that, they laughed at me. After the 1978 and the 1981 elections, they no longer had any faith in the democratic process.

I was not ready to advocate the bullet. We needed Ninoy to strengthen our cause and stop the radicalization of the people. Both extremes wanted the people to be radicalized. Marcos wanted to radicalize us so that he can tell the Americans: "You don't like me? What's your alternative? Communism. I may be a bastard, but I'm your only bastard." And the Communists also wanted that. They knew that the people were angry with Marcos. They wanted to make it seem as if only the NPA could succeed in driving Marcos out. We were trying to give them a viable alternative. That was what we were trying to do, which is why both sides wanted us erased. I felt that Ninoy had to return.

LUIS BELTRAN, journalist

A friend of Ninoy relates that a few days before the former senator went to his appointment with destiny, he was staying at the Ambassador Hotel in Los Angeles, where US Senator Bobby Kennedy was assassinated. The friend relates that on the evening before his departure, Ninoy asked his friend to accompany him to the kitchen where Kennedy was shot. Looking at the outline of the body still marked on the floor, Ninoy told his friend: "If I get shot on the head like Kennedy, I am not going to go down on my knees. If you get shot like that, you have a few seconds of life left. If that happens to me, I am going to fall straight down and spread my arms so people will know I never gave up even to the last second."

GRACIA M. CARIÑO, wife and mother

In the plane on his way to Manila, Ninoy was saying the Rosary—according to Ken Kashiwahara, who was sitting across the aisle from him. Apparently he was interrupted by someone who wanted to speak to him. When the plane landed, Ninoy realized that he had not finished the Rosary. He stayed in his seat to finish it and then prepared to go.

CORAZON C. AQUINO

I am sure that he was praying for me. His last letter to me from Taipei said: "Today is Papa's death anniversary. I offered a special prayer and you know he has never failed me."

August 21 is my father's death anniversary. Ninoy's letter on that day really helped me so much. He wrote it just hours before he was assassinated.

He also wrote to each of our children and every letter was dated August 21. Ninoy's brother-in-law, Len Oreta, was with him. Len said that after Ninoy talked to me and the children, he cried.

When Ninoy was in prison, when he was on the hunger strike, when my father died, he tended to be very emotional—not for sad things but when he was very happy or when somebody did something special. All of a sudden, tears just came. When we got to Dallas (for his heart surgery), he was so grateful to the people there that he just cried.

When I first heard about the assassination, I tried to believe that it was a false report. But I think it wasn't even an hour before I had to accept it as fact.

In the United States, of course, in the two days that we were still there (I found out Sunday morning and we left Tuesday morning), we were besieged by the media. In fact, it was forever on television. My children even remarked that it was on more often than the Sadat assassination.

At that time I did not think about the attention given to us. My main concern was how to get home as soon as possible. I had already told my relatives here that I wanted Ninoy [to be] buried in Manila. So, when my brother Peping said: "We will be bringing Ninoy to Tarlac," my words to him were: "*Kaya ba natin iyon?*" (Can we do that?) And he said: "Yes, don't worry about it." So I said: "Well, if you think people will go, then okay." I had serious doubts. In fact, the first thing I told one of my sisters was just to bring Ninoy's body to Times Street because I was not really sure how many people would go. I figured that at least it was my house and no one could do anything there. I felt, after all we had gone through from 1972 to 1983, we really had very few friends.

It was unbelievable when my sister said that people were coming in at the rate of forty or fifty per minute. So she asked me: "When you come back, will you agree to our bringing him to another place? This house of yours is too small for all the people."

It was really amazing. I felt relieved. In fact, one of my questions was: Do the people know? Knowing the strict censorship of the media, I was afraid that the people did not even know that Ninoy had been assassinated.

AURORA A. AQUINO

Nobody told me directly. I saw people talking in whispers. Perhaps they were trying to save me from shock, but I suspected something serious. I saw Ken with his head in his hands. He was so depressed. Somebody whispered to Tessie, my daughter, and she cried: "Huh?" She looked so shocked. I felt that surely, something was very wrong. "What is it?" I asked. Tessie replied: "Nothing is sure, Mommy. There was some shooting, but nothing is certain."

We had a welcome program planned for Ninoy, who had different scenarios in mind about how he would be received. In one of the scenarios, he thought that he would be permitted to go to his house, perhaps to rest a little bit, meet some people, and then be taken back to prison again.

In this scenario, the first thing he wanted to do on his way home was to greet the Blessed Mother in her shrine in Baclaran. So, from the airport, even though he was not with us, we went to Baclaran to pray. On our way over, I was still not sure if he was really dead.

In the Baclaran church, Eva Kalaw was using the mike and she was telling the people that something had happened in the airport. I could not understand her, because she was crying so bitterly. To tell you the truth, I don't think I prayed in Baclaran. I was numb. I was in shock.

From Baclaran, we went to Ninoy's house in Quezon City. There were many cars parked near his house and on top of one car, a radio was on full blast. That was how I learned that Ninoy was dead.

FRANCISCO RODRIGO (SOC)

We were there at the airport: Doy, Mrs. Aurora Aquino, and I. They gave us the run-around. They would not let us in. We told them: "This is his mother. If you will not let us in, then at least let her in. At least let her in the tube." They said no. Finally we saw Ken Kashiwahara. He ran to us. We talked in the VIP Lounge. Mrs. Aurora Aquino was there.

That night we were at Times Street. Mrs. Aurora Aquino was inconsolable. She had to be sedated. I told her: "Think of this: God writes straight with crooked lines. We all die. If Ninoy were asked to choose the way he would die, he would choose this. Even if Ninoy were to live a hundred years, he could never accomplish what he accomplished with his dying."

AURORA A. AQUINO

I think it was faith which kept me strong. I am convinced that nothing happens without the permission of God. The whole time, I was repeating to myself: "Lord, you know best. You know best."

When I was sick with cancer, I said: "Lord, your will be done." I had to have an operation and I prayed: "Your will be done." At the back of my mind, I wanted to live, so that was really a half-hearted prayer. But when I woke up after the operation and I received Holy Communion, I was really able to say: "Your will be done!" I meant that if I died, it would really be all right with me. So I have already experienced what it means to say: "Your will be done!"

But this death of Ninoy was rather shocking. I did not expect it and all I could say was: "Lord, you know best." I could not see anything then beyond my nose. There was no enlightenment at all for me.

In our lives, there are many truths that come to us—through the Scriptures, through what we read, through what we hear—but they remain dim in our minds. But the time comes when we are enlightened. I hoped to be enlightened about Ninoy's death, so I kept saying: "Lord, you know best—what is best for our country, for Ninoy, for all of us."

I was numb that first day, all of Sunday evening. I could not cry. It was only the next day when I really gave way. I was alone in the room and I cried and cried. I said: "Lord, I know that something good will come out of even this."

In the Gospel, I read about the widow of Nain. The Lord met the funeral procession of her son and he went up to her and said: "Do not cry." He saw her crying bitterly. He knew that she was alone in life, that she was a widow and this dead young man was her only son. He said: "Do not cry." Then he went to the bier and touched the young man. He sat up and Jesus gave him to his mother.

I told our Lord: "I don't expect you to give my son back to me right now, in flesh and blood. But I know that he will rise again in the next life with you." And I told him again: "Lord, you know best and someday, I will probably see the light."

TEODORO BENIGNO, bureau chief of Agence France Presse

Our reporter, Bobby Coloma, was able to get in. At the hospital entrance, they saw him with a camera and stopped him. But he had already talked to the military chaplain, who told him that Ninoy was dead. That was how I flashed the news to the whole world. That was why Agence France was ahead of everybody.

From there, I went to Times Street and waited. It was like entering a mausoleum. Everybody was quiet or talking in whispers. You couldn't get a peep out of Tañada or Diokno. The intention of the government was to sow terror. It succeeded that first night. Nobody wanted to talk. Tañada was even angry with Bobby Coloma, who wanted a reaction from him. He said: "Let's not talk about reaction." And then I talked to Pepe Diokno—in whispers.

JOHN CHUA, photographer

The following day, Monday, there was panic. People were really scared. They were withdrawing their money from the banks. I thought of doing that too, and also buying more groceries.

People were afraid to go see Ninoy's body. I was scared too. Just being near his house might be considered a crime by the government. But I went. There were hundreds of people lined up along Times Street. I didn't have the emotion they had. I just wanted to look. I wanted to see what was happening.

My involvement began then. I felt I had to record this. So I did. But my attitude changed, though very slowly.

In the beginning, I would tell myself: "You have to be neutral. You cannot even make the *Laban* sign. You are the photographer, the guy who records this event. You cannot take sides no matter what you feel. You are a photographer, not a participant."

GRACIA M. CARIÑO
(From a letter dated 22 August 1983)

Very early this morning, I went to Ninoy Aquino's house to pay my respects. I heard over Radio Veritas that his body had been brought home. The information was also in the papers, which I bought on my way to Times Street.

That was my downfall: reading the newspapers. I found out that Doña Aurora had asked that the body of Ninoy be left as it was when she claimed him last night from the Army General Hospital: the same bloody clothes, the face left without cosmetics. He was in an open coffin.

There were not many people when I got to Ninoy's house. There were some cars. There were some men on the driveway—they looked like family retainers. The gate was open and I could easily have entered.

Through the picture window, I could see the coffin. I could see the bright funerary chandeliers. All I had to do was get out of the car and walk right in.

I froze. I was too scared. I could not get enough courage to see his bloodied corpse.

I parked the car and sat there across the street and looked at the coffin from a safe distance. I prayed very hard for Ninoy. And then I said to him: "Now you know. Now you know what a big coward I am."

FREDDIE AGUILAR, singer

I went to Times Street but I don't remember if it was the first or the second night of Ninoy's wake. I offered my condolences to Doña Aurora. And Doña Aurora asked if I could sing. She asked me to sing *Bayan Ko* (My Homeland). She said it was one of Ninoy's favorite songs. So after some prayers led by Cardinal Sin, I sang *Bayan Ko*.

AURORA A. AQUINO

At about 3:00 a.m. one morning during Ninoy's wake, when Cory had not yet arrived from Boston, I was feeling very lonely. I got up and went down to where Ninoy's body was lying in state in the living room. To get there, I had to go down about four steps from the bedroom area. I thought there would be no one around at that hour, but to my surprise, there were many people still taking their turn to look at Ninoy. I saw a priest praying and I went to him. It was Father Araneta. I asked him: "Who are these people, Father?" He said that he did not know them.

I went up to some of the men and remarked: "You're here so early." They replied that they were taxi drivers. They had to report for work at 6:00 a.m. and this was the only time they could line up and pay their respects. I was very touched.

A little later, but still in the wee hours of the morning, I saw some women with big baskets. They too came to see Ninoy. I went up to them and they told me that they were fish venders. This was the only time they had to line up.

In the afternoon of the same day, I saw the Zobels and the Makati businessmen, then I also saw the humbler people. The rich and the poor came to see Ninoy. I was so touched. Ninoy is a man of the people, the poor and the rich, I said to myself.

Before Ninoy was buried, a sculptor came to do his death mask and this man told me: "It is very significant that Ninoy came down from the plane to meet the people. He had to do that because he is a man of the people."

VICENTE T. PATERNO, Member of Parliament

I did not go to Times Street until Tuesday (the killing was on Sunday). But on Monday, the day after the assassination, I was so revolted by what some of the KBL assemblymen said. They were saying: "He died because he was hard-headed. He was told not to come home. He came home; he was shot. It's his fault." The Batasan was in session that Monday. One person, Gerry Espina, even said that he had been at the cockpit that night between 9:00 and 10:00, and he said that was the popular reaction—"Ninoy's assassination was his own fault because he had been told not to come home. He was hard-headed."

I don't think they understood what the reaction of the people was. I was saying: "How can you say that? The reaction of the people was different. Not like that. 'Why did they do that to Ninoy?'"

I recounted the words of one old woman: "They are so cruel. He was returning to his country; they did not even let him step on the soil of his native land." There was a symbolism there. They were in such a hurry to kill him, they did not even allow him to see his native land, his mother. When I heard what the KBL people said, I was struck by how insensitive, how out of touch with the people, how blind they were.

In other words, it was being shrugged off. It was being dismissed. I was really getting more and more distraught by this. I was already mad about corruption, and here was a clear injustice that had been perpetrated—it was a clear murder.

All the cover-up—the lack of mention in the radio, when the world press was full of the news of what had happened—to me, this was a big reason why Metro Manila turned out in full force. They were being denied the news, so they went to see for themselves. They were witnesses. It was not being reported to them. They were seeing it and they were reinforcing one another in their comments. They felt real outrage, indignation, and anger. These feelings started swelling inside me. Remember, I was still a member of the KBL.

CORAZON C. AQUINO

My first contact with people power was when we finally got to Manila. When we were still in the airport it was still very tense. It was really the media more than anybody else. They were crowding around us. It was a little frightening and I thought: "What on earth is this?"

Before we arrived, I had asked them to give us some time alone with Ninoy—just the children and I. So nobody was inside when we arrived. They were all outside. But when I saw such a huge crowd, even if I had wanted to be alone with Ninoy, I said: "Tell them to come in." I did not feel it was right that they should be waiting so long.

Seeing the crowd did not really make me happy. How could I be happy? But it made me less sad.

The next day, when we transferred Ninoy to Sto. Domingo, was the first really big rally that I attended. Before, if we could get five hundred people it was already considered a big crowd. For the first few days—or perhaps the first two weeks—every time something struck me, I thought: "I should tell Ninoy about this." You see, when Ninoy was in prison, whatever good thing happened to me I used to think: "Ah, I have to tell this to Ninoy." Even when we were living in the States, if he was out of town, I told him all of these things when he called. So when I was walking to Sto. Domingo I thought: "I have to tell this to Ninoy." Then I realized that that was no longer possible.

JAMES B. REUTER, S.J.

I went to the house of Ninoy Aquino then. I knew him well and, of course, I knew Lupita, his sister. There were some women in black, talking, and I suspected that one of them was Cory Aquino. I wasn't very sure. I really had not met her before, but she broke away from the other women and came to me. She spoke first. "You are here for Lupita, aren't you?" she said. I said I was. She said that Lupita was upstairs and that she was going to go and get her. And she did. She went and got Lupita. And then I knew for sure that it was Cory.

CORAZON C. AQUINO

The crowd in Tarlac struck me as frightening. It was fanaticism. People just climbed on top of the hearse. I was so afraid that the top of the hearse would collapse and people would crash onto Ninoy. We were in the car following the hearse and I said: "Please ask them to get off." I was thinking: "What do they want?" I mean, it was the last thing you would expect. Gosh, where do you see things like this?

My children and I were just praying in the car: "Dear Lord, please make sure that nothing happens." The people were just all over the hearse. First, they were able to tear off the bumpers of the hearse—and they did more. It looked like a mob. I was not prepared for that.

Tarlac was my first encounter with the problem of getting through a crowd. I thought: "How do I get up there with people everywhere?" The security was saying: "How can we bring you up there when everybody just wants to get near the coffin?" So finally we decided: "Iwanan mo na si Ninoy," to leave the hearse and let the family go up to the provincial capitol. The people were just crushing us. That was my first encounter with a pushing and shoving crowd. Well, there was also pushing in Sto. Domingo, so it was not really my first time.

It was just amazing. I thought: "Widows don't normally go through this." It was just totally different from what a regular widow goes through.

Coming from Tarlac took us eleven hours. We followed the hearse from Tarlac to Sto. Domingo. At a certain point, they were insisting that we go inside a certain church and bring him in. I said: "We can't do that." It was just so late. To tell you frankly, I didn't know how I survived those days. I was eating minimally and sleep was not possible.

When we got to Tarlac, I told my children after lunch: "Get some sleep. Maybe when you wake up this afternoon, I want to go back to the church." A little later, I looked into their rooms: they were all fast asleep. You see, none of us had slept since Boston. I was awakened at midnight on Sunday and did not get to sleep even until Tarlac. I did not even feel the jet lag—it was the least of my problems. There were just so many things to do. My children slept sixteen hours straight in Tarlac. When they woke up, they were surprised that it was morning already. They just collapsed from exhaustion.

AURORA A. AQUINO

I was not surprised, of course, when many people came to meet Ninoy's body in Concepcion, our hometown. One of the farmers told me: "He was our best bet. Why did he die?"

There are still some old people in Concepcion who remember Ninoy as a little boy. How could they help not remembering him? When he was still in short pants, he liked to go with the team that announced the movies. They carried a big placard with the name of the movie and they had a ragtag band: a drum, a pair of cymbals, a fiddle.

Ninoy went around with them and soon persuaded them to let him play the drum. He was crazy about playing the drum. One day he came running to his father and said: "More than anything else, I want to be a drummer." His father was very amused and he said to me: "What for am I working so hard when all your son wants is to be is a drummer?"

That was his ambition: to be a drummer, to call all the people. I think he really became a drummer. Wherever he went as a candidate, people came to him, people flocked over to him. Perhaps eventually to the Filipino people, he became the drummer. That could be another meaning to his life.

CORAZON C. AQUINO

Coming back from Tarlac—that was the miracle. Along the way, people especially in Pampanga—you know how the people in Pampanga are when it comes to food—gave us canned Coke or 7-Up. Pampanga always considered Ninoy special. So they gave us drinks and I took some, just to put some liquid in me. After eleven hours we got to Santo Domingo, and really, we just dragged our bodies in.

I was just amazed that I didn't have a headache or anything.

The funeral was scheduled for Tuesday. But a friend told me: "Cory, I know you don't believe in these things, but it's not good for the family to have the funeral on Tuesday. Have it on Wednesday." I said: "No, never mind." But she said: "Cory, this is the only thing I am asking you, for the sake of the children. Imagine if something else happens to you." I think from sheer exhaustion, rather than argue with her I said: "Okay, Wednesday." Well, I'm glad I agreed. We arrived Monday from Tarlac. Imagine if we had the funeral Tuesday, our bodies would not have been able to take it.

Tuesday was relatively easy. I slept very late because I had to write my response and I also did something for Kris which she could say at the Mass. Somebody wrote something for her, and I said: "This isn't Kris." So I said: "Kris, what do you want to say?" So she told me, and I wrote it down, and gave it to her and said: "Is this how you want to say it?" She said: "Well, Mom, can I correct it?" I said: "Sure, do whatever you think you should." I wanted all of us to do something, whatever it was. My two daughters took part in the readings. I said: "Let's all do something because I think that's what Dad would like." Before the funeral, I think I had a cup of coffee, that's all. And a tranquilizer. The cardiologist of

Ninoy from Dallas was with us. He came back with us from Boston. I said: "Rolly, this is too much!" He said: "When your husband was alive, he always said: 'If anything happens to me, please take care of my family.'" He said he would never be able to live with it if he didn't come with us. We all rode together. I asked Father Olaguer to ride with us. With all these crowds, I just wanted to make sure there would be a priest when we got to Manila Memorial Park. But gosh, I didn't think it would take that long.

People banged at the window. We had food in the Hi-Ace but how could we eat when all these people were not eating? I told Kris: "If you feel like eating, bend over a little so the people will not see you." But she said: "Mom, I don't really feel like eating." Most of the time, my daughters were asleep.

Noynoy was on the truck. I hadn't asked him to do that. It was just that when they were carrying Ninoy's coffin, the crowd just brought him up. He and my brother-in-law Paul were both up on the truck. They got rained on. They were drenched.

It was not scary then, as it was on the way to Tarlac. It was different. At the funeral I could see that people gave water but then, instead of drinking that whole glass or whatever container they had, they passed it on to others. I said to myself: "This is so different, people care about the others."

There were two people who decided to get under that ten-wheeler. I don't know if there is any superstition about that, but I said: "Oh no, please," and told one of the security guards to ask them to come down. I didn't want anybody getting hurt. I was very upset when I learned that someone was struck dead by lightning.

All along the way, I was praying. I was no longer praying for Ninoy but just saying: "Dear God, please make everything go right." With people darting in and out, if no one gets run over, I thought this would really be a miracle. It was a miracle that nobody was hurt.

When we got to the grave, people surged forward. I hadn't intended for Ninoy's coffin to be opened again, but Noynoy said: "Mom, I want to see Dad one last time." So I asked them to open it and people thought that they could see the body again. I had to ask them to please keep back. It was getting to be too much already.

I was so exhausted, I couldn't even cry anymore. I was feeling a little dizzy, not having eaten anything, but I thought I could still manage. I said: "I've never fainted in my life, and I don't want to faint now."

That was for me really huge people power. I kept thinking then: "Ninoy is really so happy, now that people really care." I think I would have collapsed if it was just my family and I who had taken care of this. I would have said that I was right after all, because I had earlier been telling Ninoy: "Filipinos are cowards." He said: "No, all they need is a leader."

AURORA A. AQUINO

I was amazed at how many people came to the wake and to the funeral. I saw the hand of the Lord in this, because most of the mass media, especially television, did not cover it. Because the people did not see what was going on over television, they went out to see for themselves.

During the funeral, the people were a great comfort to me. I was in a van and it was going at an ant's pace. People talked to me as we each went along, they on foot and me in the van.

JOHN CHUA

So I began to take pictures. I went to the funeral Mass in Santo Domingo; I went there at 5:00 a.m. to make sure I could get a good position to take photographs. The church was full and there was a huge crowd outside trying to get in.

After the Mass, I went with the funeral procession. I got rained on twice, first in Lawton and then in Luneta. I had to go home and get more film. If this had been just any other event, I would have quit and gone home.

I saw this guy in a wheelchair who went from Santo Domingo to the cemetery. By the time we got to Luneta, he was exhausted, but he kept going.

The people who went would not give up and leave, no matter how tired or uncomfortable they were. It was as if they had made a vow or thought of what they were doing as penitence. That was really an emotional event, one of the most emotional events I have covered.

EUGENIA APOSTOL, publisher

Mr. & Ms. did not cover the funeral but I had deployed five photographers along the route. And I had my ears glued to Radio Veritas.

Next day, I said: "What's this? Not a single photo of the funeral in the papers, as if nothing happened." What really got me was the *Times Journal.* What they printed was the photo of the spectator who was hit by lightning—that was their top news! The next morning, I brought all our photos and printed everything. I handled it myself. It was like I put in everything, the past 35 years, all in one afternoon, into that special edition.

TEODORO BENIGNO

What struck me about the assassination of Ninoy was the animal savagery and the brutality. It was like an ominous scream, something that you had never heard in this country. You're so mad. Shot in the tarmac! It was not in accordance with anything that a Filipino was ever used to. We're Christians. Whatever our enmity, whatever our rivalry, whatever our differences, there are some limits to what we can do. Beneath every human being lurks a savage. Christianity, culture, civilization, the patina of everything we have ever learned ever since we were kids are supposed to cover that. But then the assassination tore the whole thing up. So it certainly touched off a wave of, initially, numbness in the Filipino people. Then shock, stupefaction, hurt, bitterness. And outrage and anger.

The death of Ninoy opened up a long gash of wound upon the Filipino nation. The unifying element was the Roman Catholic religion. It was a conscience brutalized and violated. All the things that made Jesus Christ a great leader of men and a great apostle at the same time—the values of human kindness, the values of Christian compassion—were brutalized with the death of Ninoy. All the people who had been going to church for years and years realized that their values as Christians would only be redeemed if they went out into the streets. So they went out.

In all my career as a journalist, I had not seen such crowds. The crowd of Mahatma Gandhi was only one million. Ninoy's crowd was a very exceptional crowd, not only in size but also in reaction—a cry of lament, a cry of sadness. It was a cry of anger and it was a cry of outrage; it was a cry of being orphaned. It was a cry of distress. It was also a cry of courage. And Ninoy's death did the trick. They gained courage to face the future that they were not sure of. It was formless, in the very beginning—the Catholic population finally was able to get it into their system to say something, to do something, to react, to show their anger and their outrage against the government. Many kept saying that if the funeral only headed for Malacañang, the government of Marcos could have been overthrown. They wouldn't have had the guts to stop those millions of people headed for Malacañang.

VICENTE T. PATERNO

The funeral procession finally came at about six in the evening. That, for me, was a very moving thing: people lined up from eleven in the morning and waited until almost six. And I asked myself: "Why? Why are we doing this? Why are we here?" And when the coffin passed, people were not crying, they were not laughing, they were not silent. They were clapping!

A Japanese reporter asked me two days later: "Please, tell me, is this the normal reaction, that when there is a funeral people clap and chant?" I said: "No. I think it was, first, because they stayed for a long time as an act of expiation. It was an act of penitence. They were trying to show their contrition for having allowed such a thing to happen. They were chanting and applauding not because it was a funeral procession, but because it was a hero's procession. In a sense it was a triumphal procession. You have to understand that the greatest heroes in Filipino culture are the martyrs. Ninoy is a hero in the most accepted Filipino sense, that he achieved, by his death, an awakening of the Filipino conscience." I said this again in the *Batasan* during an interpellation.

People were there shouting: "Ninoy!" They stood in the rain and in the sun. For them, it was an expiation for having allowed this to happen. Even Marcos said that Ninoy s assassination was a "national shame." For me, this was the evidence: between one and two million people of Metro Manila out there in the streets, not just for ten minutes but for hours; some of them marching for many hours. There was thunder, lightning, and rain that afternoon. But people stuck it out; they didn't leave. They stood, they waited, they shouted, and they clapped. "Put down your umbrellas. Only Imelda carries an umbrella." That was it. It was a blatant act of injustice, callousness to the feelings of the people, an attempt to hide the happenings from the rest of the people. I had already been outraged by such actions but this, to my mind, epitomized the injustice that had been perpetuated throughout this regime. I shared in that sense of shame of the people. That's why we were also there from ten in the morning to six in the evening. We stayed. We wanted to be there. For me, that was it. The regime was lost. There had to be change.

To me, Cory was a heroic figure. I realized while listening to the radio and seeing all the people there that if she had agreed to have the funeral procession pass Legarda Street, that could have toppled Marcos. The people were so mad that if they had passed by Mendiola Bridge, they would have attacked Malacañang. That was clear to me. I understood her lack of any desire for retribution or vengeance which would have been very natural at that time. I admired her character—she was grieving but she was not out to use any of the power that had been given her.

CORAZON C. AQUINO

The next day, I went back to the cemetery so I could at least be alone with Ninoy. I was so amazed at how near it was. During the funeral, the way people were shoving and all, I thought we would never make it there. It didn't seem as near then.

There were still people there. The amazing part was when we transferred Ninoy's tomb to the other place, the grass that was under it was so green. Yet the grass alongside of it was so brown, people had been stepping on it. This was amazing, because the sun had not been able to shine under the concrete vault. It was so green under the slab. What was it?

---

21 August 1983: Shot to death while in military custody, opposition leader Benigno S. Aquino, Jr., lies face down on the tarmac of the Manila International Airport only minutes after he arrived from a three-year exile in Boston. He came home to lead a non-violent reconciliation for justice and freedom, which had been increasingly suppressed in the regime of President Ferdinand E. Marcos. For millions of Filipinos, Ninoy Aquino's assassination was a shock and an awakening, particularly since a news shutdown by government-controlled media left them little information except what could be pirated from foreign publications and video. This frame came from footage taken by a Japanese television crew, who were among the international journalists asked by Aquino to accompany him as guarantee of safety and so that the world will know if assassination aborted his mission.

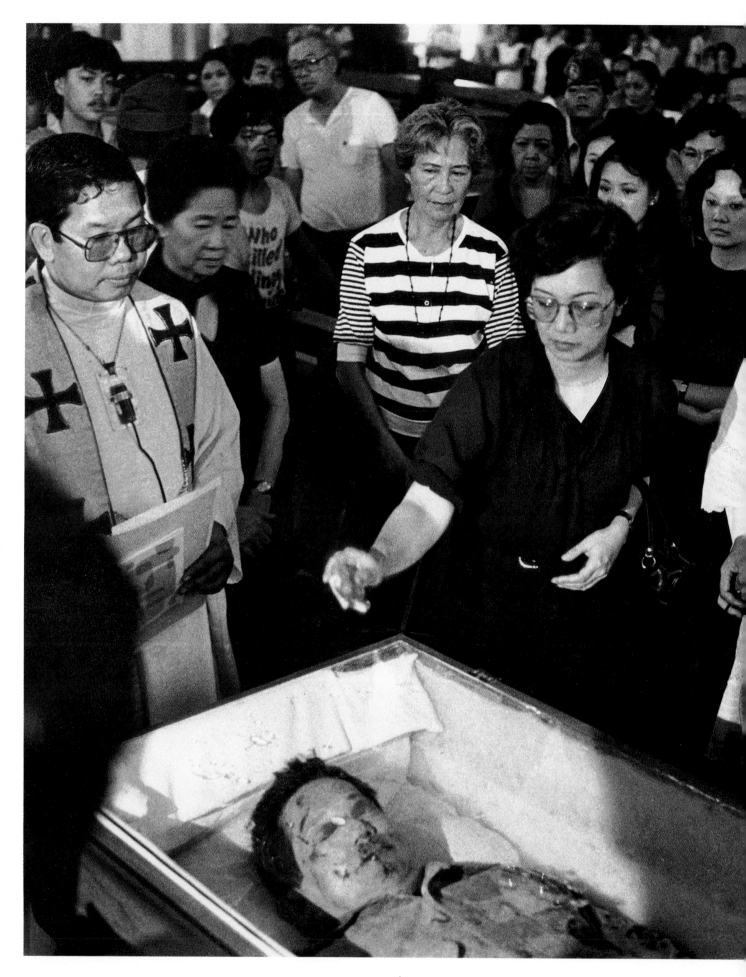

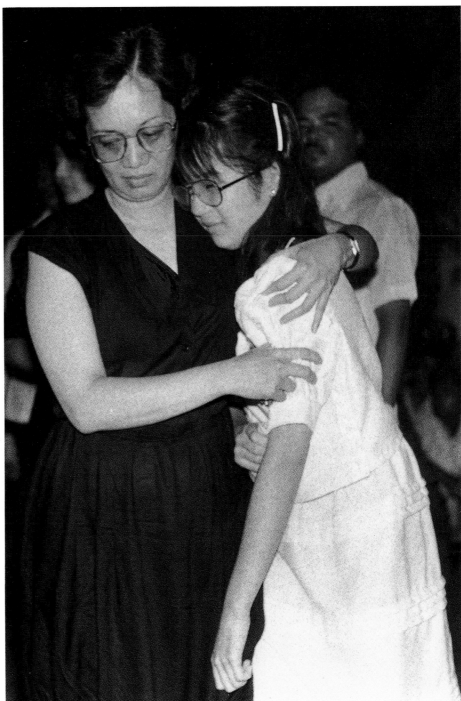

As priests say prayers for the dead, Cory Aquino sprinkles blessed water on the open casket of her slain husband, left. Neither change of clothing nor cosmetics masked the brutality of his death. His mother, Doña Aurora A. Aquino, wanted to show him as he was when she claimed his body from a military hospital. Although she said she had done all her crying in Boston from where she travelled home to bury her husband, Cory grieves with her youngest daughter Kris, 12, who was her father's kindred spirit, above. As a seven-year-old in 1978, Kris campaigned for Ninoy Aquino when, although under detention, he ran for a seat in parliament. He lost the election and remained in detention for a total of seven years and seven months until he was allowed to travel to the US for heart surgery.

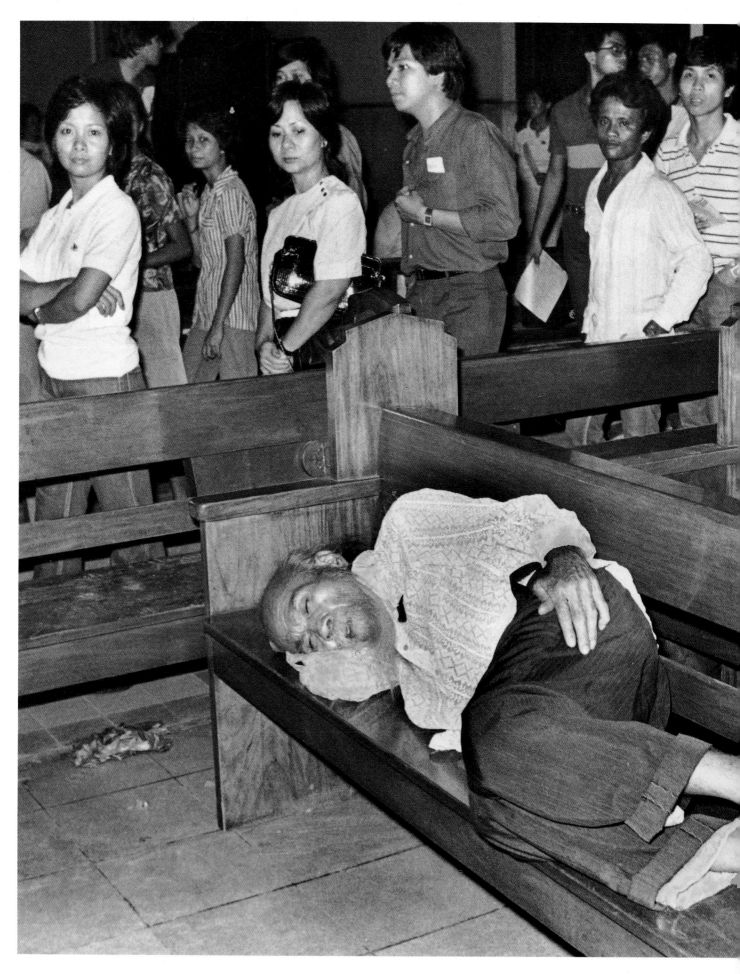

Perched on his father's shoulder the better to view Ninoy Aquino's body lying in state, a boy recoils in shock, above. Believing that history was being made, many Filipinos deliberately brought their children to the Aquino wake and funeral. They lined up even through the night during the ten-day wake. Tired after the long wait in the queue, this man appropriates a church pew, left.

Mourners surge into the churchyard on the day of Ninoy Aquino's funeral, right. Entry was restricted because the church itself, Santo Domingo—one of the biggest churches in Metro Manila —was already filled with people as early as 5 a.m. for the 9 a.m. funeral services. Unable to enter, a woman prays the Rosary, above. She wears a yellow ribbon around her forehead, the beginning of a popular emblem to signify protest against Marcos.

Over the traditional black mourning armband, a friend wrapped a yellow ribbon with Ninoy's name; he also tapes a favorite portrait of the slain leader to one of the cars in the funeral cortege, above left. Slowed down by the crowd walking with the funeral on a 30-km. route through Metro Manila, Doña Aurora Aquino — Ninoy's mother — speaks to the people, left. More than just a funeral, the procession of mourners for Ninoy Aquino

was a political demonstration, the biggest within memory, above. News about it was suppressed in the government-controlled media. One mourner, when asked why he was there, replied: "Ask the flowers." It was a statement typical of the political trepidation during the Marcos regime. Other mourners however were more vocal and said: "It is the least we could do since Ninoy gave his life for the country." Still others compared him to Dr. Jose Rizal, the national hero, who was also a martyr, and whose death—along with those of other patriots—further ignited the fervor which led to the Philippine revolution of 1896 against the colonial government of Spain. That was why Aquino's funeral procession had to pass by Rizal Park, the country's major memorial. There, amid an unseasonal downpour of rain, the cortege slowed down before the Rizal monument and mourners lowered the flag to halfmast, overleaf.

A flagbearer holds the Philippine emblem high above the casket of Ninoy Aquino upon a flowered bier, high above the black-draped flatbed of the ten-wheeler truck that was the funeral car. The burial was meant to be at high noon but the cortege finally reached the cemetery in the evening—past throngs of people and after several shifts of flagbearers had waved the flag atop the truck. "If it takes my death to waken the Filipino, so be it," Ninoy Aquino once said.

II Rallies, marches and demonstrations, 1983 to 1985

Scenario

FRANCISCO S. TATAD

Aquino's assassination lit a fire of protest which the country had not seen before. In the months ahead, its flames raged in the city and countryside. Ugarte Field in Makati, the financial district, took its place beside *Liwasang Bonifacio* (Bonifacio Plaza) in downtown Manila as a center of protest. Here, the upper and the middle class marched with the poor, the professionals with the workers and the unemployed. They came attired or ribboned in yellow—the official color of the Aquino crusade—and faced policemen's truncheons, water cannons, and tear gas. From the high-rise buildings on fashionable Ayala Avenue and Paseo de Roxas, corporate secretaries, clerks, and executives unloaded tons of yellow confetti shredded from telephone books.

Here as elsewhere, yellow banners mingled with red as the "social democrats" marched with the "national democrats," the cause-oriented with the militant Left, the laity with the religious. But whatever the size of the crowds, they remained surprisingly orderly and nonviolent.

Eventually the government complained that the marches and shower of confetti were causing capital flight and scaring the IMF, the World Bank, and the country's creditor banks. Business had ground to a standstill; there was no foreign exchange to open letters of credit; unemployment and underemployment had risen to the highest levels in postwar years; inflation was on the gallop; and armed insurgency was spreading like fire in the countryside.

The business community replied that the crisis was in direct proportion to the loss of confidence in the government. The problem had become political, no longer simply economic. Reform or change the leadership. Lead us or leave us, they told the President.

They demanded a speedy and impartial investigation of the Aquino murder; a clear and stable line of presidential succession; clean and honest elections, beginning with a reformed Commission on Elections (COMELEC); the dismantling of agricultural monopolies; and a free press. A nonbinding resolution passed by the United States Congress specified most of these points.

Thus, the regime tried to make a show of not interfering in the fact-finding work of the Agrava board on the Aquino assassination. The office of Vice President was restored in the Constitution. The age of presidential and vice presidential candidates was brought back from 50 to 40 years. New members were appointed to the Commission on Elections. The National Citizens' Movement for Free Elections (NAMFREL) was accredited as a citizen organization to police the elections.

In May, 1984, the opposition captured 59 of 183 elective parliamentary seats, winning in Manila, the seat of power, by a nearly complete shutout. By October, the Agrava Board formally sought the indictment of Armed Forces Chief of Staff General Ver, 24 other military officers and one civilian for the Aquino murder.

Voices

GRACIA M. CARIÑO, wife and mother
(From a letter dated 6 September 1983)

I am putting together for you all other clippings that you may not have read there. Among the distressing things, aspects of Ninoy's death, for me is the shrill and rampant coverage of the American press—so totally out of context in our culture and in our Christianity. The Aquino family has again and again reaffirmed that they want his death to be taken in the Christian spirit —which the American press failed utterly to capture. Some of the assassination coverage strikes me as hysterical, accusatory, and troublemongering. (Yes, I get to read everything from the foreign press, because we get the *Herald Tribune.*)

With the government propaganda machine quiet, a lot of sincere and from-the-heart writing, especially from ordinary citizens, appears in the papers and it is this kind of thoughts, ideas, and directions that better and more authentically reflects our reaction to the death of Ninoy Aquino.

We are a gentle people, as you have said. And we are Christians. Christianity imbues our culture and we react with the Christian sense of trust in God, reconciliation, forgiveness, and peace when pain and tragedy hit us.

The entire experience with its outrage, its shame, its confusion, its restlessness and insecurity, its questioning—was also cleansing and a tremendous opportunity for faith and trust in God.

Tomorrow I will visit the grave of Senator Aquino, as people continue to do so with prayers and flowers all of this week. Tomorrow it will be a week after his burial and I know that there, after all these days, I will at last cry—because we have lost an alternative.

And yet I will also cry out of joy and pride for our race, for the Filipino people who in these recent days have shown themselves people of faith and of heart, people who mourn and weep, people who pray. In all, it is the Filipino people who emerged triumphant and whole from Aquino's death—open, free, unashamed, and unafraid to grieve and to mourn.

One of my dearest friends, Poy, is typical of the mourners. She belongs to a provincial family but for the last years had been in the upper crust of Manila, being married to an executive of the Ayala Corporation. In fact, she was in Hongkong when the assassination happened. She returned as scheduled on the day that Ninoy's body returned from his province, Tarlac. That was two days before his burial. From that day onwards, Poy was a mourner—in the church for the wake, for one of the many Requiem Masses, in the funeral march from the beginning to the end, and in repeated visits to his grave nearly every day.

I tell you the story of Poy because I suspect that several hundred and thousand times, it is multiplied in the other mourners who lined up, heard Mass, prayed, and now continue to pay their respects and to think. I fear that their story is not reflected in the American press and I owe it to Aquino and to my people to say so.

TEODORO BENIGNO, bureau chief
of Agence France Presse

The mass actions after the assassination were very unprecedented.

For the first time, the middle class came out. It struck me as being very significant and crucial. You had husbands, mothers, children, teenagers, people from all professions—lawyers, doctors, engineers. And finally you had the Makati people joining in. That was the most unprecedented. They were the most conservative people in the Philippines; they couldn't care less about demonstrations. When they joined, they had to disown their own cultural reflexes, their own business interests, their own refusals to come down from their business temples. They joined because they were Roman Catholics. The brutal-

ity of the Aquino assassination hit them where it hits most effectively. The workers had come out already, the students, the middle class—but when the Makati people came out, I was convinced that it was the twilight stage of the Marcos era. It was just a matter of time before the curtains fell on his regime.

PAZ C. PASCUAL, housewife

The first rally I saw was on September 16, 1983. Before that rally, I couldn't really say anything against Marcos and his government. There was such an atmosphere of repression. I was waiting in my car in traffic when all of a sudden I saw all those people with "Marcos, Resign!" posters. It was brave of them. I was watching this. All of a sudden, everything just overflowed. My tears started to fall. After that, I was brave enough to join rallies.

JOHN CHUA, photographer

How does a security guard contribute to a rally? Once, I saw a security guard of the Bank of the Philippine Islands in Makati. As rallyists passed before him, he took out his whistle and began to play *Bayan Ko* (My Homeland). I don't know how he was able to do that with just a whistle. Everybody applauded him. He blew the whistle with all his might. A picture couldn't capture that. You had to be there to feel it.

RENE A. OCAMPO, S.J.

I joined Ninoy's funeral procession because it was an expression of grief. But I did not join the September 21, 1983 rally, because I was very conscious of various other groups that were there and the threats of violence that may erupt.

In subsequent years, however, I was a lot more at ease. Talks about active nonviolence had begun. I think that this is very important because when you are reacting against violence and possibilities of manipulation by the Left, your fears prevent you from becoming really involved. I think active nonviolence provides an alternative focus for one's own search. It is not negative fear, it is a concern for truth. So it is something positive that draws you out rather than draws you in.

FREDDIE AGUILAR, singer

I went to rallies on my own. Sometimes I was invited by Butz Aquino. But most of the time, I went even when I was not invited. I received some threats, which did not really scare me. They said to me: "Mr. Aguilar, a living hero is better than a dead hero." This was before the *Batasan* elections of 1984. People I didn't know approached me and said: "You know, Freddie, we hope that you won't be too vocal. You're not a politician.... why do you have to get involved?" But I told them: "What I do is based on my principles, my beliefs." Even before there was news of Ninoy's return, I was already protesting. I had been doing it for a long time.

JOHN CHUA

I took pictures of the rallies. When people started honking their car horns and dropping yellow confetti, my hair stood on end. I felt that the Filipino spirit was alive. You tend to drop your camera when you feel it. Although I know that as a photographer you should not feel it. If somebody shot somebody else, I'd cover it. If there's a murder, I'd cover it. I am good at that. I am used to it. When you are a photographer, you do not have to be emotional to do your job.

Once, I saw a businessman get off his car, take off his business clothes, and put on a yellow t-shirt. I thought of Superman—a businessman one minute, then all of a sudden, a rallyist.

AGAPITO AQUINO (BUTZ), opposition leader

When the IGNORE RUN was launched in Concepcion, Tarlac, on January 7, 1984, it was meant to express very specific sentiments which we felt we shared with the great majority: our contempt for Mr. Marcos' plebiscite gimmickry and the continuing esteem of the Filipinos for Ninoy. A clear majority of the people have disdained to participate in Mr. Marcos' gimmick and they laughed at the claims of his COMELEC that there was a huge turn-out for this exercise. And what better tangible evidence of the people's feelings for Ninoy than the overwhelming response to our hour of need in Meycauayan?

When I saw the phalanx of soldiers, at least six deep, in full riot gear and arms, determined to block our passage at the boundary of Malanday and Valenzuela, I suddenly smelled blood. I thought that perhaps many of our people would get hurt—or perhaps even worse—if we stood our ground. So I decided to pull back to Meycauayan to give us time to plan our move.

At that moment when I wasn't sure whether to stay put and risk violence or to retreat to Meycauayan, I prayed. In big decisions, I never do it alone.

If they had just let us through without any fuss, the whole run would have been over by Saturday afternoon. How could some 300 people—many of them young, in jogging shorts and sneakers, totally unarmed, and merely wanting to run the 145 km. stretch—be construed as revolutionary, as a threat to anyone?

GEMINO ABAD, poet

In 1984, Alran Bengzon, Noel Soriano, and Butz Aquino organized a series of seven-day fasts for justice under the spiritual direction of Father Jose Blanco. They asked for volunteers and I joined. It was the beginning of the active non-violence movement in the Philippines. Father Blanco, a strong believer in liberation theology, was its founder. Later, we met with a couple who founded an international active nonviolence movement. Soon after, we began to disseminate these ideas.

We had a group of fasters, the Community of Fasters for Justice, which coordinated activities with the group of Father Blanco.

My group came out with an issue of *Caracoa* called Sub-Ver-Su; it was made up of political poems. I had made a vow after the assassination to write 100 poems for the Filipino people on political and social issues. We also had exhibits of poetry and paintings. So that was the form my protest took—poetry and prayer and fasting.

RENE OCAMPO, S.J.

For me, the most important rallies were on the death anniversaries of Ninoy—August 21, 1984 and 1985. There must be something that makes it easier for Filipinos to express our oneness with those who were victims of injustice. I think there's a lot to say about the underdog mentality that people always talk about. It is easier to identify with the underdog, rather than with abstract issues of U.S. Imperialism and all these highfaluting words. It is another thing to be confronted by a widow or orphans. Your whole heart goes out to them. It is much easier to identify with them.

FREDDIE AGUILAR

My most memorable rally was on the first anniversary of Ninoy's death in *Liwasang Bonifacio* (Bonifacio Plaza). People wanted to attack Marcos in Malacañang. They were burning his effigy and cursing him. The politicians spoke but the people did not listen. When I went up the stage to sing, everybody was suddenly quiet and calm. I felt like I was singing in a cemetery. Music is powerful. It can calm down people's anger. I saw this wherever I went, even in the provinces.

CORAZON C. AQUINO, widow of Benigno S. Aquino, Jr. (Ninoy)
(From a speech delivered on 10 March 1984)

When Ninoy emerged from prison, it seemed clear to those who knew him that much had changed in him. The superb political animal—shrewd, fast, eloquent, and brave—who had placed his immense talents in the service of the Republic in the hope of public honors, had evolved into a man for whom love of country was only the other face of his love for God. And I think this is the truest and best kind of patriotism. It is only on this plane that patriotism ceases to be, as they say, the refuge of scoundrels and becomes, instead, the obligation of a Christian.

A man or a woman reaches this plane only when he or she ceases to be the "hero" playing to the gallery and becomes the humble Christian praying to God, using only the words of our Lord to fix the direction of his or her actions. It is upon such men and women, rather than merely upon unity pure and simple, that we should rely to bring about the changes, especially the political changes that we all desire.

We cannot, of course, just place an order for such men and women to be or to lead the opposition. Such people are not made to order. They make themselves that way.

If you share, therefore, my growing conviction that it is only by such people that the changes we want will be brought about, then you must also share the conclusion I have come to: the changes will come and victory will be attained—a victory that will mean more than a change of faces—only when there are enough of us who have become like that.

I think, if that happens, we shall have more strength to resist and overcome evil than any superficial unity of opinion can achieve. We shall probably continue to entertain a wide and contradictory variety of opinions.

However, our fundamental direction will have been fixed by faith—faith in the ultimate things about which we cannot possibly disagree.

These are the things that we hope God will reveal to us, as He revealed them to Ninoy, in the course of our transformation.

VICENTE PATERNO, businessman

My first rally was on October 7, 1984—to protest the brutality by which a previous rally was dispersed. It was a rally to protest violence and I thought that this was one rally I should attend.

In that rally, for the first time, Jimmy Ongpin gave a talk. He said: "There is nothing more important for me than to be here with you."

A number of other people marched in that rally for the first time. There were many people from the business community. In a sense, perhaps October 7, 1984, was a significant event if only because more people felt that they had to stand up and be counted.

Throughout all of this, it seemed to me that the people in Malacañang did not appreciate what was going on. Do you remember that remark by one of Mrs. Marcos' Blue Ladies: "The Aquino funeral must have cost a lot of money, because of all the people who were paid to attend"? That mentality, the idea of hauling people to rallies, continued in their minds. I guess they could not imagine that all this was happening spontaneously.

While the participation of some organizations like *Bayan* was clearly organized, there was much spontaneous participation by others. There wasn't much calling and mustering of people. People joined because they wanted to be there. They felt that they must be there.

The business community became more and more open in denouncing and starting to make their sentiments known—still not in large numbers, but there was a growing sentiment.

AURORA A. AQUINO, mother of Benigno S. Aquino, Jr. (Ninoy)

I was invited to many rallies—in Mati, in Tagum, everywhere in Mindanao. I took the plane by myself rather than pay for the ticket of a companion. They just called me on the phone, or sometimes they came to my house. Once Mr. Zabala came here from Mati, and I did not know him from Adam. He wrote down the date of my going there, and the flight number, and the itinerary. And I said yes. So I flew there all by myself. Thank God, the mother-in-law of my son Paul was there to meet me.

Five men took me to Mati, and it turned out

that Mr. Zabala was a Protestant pastor. We had breakfast at a house on the way and their prayers were not our prayers. They prayed the Protestant way. I was glad that all over, anywhere, they expected me to go.

I was also taken to Cebu by the people. They wanted to hear all about Ninoy. One day the Cardinal called me to a meeting and said: "Were you in Tagbilaran, Bohol?" I said: "Yes." He continued: "The one who told me was the mayor of Tagbilaran. He could not go to the rally, so he just stayed in his house, and turned on the radio and he heard you speaking. He cried like a child when he heard you."

I did not realize that by being there, by speaking, I helped people. I said of course, that there must be forgiveness in our hearts. Whenever I was invited by the Knights of Columbus, they asked me: "Is there any bitterness in your heart?" I said: "No, I have forgiven, because if we cannot forgive, we can never have peace in our hearts."

Of course, justice must prevail. But deep in my heart, I have no hatred. I have no vengeance. I'm already in the sunset of my life. I'm 76, and soon I will be leaving this world. I don't want to take with me a load of hatred in my heart. That's not in the list of God's imperatives. We must love one another, and must even love our enemies. In fact, I prayed for Marcos and his wife.

MARGARITA COJUANGCO (TINGTING), opposition leader

I'm writing you while events are still vivid in my mind. In history, this would be termed a primary source. I wish to put down my experience for future writers. I am writing about the Quezon Boulevard rally.

I arrived with my other AWARE friends (Alliance of Women Towards Action and Reconciliation)—Mariel Tolentino, Narz Lim, Guila Maramba, Ching Escaler, Dede Quiroz, Winnie Monsod, Betty Nelle and Phyllis Zaballero—with KAAKBAY's Daphne Ceniza. I had a borrowed gas mask. The others brought theirs, too, along with lemon juice and water to protect their faces from tear gas.

We immediately lined up in our assigned places. We were in the third and fourth rows, behind the composites (the urban poor and students) who stood behind Butz Aquino, Senator Tañada, Chino Roces, and other rallyists.

We locked our arms tightly to keep from breaking ranks. I prayed my novena to the Infant Jesus of Prague but couldn't quite get on with it. Suddenly, the water hoses were turned on us. We did not break formation. A few minutes later, I heard cans fall on the pavement. Smoke blocked my vision—Elmer Mercado, the president of the League of Filipino Students (LFS), shouted "Retreat!" We ran. Our first dispersal was successful. It took us one hour to re-group. Our leaders began to negotiate with General Yson. In the meantime, we were told that those who wished to leave could do so. We of AWARE—Karina, Odette, Maita, Nelia, Nikki—opted to stay. We had committed ourselves to be front liners. How could I let the students and the urban poor fight my fight? I fight my own battles.

We returned to our places. Each group we passed shouted: "Long Live the Women!" I answered sadly: "Thank you." I wasn't my usual self. I knew there would be more to come. This was an indignation rally for the waterhosing and tear gassing at dawn on September 22, 1984, at Mendiola. I had to be alert.

It was now 4:30 p.m. We in the third row put lemon on our faces for tear gas protection and passed them on to the composite group behind us. One of them lost his handkerchief. I gave him mine, wet from the first water hosing. It had tiny, multi-colored hearts. That made me smile. A toughie with colored hearts on his face.

Suddenly, a composite shouted: "Armalites!" I saw a long gun behind a military man's shield on the left side of Quezon Boulevard. The military now occupied both lanes, the left lane and the right side of Quezon Boulevard. We were boxed in from behind by the other rallyists as well. I took a deep breath and remained unafraid. I cannot explain how I mustered all that courage. Then, fire trucks and truncheon-and-shield-bearing soldiers came at us.

A stone wrapped in newspaper was thrown in front of me. "Infiltrators!" shouted someone. A man from ATOM shouted: "Go after them!" The rocks were thrown by the military. They were big stones. They fell on the first group of leaders. I saw Butz Aquino being covered by at least four or five men. None of them wore helmets, except 86-year-old Senator Tañada.

The fire trucks continued advancing on us and were now 35 meters away. The soldiers were positioned on both sides of the fire trucks with their shields and truncheons. They came at us, keeping pace with the fire truck. I heard cans fall on the ground and I saw smoke rising. Still, we didn't move. More smoke bombs were hurled at us, along with some rocks. Gunshots were fired. The order came: "Run!" My partner, Guila Maramba, and I ran, arm in arm. Ray from PDP (Philippine Democratic Party)-LABAN, Q.C., saw me and linked arms with me. We ran past Kanlaon Street, Apo Street, into Speaker Perez Street, about 1,000 of us. The others, without our knowledge, had run inside buildings in Kanlaon and Apo Streets, but we kept running for our lives.

I was running with tears rolling down my cheeks, thinking: Why is this Filipino shooting at us Filipinos? I heard: Pop-pop-pop-pop-pop-pop! like popcorn from my kitchen. These can't be smoke bombs. They're guns firing at us. God! I remembered that I received Communion yesterday. Then, I remembered my small children vividly, Tsina and Mai and Mikee. Liaa and Pin are grown up, they can take care of themselves. Then, more: Pop-pop-pop-pop! Again, my choppy thoughts: Peping and his sisters will take care of them… I can get shot in the back! I'm wearing a thin T-shirt.

At this point, UP student Fidel Nemenzo was running behind us. He overtook us. The bullet hit him on the back. He fell ten feet away and turned around. Rocks were being hurled at us. He saw blood gushing from his chest and collapsed. Two men picked him up and dragged him to where we were. A young student with us kicked a gate open. Twelve of us ran over to the gate. We ran further inside for cover between two apartment houses. We leaned on the walls. I heard soldiers' feet thumping on the asphalt road.

All the apartments were locked and seemed empty except for the last. Its owner was closing the door hurriedly when I shouted, my hands on her screen door: "I beg you, let us in!" I said: "I'm Tingting Cojuangco." I said: "Please, Please." She recognized me and answered: "Okay, but only you. Only you. Someone called earlier not to let anyone in." "No, no, I have an injured boy with me." I opened the door wide before she could answer, and Art and Maricor carried Fidel inside. I saw blood all over Fidel's white pants. I sat him on a chair, and the only sound he made was one long "Ayee." I found a folding bed. The lady of the house asked her maid to help me lay it down in her sala. Art, Maricor, Bernarao, and Dingdong removed Fidel's shirt. Art had bandages.

We must have been hiding for 30 to 40 minutes. I ran to open the gate with the others and saw the soldiers walking back to Quezon Boulevard. They were about ten feet away. I hid behind the gate. Sonny pulled me by the arm, shoved me into the front seat of the van. The boys carried Fidel on the folding bed, and laid him gently at the back.

United Doctors Medical Center was waiting for us. On the second floor, Fidel was whisked to the operating room. We saw UP student leader Lean Alejandro in UDMC checking on other casualties, and he asked that we walk around to check on anyone being picked up at random. We did, with Wally of PDP-LABAN. The military stared at us — it must have been my necklace (a tear gas mask around my neck!).

The brutal and unchristian manner of dispersal that September day — September 24, 1984 — taught me a lesson, for which I am grateful to the uniformed men.

The military are powerful because they have their Armalites, .38s, .45s, shields, truncheons, tear gas, protective masks, smoke grenades, so on and so forth. Courage comes easy with them because of what they possess.

For my part, I discovered an inner quality I did not know I possessed, the inner spirit of courage without outside, material support. Consequently, I have begun to feel less burdened and to be filled with Christian forgiveness for the uniformed aggressors because I know I have come out the victor.

My determination towards peaceful, nonviolent demonstrations is stronger than ever. I am more resolute in my commitment to help the urban poor, students, families of political prisoners and the elite, in the restoration of our rights and freedom for my country.

A candle stuck into a bamboo tube is a light of tribute to Ninoy Aquino, memorialized with a statue within the year after his death. A street parliamentarian—as protesters against the Marcos regime came to be known— holds the candle during a rally. With the death of Aquino, a fever of protest rose and gripped, not just the predictable activists like students and workers but the middle class and the professionals, a segment of the population frequently inclined to keep the status quo. Not this time, however—and the protest rallies swept major cities and towns of the nation.

NO BULLET CAN KILL THE SPIRIT

Never the scene of rallies before, Ayala Avenue in the country's major financial and business district became the setting of protest marches and meetings. Held on a regular weekly schedule after the Aquino assassination, the protest rallies were invariably announced by a blizzard of yellow confetti from the buildings on Ayala Avenue, above. The protest was thus oddly lighthearted while given to major issues of justice, human rights and the restoration of democracy to the Philippines. Mendiola street in downtown Manila seethes with marchers, right. It is the street which leads to Malacañang, the traditional residence of the president of the Philippines. There, Marcos had entrenched himself for two four-year terms and further tenure through martial law and the complex weaving of support from the military, crony businessmen, a controlled press and wily presidential decrees that had the force of law. When protest marches were held in Mendiola, they were understood as a siege on Malacanang's prime resident.

Cory Aquino speaks during one of the
major rallies of the protest movement,
left. It was held on the anniversary
of the declaration of martial law,
September 21, 1983. Marching with
the people, always with characteristic
serenity, she silently stood as the
symbol of the victims of the Marcos
regime. That was eloquent enough
and, when she had to speak, she simply
said that she had made a promise to
Ninoy Aquino that she would do everything she could to restore democracy in
the Philippines. Her resolve is on the
placard held by a mother who took her
children to a Children's Rally which
was held on Ayala Avenue, above.

With hands lifted, a woman prays the Lord's Prayer during a rally. Against repressive police measures that in the history of rallies after the Aquino assassination resulted in several deaths from gunfire, the protesters turned more and more to prayer rallies instead.

III   The Election Campaign, 1986

Scenario

FRANCISCO S. TATAD

After 20 years in power, Ferdinand Marcos had one proud boast. He believed he alone could run the Philippines. Many, of course, questioned it. The economy was in shambles, political institutions lay in disarray, the communist-led insurgency threatened most of the countryside — what was once democracy's pride in Asia had become a basket case. Events beyond the government's control had brought many of its woes. But poor management was an important cause. And now, upon Aquino's death, the regime faced an unprecedented confidence crisis.

So long as he remained in control of the military, parliament, the courts, the bureaucracy, the electoral process, most of the press, and the agricultural monopolies, and reasonably assured of continued American support, Marcos thought he could survive any crisis. Having won his last six-year term in 1981, he found it absurd that he should be under so much pressure to call elections in 1986. And yet he was.

Pro-Marcos politicians had publicly denounced this pressure, and this had appeared to help. But the issue of ill-gotten wealth suddenly came up in the *San Jose Mercury News*, and was immediately made the basis of an impeachment move against the president by the opposition MPs. The *Batasan* threw out the complaint in less than 24 hours, but the issue remained. Some predicted it would be Marcos' Watergate. President Reagan sent Senator Paul Laxalt, a Republican from Nevada, to Manila for secret conversations; and, not long after, Marcos announced in a satellite TV interview with David Brinkley that he had decided to call a new presidential election. Washington was welcome to send observers, he said. And so was everyone else.

Immediately, he wrote the *Batasan* a letter saying that a vacancy would occur in his office upon the election and assumption of a new President. The *Batasan* then passed the law calling special elections for President and Vice President to be held on February 7, 1986.

This law clearly violated the constitutional requirement that the vacancy should first occur before any such law may be enacted. And many went to the Supreme Court to question it. But most of them realized that although the law was defective, the people wanted an election, and they did not want to prevent it. In the end, the court decided that the issue had become political, and no longer for the justices to decide.

Marcos had earlier calculated that the opposition would field not one, but two separate tickets. And very few doubted it. Efforts to bring together Corazon Aquino, the martyred politician's widow, and Salvador Laurel, the leading presidential aspirant, had come to a dead-end when the then partyless Aquino refused to run under Laurel's UNIDO party as a condition for his giving up his presidential bid and running as her vice president. At the close of working hours on the last day for the filing of candidacies, the opposition had two presidential candidates. Before the midnight deadline struck, however, they forged their unity ticket: Aquino for president, Laurel for vice president.

Ranged against this ticket was Marcos' well-oiled machine. It counted on men, money, the media, a historic vote, and 20 years of presidential experience. Aquino had nothing. No campaign organization worth its name, no campaign manager to the very end, no spokesman until a couple of days before the elections, no personal contact with most of the local leaders, none of Marcos' unlimited resources, no experience. But her husband's brutal murder and the scandalous acquittal of all the accused after a year of farcical trial had made her a symbol to the entire nation.

She spoke in a soft monotone about opening Malacañang to the people rather than about any large issues, and the crowds hung on her every word as though she was reciting the Beatitudes. Men, women, and children marched on foot and stood at the plaza for hours waiting for her to come and speak; flashing the L-sign for *Laban* (her late husband's party, which means fight) with their thumb and forefinger, they swooned and danced and shouted in the streets, "Cory, Cory!" Whole cities overflowed.

The nation was in love, a love affair had swept the nation, and it would transform the self-image of the Filipinos.

Voices

CORAZON C. AQUINO, opposition leader
(From a paper read on 1 October 1985)

If we were to characterize the style of leadership of Mr. Marcos, the phrase that would best describe it is "management by illusion." But the reality is that the regime of Mr. Marcos is finished. No amount of media manipulation or officious bravado can change the reality of our economic and moral desolation. Mr. Marcos faces the classic dilemma that every dictator must eventually reach, he is running out of illusions and of options, and can only continue in power by the use of force or fraud.

We are certain that Mr. Marcos has his back against the wall. Is it possible then to displace him without resorting to the use of violence and thereby triggering the cycles of instability and suppression that his removal seeks to avoid? Those of us who believe in the peaceful processes know that this is a difficult middle ground to take. But we have to hope.

For the sake of our country, we have to hope that a safe passage is possible. I am confident that a peaceful political solution still is possible. I base my confidence principally on four factors: first, the capacity of opposition parties to unite; second, the electoral militancy of the awakened Filipino; third, the moral leadership of the Church; fourth, the reform movement in the military.

I am confident that the opposition will unite under one candidate when the presidential elections are held. For there are more shared values than personal ambition which are deeply felt and will ultimately prevail. I am confident that, as in the 1984 elections, the ordinary citizen will appear in great numbers to support the National Movement for Free Elections and the public school teachers in safeguarding the ballot. I am also confident that political parties and the citizenry will be able to draw support from two important sectors of society—the church and the military. Both have a dominating presence in the countryside, and this is where the insurgency problem is critical, and where sixty per cent of the voters reside. We have reason to hope that both sectors will play their rightful role at the proper time.

VICENTE T. PATERNO, businessman

If somebody else other than Cory had been the candidate, if it had been an old politician, I'm not sure if I would have been as enthusiastic.

On October 1984, I told Jimmy Ongpin that the president we needed was someone who did not want to be president. We needed a person who would not have re-election in his mind. We needed a person who did not have political debts. We needed a person who would do what was needed to be done because he wanted to do it, not because he wanted to be re-elected.

By October or November of 1984, I felt that Cory was the only person who filled my bill.

As early as May 1985, I was telling the people, such as the members of the Board of Trustees of the Makati Business Club when we attended a number of conferences with people who had come from Washington, that Cory was my candidate for president.

In August 1985, when she talked to the business community, I told her: "I do not mean to put any pressure on you but if others are the candidates, I will not help; if you are the candidate I will join." Cory said: "Thank you." At that time people were already urging her to run.

Sometime between June and September 1985, she spoke before the Management Association of the Philippines. Somebody asked her a question about her economic program. She said that she was only a housewife but there were three things that she could tell us: first, the government must be credible to the people; second, we should not spend more than we earn; and third, the government must be honest. She said she was not well versed in economics and that that was a housewife's view of an economic program.

I stood up because I was worried that some KBL types might push and press her on that. I said that I thought that that was a very sound economic philosophy. After the forum, I went up to her and said: "Cory, please don't underestimate yourself." In effect, I was trying to convey to her that she had far more to offer than what she thought she had. And she said: "Well, you have to teach me about economics."

At that time, people were already pushing her to be president. Probably, she was already thinking of what her reaction should be. A few weeks later, she spoke to her sorority and enumerated her conditions — conditions which, I believe, she did not believe would come true. At that time, Cory was the only candidate that I would even consider supporting.

Back in June or July of 1985, there were not too many people who thought she should be seriously considered. She had never presented herself and she underestimated her own capabilities — not only her vote-getting capability but also her personal capability to run the country. I know that she was very sincere in thinking that her conditions were impossible to fulfill.

Cory had several things that swung people towards her. First, her honesty. Second, her dignity. And third, her strength. Here was a person who said something that people could believe. She did not even begin to consider running until the million signatures came forward. Here was a person who consistently did not want to be president. And as Ninoy's widow, she had paid her dues. Unquestionably, here was a person with moral authority. For me, that was something important. Her being a widow was important, not to her winning but to her being a candidate. It was important but it was not crucial to her winning. It was important to her credibility. Here was someone who had suffered under Marcos. And she was credible speaking against Marcos. After she gained entry, her own self began to come out.

JOAQUIN ROCES (CHINO), chairman of the Cory Aquino for President Movement
(From a speech delivered on 15 October 1985)

At the very outset, I should like to emphasize that our gathering here this afternoon could be a great moment in our history. We are here for the purpose of launching the Draft Cory Aquino for President Movement, an event fraught with great significance, great hopes and great expectations.

We are doing so at a time when the nation is torn, anguished, and bleeding, when 54 million Filipinos cry for succor, when our countrymen are fast losing hope that nonviolent means can restore those freedoms.

And somehow they cannot entirely be blamed.

Our traditional political parties largely remain in disarray. The majority of our political leaders continue to bicker. Theirs is a cacophony of voices expended mostly on trivial issues when what the country needs is the healing, inspiring, unifying voice of a revered and respected leader.

After groping for more than two years following the death of Ninoy Aquino, we have no doubt in our minds that Cory Aquino is that leader. There is of course no certainty that she will heed our appeal, that this still sorrowing widow will shed her mother's garments for the battle tunic of a political warrior.

But because Cory Aquino is our only hope, our movement is worth launching.

And it is worth launching for the following reasons:

First, Cory incarnates the Aquino legacy. This is the legacy of blood, courage, integrity, and martyrdom that Ninoy Aquino bequeathed to the Philippines at high noon on a lonely tarmac, August 21, 1983, at the Manila International Airport. Also in the slipstream of this legacy is the blood shed by all Filipinos who have died in defense of their freedoms since martial rule fell on the Philippines in 1972.

Second, only Cory can bind the factional wounds of the opposition, persuade it to close ranks, bestir it to march for the country, and rouse the Filipino people to feats of dignity, honor, and courage. Foremost of these is the immediate task to snatch the nation from the brink of the precipice.

Third, Cory's moral stature is such that even the ranks of Ferdinand Marcos' authoritarian regime harbor many people — among them men of valor in the armed forces — who would recoil from desecrating and brutalizing the elections if she were a candidate.

Fourth, Cory Aquino can certainly bring to the government the best minds that the nation can offer in terms of dedication, sincerity, and integrity, talent and patriotism.

We have all to link arms and expand our ranks till the entire country is bound together with the strength and the ardor of our resolve.

· I do not exaggerate when I say this could be our last chance to save democracy in the Philippines. The darkness thickens and we have to move.

To Cory, we therefore pledge to persevere in this crusade to gather the signatures of one million Filipinos. This would mark the first time in our history that a presidential candidate would be drafted by the Filipino people.

To Ninoy, we pledge that the fight not only continues but rages on, and will continue to rage till the Filipino people themselves bring back to life everything noble that he stood for.

To the nation, we pledge our honor and sincerity of purpose.

VIC SISON, Secretary-General of the Cory Aquino for President Movement

About a week after the launching of the Cory Aquino for President Movement, Cory was invited by the Sigma Delta Phi Alumni Sorority at the Century Park Sheraton as guest speaker at their luncheon. She talked about widowhood, motherhood, and grandmotherhood.

In the open forum, the first question was, "Cory, when will you finally tell us if you will run for President or not?" And she answered: "I have two conditions before giving my answer. First, if Mr. Marcos calls for snap elections, which he probably won't, anyway; and second, if Mr. Vic Sison, who is I think sitting there, can produce the million signatures that they promised." That was exactly how she put it. And she said: "I consider these two conditions as joint conditions, not one or the other." There was a tremendous roar. People sitting at the table with me said that my blood pressure must have dropped a hundred points.

That scared me. We were just starting and here she makes it a condition. Anyway, that in itself gave us a boost. It became a challenge not only to us but also to all the people who heard and read about it.

At that point, I didn't know if it was finally an endorsement from her or if she was just saying it wouldn't happen anyway — Marcos won't call the snap elections or you won't have the million signatures. It was significant that she made it a joint condition because that made it harder to achieve.

FRANCISCO RODRIGO (SOC), opposition leader

I never expected Cory to be a candidate. Butz was the Aquino whose name came up as a possible candidate, not Cory. The Convenor Group came up with a list: Jose Diokno, Jovito Salonga, Eva Kalaw, and Doy Laurel.

We put up the National Unification Council to unify all the opposition groups: UNIDO, PDP-LABAN, Panaghiusa, and the other groups. Doy Laurel led it at first. When he indicated an interest in running, he resigned. He recommended Celing Muñoz Palma to replace him. I was elected vice chairman.

We called a big convention at Valle Verde Country Club; the whole country was represented. We drew up plans to organize from the grassroots and we named leaders for each province. We began but it was slow going. People were getting impatient.

Then the Convenor Group surfaced. They proposed a shortcut just in case there would be snap elections. They put up a list, but Cory was not among them.

The front-runners at the time were Laurel, Salonga, and Kalaw. But the feedback was that we would have trouble winning with Laurel. The other two would also have problems getting the sort of popular support we needed. People began to think: only Cory can do it.

She was reluctant. She imposed two conditions: one, that she would run only in snap elections, and two, that one million signatures be collected. We all thought that these were impossible conditions. Nobody was seriously thinking of snap elections. We were thinking in terms of 1987.

Then Chino Roces came up with one million signatures.

Then Marcos called the snap elections.

I was vice chairman of the NUC. I became chairman through that famous shouting incident. In fairness to Doy Laurel, the newspapers exaggerated the incident. He raised his voice, but he did not shout. He learned that Celing Muñoz Palma was becoming part of the draft-Cory movement. He lost his temper. Celing resigned. I took over. The NUC then made me the mediator between the contenders: Doy, Jovy, Eva, and now Cory.

I talked to Jovy Salonga first. Jovy is very easy to talk to; he said that he would readily give way to Cory if she would run, but otherwise he would reserve his party's right to field a candidate.

Then I talked to Eva Kalaw. She was harder to deal with. I told her: "Time is of the essence. I'll tell you the truth: the feedback we receive indicates that in the minds of the people there are only two candidates—Cory and Doy. Why don't you make a graceful exit? People will even praise you for your sacrifice." She said: "I have my party to answer to. I have worked hard for this." Finally she said: "Whatever Doy and Cory decide, we will abide by."

So I began to talk only to Cory and Doy. When I began, the one million signatures had not yet been collected.

I told Cory: "What's going on? Will you be a candidate or not?" She said: "I do not want it. If it were only me involved I would refuse. Four of my children are against it. Only Kris is for it. I feel that this is a cross for me; it is very heavy, but I cannot drop it."

Even if the one million signatures were not in, I knew that it was just a matter of time before Chino brought them in.

I was going back and forth. I had to be frank with both of them. I told Doy: "I don't understand it. You're a nice fellow, one of the easiest people to deal with. But the public perception of you is that you are abrasive and brusque. It will be hard to win with you."

The shouting incident with Celing Palma only made things worse. The people around him told him that it was nothing, that people would soon forget it. "No," I said: "Let's not lie to ourselves here. That was a big setback. Doy, it's Celing's birthday three days from now. Go to her and wear rags." He went and he apologized.

I went to Cory next. Her advisers were adamantly against any team-up with Doy. "Cory," I told her: "What's our alternative? If we have both of you run for president, we're finished." Some of those around her said that there was a chance for a victory even if the two of them did run separately. I said: "Look, if there are two of you running, even if you win, you will be cheated massively and your loss will look credible before the eyes of the people and the eyes of the world. And the people will blame both of you. Of course, Marcos will win if the two of you run. This is my conviction: Marcos will under no circumstances allow himself to lose these elections — not for lust for power, but because of fear of retribution. And not just Marcos — the people around him, the cronies, the generals — they have too much to lose."

I told Cory: "I must warn you: the memory of Ninoy will be dragged into this campaign and be desecrated. If Marcos wins, it will look as if the people had rejected Ninoy."

Cory said: "Now I'm beginning to have doubts about you." That was only natural. When I took the job of mediator I expected to come under suspicion from both sides. It's hard being caught in the middle.

AURORA A. AQUINO, mother of Benigno S. Aquino, Jr. (Ninoy)

In the beginning, I went to Cory and said: "Cory, I have been hearing that they will make you the candidate of the opposition. Did you agree?" And she said: "No, Mommy, I know what politics is. After the rallies, we could come home and sleep well. But if I'm president, my goodness, there will be so many problems. And as Ninoy said, the one who will take over after Marcos will have a big, big problem. So I know what politics is."

She had been exposed to all this for 29 years; so she must know. So I went home rather happy. But then I read in the newspapers that she was cornered by the ladies. "If there were snap elections and if there were a million signatures endorsing me, I would consider," she said. And so I went to her that morning after I went to Mass and said: "Cory, what's this in the papers?" She said: "Yes, Mommy. But don't worry, Marcos says there will be no snap elections. And the one million signatures, ah, it won't come about. Many are very vocal against the Administration, but when it comes to signing, they are afraid to sign. So do not worry about that." But then Chino Roces kept calling us: "They're rising, rising, the signatures…"

And when the snap elections were announced, I asked Cory: "What is this? It seems to me that they are really asking you to run." She said: "That's it. It's ringing in my ears, what Ninoy said: 'If during my lifetime I could have done something, and didn't do it' … it's ringing in my ears. And besides, I have been telling the people: Be involved, be involved. And now that they ask me to be involved, what shall I say now?"

So I told her: "Well, if you decide, it's a big jump. What I know is that they might eliminate you, my daughter. I don't want any more sacrifices. Why, are we the only Filipinos to make sacrifices? Why Ninoy?" She said: "Don't worry, Mommy. That probably won't happen." "Anyhow," I said: "If you decide, remember I am behind you one hundred per cent. Perhaps that's what Ninoy would like. Let's pray about it." And so she went to the Pink Sisters. It was not my recommendation. It was, I think, her own desire to get more light. I knew about it; she decided, but did not want anybody to know about it.

I think it was Father Arevalo who suggested that she should go to the Pink Sisters. She stayed one whole day; they gave her a room. Afterwards I asked her: "How was your recollection?" She said: "Very good, Mommy. You know, when I was praying there, I asked the Lord to forgive Marcos, to forgive Ver, so that I could forgive them, too. I asked only for forgiveness."

When she decided to pray, her mind became very clear. It was so clear that she said: "I have nothing to give to the people except my sincerity, my determination to really clean the government. If we can clean it up, that is what we must do." I said: "How, my daughter?" She said: "Perhaps that is the only thing they would believe from me. I might sound like a politician, promising this, promising that. I don't want to promise what I cannot do. What I will tell them is that I have been a victim of this regime." She said this so clearly, so well and she was very logical.

She said that her strength would be in prayers, in closeness to God. She said: "The people will believe me, Mommy. I am a victim; we are victims of this regime. We have suffered a lot. I can say that I am with them in their sufferings. My sincerity will be real and will make people free from fear. We have not lost our freedom from fear, freedom from hunger, freedom from all of these lies they give us."

I told her: "My daughter, you have our one hundred per cent support. Although I fear for your life, we will pray, because as you say you are ready for any eventuality." That was it.

Before this happened, Cardinal Sin told me: "Don't cry; just let the plan of God go on." I said: "How do we know the plan of God?" "You pray. We pray. Let us pray," said the Cardinal. "Aurora, if Cory wins, it would be the greatest humiliation of Marcos. Imagine, a housewife, not a politician at all, winning over him. That would be the greatest vindication of Ninoy."

I think Cory was conscious that she might lose the elections because of the odds — facing the guns, the goons, and the gold. How could we win? I always told her. How could we win? They would use massive cheating, vote-buying. Cory said: "But let's see what we can do, Mommy. We can expose things and make sure people know what is happening in the country." I think that is what pushed her on. And when she saw the difficulties — many people being "salvaged" — nothing could hold her back.

JAIME CARDINAL SIN, Archbishop of Manila

Cory said to me: "Cardinal, Ninoy is inspiring me. It seems that he is talking to me, telling me that I should run."

"When did you have that inspiration?" I asked.

"When I was praying at the Pink Sisters' Convent in Hemady."

"All right," I said. "Pray more. It is not a joke to go against Marcos."

One day, she came here and said: "All right, I will run. I have decided. My decision was made on December 8." That was the closing day of the Marian Year. She was on a retreat at the Pink Sisters Convent. "I am now sure to run. It is God's will," she said.

"All right, kneel down," I said. "I will bless you. You are going to be president. You are the Joan of Arc." At that moment I thought God answered the prayers of our people. He chooses weaklings. And why weaklings? Why a weak woman? We have never been gifted with a president who is a woman. That is how the Lord confounds the strong. When Our Lady appeared in Lourdes, she appeared to a girl who was weak. And in Fatima she appeared to three children.

"This is what will happen. And you will win. We'll see the hand of God, one miracle after another. God bless you," I said to Cory.

I was sure of it because God could not refuse the prayers of the people, the fasting, the crying. All day long, we were praying, day in and day out. Children, old people. How could God refuse our prayers?

NENI STA. ROMANA-CRUZ, journalist

At the first meeting of Cory's Crusaders, obviously overwhelmed by an attendance that filled the building cafeteria of the Mondragon Building to SRO capacity, with many others left to linger by the doorway, Cory thanked the audience: "Because of your show of support today, I will have fewer sleepless nights."

The night before had been such a night, but her wakefulness had produced a short and simple campaign jingle which she herself had thought of, to the tune of *Leron, Leron Sinta* (a popular folk song). Announcing that she was no singer like Imelda Marcos, she went on just the same to test it out on her friends who, like children, immediately joined in.

VIC SISON

I saw the growth of the support of the people for Cory from almost nothing, from fear to absolute courage. In Cebu, the drive from Mactan Airport to Cebu City normally takes 20 minutes of easy driving, with or without traffic. It's quite a long drive. You go through the whole island, cross the bridge and pass through several towns first before reaching Cebu City. Can you imagine that whole stretch lined up with people, at least from one abreast to perhaps thirty deep on both sides? The open jeep Cory was riding on could not move anymore. The jeep got as far as four kilometers and then conked out. It had taken two and a half hours to cover four kilometers running at probably an inch per minute.

On our way to Cardinal Vidal's house, I was in the coaster with Cory and I kidded her: "Cory, perhaps you should ask the Cardinal to forgive all of his people here in Cebu." "Why?" she asked. "They are beginning to commit the sin of idolatry." She just laughed.

FERDINAND E. MARCOS, President of the Philippines

What qualifications does she have except that her husband was killed?... She always stands up and asks for pity, making believe that there was no reason for her husband's arrest.

GLORY CHANCO, wife and mother

Our son Jeffrey's admiration for Cory began when Ninoy was assassinated. He asked me to buy yellow Ninoy ribbons, flags, t-shirts and visors. And when the election campaign began, he also collected Cory-Doy paraphernalia. Everytime he wore his Cory-Doy t-shirt, he covered it with the numerous pins and stickers he bought with his own allowance.

One day, the ladies of Cory's Crusaders visited the Benedictine Abbey School, where Jeffrey studies. That evening, Jeffrey went home complaining that he was very hungry. His younger brother Bryan said that they donated their lunch money to Cory's Crusaders. Then I asked Bryan: "How come you are not as hungry as your brother?" The child smiled at me and said: "Because after I donated my lunch money, I borrowed money from my teacher."

YOLANDA L. LACUESTA, bank employee

I lost all my savings. During the campaign, I bought so many pins, t-shirts and stickers, not only for myself but also for my friends. I think I ended up supplying my whole neighborhood with campaign materials.

SYLVIA MAYUGA, journalist

Yellow was the color of this longing and this warmth, yellow like the ribbons tied around old trees, not oak but mango, acacia, and *banaba* standing along Ninoy Aquino's homecoming route, yellow like the sun and stars of the Philippine flag vanished in the black of mourning, always that black of mourning, where Marcos and the military ruled in viselike grip.

In this campaign, Cory always wore yellow, radiant Child of the Sun returning to the Land of Morning and yellow the towels and dishcloths,

umbrellas, dried leaves, raincoats, fans the people waved back at her in a rising tide like light as they waved the L-sign — for *Laban*! Fight! — against the black of mourning that had claimed the red, white, and blue of the Philippine flag for its own.

Red, white, and blue were the ribbons tied to Armalites and AK-47's that threatened frightened oppositionist voters with death if they did not stay home on Election Day. Red, white, and blue those t-shirts saying *Marcos Pa Rin* (Still Marcos) tied banditlike around the faces of armed goons snatching, running away with ballot boxes all over the country.

CONSUELO LOVERIA, government employee

Civil servants like me have not been given the proper chance to lead dignified lives. We have not been given salary increases and our supervisors are mean to us.

We were told to vote for Marcos. But most of us were for Cory. I was unhappy when I could not campaign for Cory, since civil servants were prohibited from campaigning. Nonetheless, I campaigned secretly with my mother's circle of friends. We went around telling people to vote for Cory. We felt she was the only one who could save the country.

ANTONIO MAPA, shipping executive

My wife Marilyn and I were out of the country when Marcos was needled by a panel of American TV anchormen into announcing the snap elections. We had our first glimpse of the reach of people power after a Sunday Mass in Los Angeles when we were met outside the church by volunteers soliciting signatures for Cory Aquino.

The Marian Year was about to end when we returned home; we prayed that the opposition would be able to unite and come up with the candidate who had the best chance of beating Marcos. We were sure we were united in our prayers with millions of other Filipinos because shortly after the feast of the Immaculate Conception, the dream ticket of Cory and Doy was finalized. Christmas came and went quite fast as the nation eagerly looked forward to the bright prospects that the New Year could bring.

The willingness and the readiness of ordinary, private citizens to be involved in the coming elections quickly showed itself when Marilyn and other housewives from our village volunteered as UNIDO inspectors and watchers.

In between Registration and Election Day, Marilyn joined the Cory Aquino for President Movement in Makati, and did volunteer work at the office, sorting out and handling campaign materials as well as selling various elections paraphernalia, often on Ayala Avenue. Once her group was intimidated and threatened by KBL volunteers, only to find scores of office people from the nearby buildings immediately come to their rescue.

We spent evenings working on voters' lists, pasting campaign posters and attending seminars on polling duties in outlying barangays. We asked our children to make car stickers, specially worded and meant to keep political agitation at a high level. Using campaign contributions, we eventually came out with a properly printed car sticker that read: "Cory a Bright Hope; Marcos a Proven Failure" to focus on what we thought the election was all about.

We joined opposition rallies in Antipolo, Muntinglupa, Makati and the *miting de avance* in Luneta. Judging from the enthusiasm and mood of the huge crowds, we were convinced that Cory and Doy couldn't lose. On the other hand, we saw KBL motorcades in Makati and Pasay being laughed at, jeered, or scorned by onlookers, pedestrians, sidewalk habitues, and bus riders. We didn't see how Marcos could win. A hapless bank employee inside an air-conditioned bus flashed several new bank bills to show that they were being paid and herded to attend the KBL rally, while a Makati traffic cop furtively waved us through traffic using the *Laban* sign.

PORFIRIO P. CASAPAO

His hair bleached from constant exposure to the unmerciful sun, his face wrinkled, a toothless grin from ear to ear adorning his face, he waited patiently by the roadside for a glimpse of his hope for deliverance from endless toil.

He came empty-handed, no banner, no pin, not even a wisp of a ribbon, a few pesos in his pocket reserved for the long tricycle ride to his barangay several kilometers away.

Sensing that he somehow looked out of place in the yellow sea of decorations, he scrounged around for anything yellow. He was able to get some yellow banana leaves. He waved them proudly. He was happy.

To him, the yellow leaves are an expression of long-repressed feelings. Now, he can face the mysterious men that visit his barangay in the dead of night to convince him that all is lost and their way is the only way.

He will tell them that there is hope, that this lady in yellow offers a better alternative to their idea. Also perhaps he will finally know whatever happened to his son, missing for the last three years because his son was more vocal than the rest of the barrio folk.

At last, the white coaster passed, the bespectacled lady waving at him. Just a glimpse, but it was enough. The sun had already set, he would probably miss his ride back home, but no matter, he would walk knowing that, after a long, long night, dawn will come.

Mr. Marcos should not be afraid of the suburban elite, nor the nuns and priests, nor the students. He should be afraid of this man. For if he feels that he has been cheated of his last remaining hope, the same gnarled hands that held the yellow leaves would be holding something else.

AURORA A. AQUINO

During the election campaign, Cory and I agreed that I should go to the places to which she could not go. She only went to the big towns, big cities, and made whistle stops in the little towns. I went to the small towns.

Headquarters told me, for example: "Mama, you go to Zamboanga." The last one was: "Mama, you have to go to Sorsogon, because Cory cannot go there. Go with Celia Laurel." So I went to Sorsogon, and a beautiful thing happened. I was getting down from the stage and I fell. I was wearing low-heeled slippers, and they flew. If I had been in heels, the heels would have caught. But I slid and someone caught me at the foot of the stairs, high off the ground.

When I went home, I realized that I could have been crippled. At this age, 76, my bones are brittle, and it would be hard for me to heal. And I said: "Oh goodness, thank God," and I shuddered at the thought that I could have been crippled — possibly for life. I had a sister who died when she fell, she never got up. And so I prayed for the man who caught me. I said: "Lord, he needs You." He was one of the leaders; perhaps he needed prayers. I was so grateful.

And then later I saw the man who saved me. "If it hadn't been for you, I would have been crippled," I said. "Yes, ma'am," he answered. "When the rally was over, my body hurt." I had never thought of that.

We have to be broken in order to serve the people. We are broken because the Lord broke the bread and gave it to us in communion. This is the way to be broken; we have to attend the needs of others whom we might be able to help.

JOB S. DE JESUS

My brother Jeremias S. de Jesus was the PDP-LABAN campaign chairman for Capas, Tarlac. Memeng, as he was fondly called, was gunned down together with his driver, Alberto Briones, by men from the Civilian Home Defense Force. The killers cut off Memeng's thumb and forefinger — the fingers used to make the *Laban* L sign—as a warning to other LABAN supporters.

Memeng was so effective as a campaign manager that the KBL had to send an emissary to warn him. He was offered a big sum of money by the ruling party and was given up to January 12 to stop campaigning. But Memeng was a man of principle, a man of integrity and honesty. He refused the tempting offer, shrugged off the death threats, worked even harder for the Cory-Doy ticket. And so, true to their word, Memeng was killed on January 15—exactly three days after his ultimatum ran out.

GEMINO ABAD, poet

On January 18, we put up this "Tent City" in Ugarte Field. There, we fasted and prayed in anticipation of the coming elections. Some of us stayed overnight. The size of the crowd varied, from ten or twenty to a large crowd whenever the office workers could join us—which was usually around noon. We recited the Rosary and did private prayers.

We derived much of our support from the poor and their people power. Without them and AKKAP-KA, a foundation for nonviolence, Tent City would have folded up. They were the ones who stayed during the night. They took care of security.

Even though some of us chafed at times, there was still a constant atmosphere of prayer and re-collection. This was primarily due to the nuns. They took care of the liturgy and of organizing prayer groups. There were so many of them there.

This was one Filipino gathering without food. A Filipino gathering for prayer or the Mass is ordinary, but a Filipino gathering without food is unusual. And it went on from January 18 to March 21.

We did have a bit of trouble. Some people were to set up their own tents in Ugarte. They began passing out anti-Cory leaflets. We invited them over but they always refused. It was a little tense for a while, but fortunately, nothing happened.

During the campaign, we felt sure that God would take a hand. That was why we felt so strongly about fasting and prayer. As Cardinal Sin said, this was a battle between good and evil, as simple as that—so we kept on.

RENE A. OCAMPO, S.J., Superior of Jesuit Juniors and Philosophers

What struck me most about the campaign was Cory's sheer energy as she tried to cover all the provinces. Although the crony press gave her very limited space and time, the coverage of the "alternative" press was extensive enough to give readers a sense of the response Cory received in the provinces.

Certainly, the reception in Davao City was the first of its kind. The coalesced opposition was able to work together and prepare for that rally—the biggest ever staged in Davao.

JUN ZAMORA, hospital employee

I had just gotten a new job in a hospital in Davao. I was very conscious about absences because I was still on probation. Luckily, we were given two days off when Cory arrived in Davao to campaign. My friends and I grouped together to make placards and confetti and we went around Toril and MacArthur Highway. We led the march.

We all listened very attentively to Cory as she delivered her speech in the main plaza. Suddenly there was panic in the crowd. People were pushing and shoving. I tried hard to keep Cory in sight, as security men surrounded her. We later found out that the commotion was caused by a little boy who, in his eagerness to get a closer look at President Aquino, fell from a banana tree.

MARGARITA COJUANGCO (TINGTING), opposition leader

I was not part of Cory's entourage. (I was with her in Zamboanga, Basilan, Lanao and Cotabato because these were the regions of which I was in charge.) The areas I went to were generally not peaceful. They tried to harass me directly in TawiTawi. The Governor arranged for some kind of rally while we were in the municipal hall. He thought we represented NAMFREL.

It was a misconstrued rally that nonetheless turned out to be quite noisy. The situation grew tense. There were soldiers in the capitol and resistant COMELEC people.

I don't run scared easily. When it's time to die, it's time to die. I joined the cause knowing what the consequences are—harassment, even death, but I had to take the chance.

CORAZON C. AQUINO, presidential candidate

After Mindanao, I came back and told my children: "We have won." I had never seen such crowds before. People were waiting for me. They were not just waiting and listening, but also contributing whatever little money they had.

After I got back from the Visayas, I was so confident. I just couldn't believe how I could still lose. At every airport where I stopped, there were such huge crowds. I said to myself: "Here we go again, pushing and shoving." I had about ten security people, but they were hardly enough.

I don't know why the crowd kept touching me. Lupita told me she saw the same thing before with Nora Aunor. It is something in Filipino culture —the need to touch. They were touching me. It was getting to be too much. Sometimes I didn't even feel it when there was a huge crowd around me. I felt that we would win by a landslide.

Of course, I changed. It is impossible not to change. I think the confidence of the people did it. I told my children: "The people will fight for me." I was so convinced of that. I did not have a political party, although members of the *Batasan* were there throughout the campaign. Many of them told me when I thanked them after a meeting, "We cannot take credit for this, we just announced that you will be here." Before, crowds had to be paid to come to rallies. But how could we pay the crowds when we had no money? There were so many of them. Once, Jimmy Ferrer told me: "Cory, you are bringing the crowds in." How could I not be confident?

SYLVIA MAYUGA

That campaign could only be a study in sharp contrast to delight any newcomer to the Philippines. Marcos, a sick old man, often had to be carried by bodyguards through the crowd, subtly heaved up the rally stage. The rumor mill went wild about his aging kidneys.

Weak kidneys or no, Marcos proceeded to recapture the extravagant campaign style of his yesteryears. He promised astronomical sums of civic improvements, bared fangs at the communists, promised land titles to property the government did not own. The alternative press mixed all its metaphors with eager accounts of truckloads of goons, local officials, government employees in brand-new Marcos t-shirts, pocketing crisp bills and being ferried to Marcos rallies on army trucks. Goodies flowed in the KBL (Kilusang Bagong Lipunan, Marcos' party) camp, in clear violation of Marcos' own Electoral Code.

Most of these rallies took place under control —the military likes to call it "sanitized"— conditions, heavily secured, awash with neat placards bearing identical letterings of slogans of trust, faith, and adulation for a continuation of Marcos in the partnership with the "oppositionist" Tolentino (who had ended many years of public respect for his brilliant legal mind by consenting to run with a man he had roundly criticized on so many occasions in the past). Coverage on the four government-owned TV channels was long and lingering, if selective in its angles, panning only over thickly populated segments of the audience but unavoidably passing over bored and inattentive faces inured to the Marcos monotone.

Meanwhile, despite an inch-by-inch struggle for equal TV time, no media stranglehold by the government could hide the fact that when a radiant Aquino and a grinning Laurel hit the campaign trail, they were met by exuberant, chanting crowds whose volume surprised both Cory and Doy. Gradually, the people themselves were proving to a once hesitant Cory that Marcos could do nothing to keep their tide from engulfing his throne.

CECILIA MUÑOZ PALMA, member of parliament

During the campaign, what struck us was the response of the people. Wherever we went, people lined up in the streets chanting "Cory, Cory." It was almost like hero worship. The campaign tours lasted beyond our schedule. Cory and Doy sometimes arrived hours late, but people stayed to wait for them. That's the beautiful part of it. The people did not leave. In Quezon City, it was almost midnight and it was raining cats and dogs. The people said: "Nobody should leave." Nobody left until she arrived at about midnight.

The crowds were very spontaneous; they said: "We were not paid to come and see you."

Some people came to see Cory because they did not see her on TV. It was the only way they could see her. But there were meetings of the opposition where she could not be present and the crowds still came. They wanted to know from us how Cory would respond to the attacks of Marcos about her being a communist and being incompetent.

CORAZON C. AQUINO
(From a speech delivered on 6 January 1986)

Some who support my candidacy say that if I am elected my role will be that of Mother of the Nation. I am honored by the title, but I am campaigning to be president of our country. It is in that capacity that I shall serve. And as president, I assure you, I shall lead. If elected I will remain a mother to my children, but I intend to be Chief Executive of this nation. And for the male chauvinists in the audience, I intend as well to be the Commander-in-Chief of the Armed Forces of the Philippines.

GRACIA M. CARIÑO, wife and mother
(From a letter written February 5, 1986)

Why this allowance, why this lack of discomfort that a woman is doing the fighting for the Filipino men? More than this, Cory is most credible in her fighting stance—credible both to men and to women.

Why so? Perhaps it is because the Filipino women have always and frequently done the fighting for their men. The Filipino mother fights for her son, the Filipino wife fights for her husband. We take up the cudgels. We sail to the unpleasant duty. It is not that the Filipino man is less of a man for this—it is just that the Filipino woman is a darn good fighter. Believe me.

I have always told you that Filipino women run everything, but we have always done it in guerrilla fashion—hidden, unacclaimed, but strong. I was worried that Cory would let out that secret and men would resent it and so would the women. It seems not so.

The children and the young people—how well and enthusiastically they take to Cory, just as they take to their mothers leading the fight. The most moving thing that my young son said when he first saw Cory in triumph while campaigning was: "Mom, she looks just like you!" But, of course! Cory looks and sounds like the quintessential mother, especially when—in her campaign slogan—she says: "Tama na, sobra na! That is too much." She sounds like all mothers who are just up to here with her children's rowdiness. But of course, in this political campaign she is saying Stop to more than rowdiness. It is only as it should be: the mothers take on causes, fights, and campaigns.

From Mindanao, Cory tells an anecdote. Two women with children came to her and said: "Cory, we have to vote for you. Our children wouldn't leave us alone." And the children were four and five years old.

It is most exciting to be alive at this time in Philippine history. Whatever the ballot count shows, the victory has happened. People are involved. Youth is involved. We have found our voices and we are saying: "Tama na, sobra na." That is too much. We are saying: No more lies, no more dissembling, no more hoodwinking.

Through Cory, we have found expression for all our wishes and desires and values. My husband asks me why I go to rally after rally. It isn't the speeches that I want to hear. It is the spirit that I seek. I want to be part of the hope and the reaching out for sincerity, for honesty, for truth. I want to be part of the jubilation because we have at last a spokesperson, a rallying point, a champion. I want to be counted. I want to be part of the protest as much as I want to be part of the affirmation.

ANTONIO MAPA

The weekend before elections, I flew south to campaign among the workers and personnel of our farms in Negros. In the past elections, they had always been "instructed" to vote for Administration candidates, and were expecting to be similarly "instructed" this time.

We told them they were free to vote for whomever they wished, but we asked them to listen to our campaign. In one large field, I anxiously waited as more than 160 laborers emerged from the tall cane stalks and gathered to hear my plea. I was deeply moved when, at the end of my short speech, an elderly worker stood up to say how greatly pleased they were to learn that the owners had come to ask them—instead of ordering them—to vote for the same candidate they had set their hearts on. In the past, these people simply nodded obediently or passively to similar exhortations. This time, they responded with outright cheers, jubilation, and emphatic *Laban* signs—and they were a good 600 kilometers away from the influence of Makati.

Heading further south, I could only shake my head in admiration for the Cory-Doy posters that practically every house displayed all throughout the 120-kilometer stretch of scenic road that runs down the eastern coastline of Negros. Enthusiastically outstretched arms flashed the familiar *Laban* sign when our Cory-Doy banner caught the attention of folk by the roadside, as well as drivers, passengers, and roof-riders of oncoming vehicles. Even fishermen 160 yards out at sea frantically waved their hands at us. That evening, during a rally, schoolteachers, farm accountants, tractor drivers—some very eloquently, others forcefully, and still others pleading in near tears—were telling their rapt listeners to realize that selling their votes for a measly two to three days of temporary "happiness" would lead to another six years of tyranny, ruin, and suffering. While Metro Manila had its "Peso for Cory" people's contribution, Poblacion Palanas in Bais also had its own "Centavos for Cory" and it was a truly moving experience to see these plain, small town folk eagerly reach out to drop their few centavos into bamboo containers being passed around. I couldn't see then how Cory and Doy would lose.

CORAZON C. AQUINO
(From a speech delivered on 3 February 1986)

I say to Mr. Marcos what Moses said to the cruel, enslaving Pharaoh—Let our people go! The nation has awakened. I, like millions of Filipinos, look on this awakening as the dawning of a new day.

Less than two months ago, I said yes to a million signatures that asked me to run; the people power phenomenon began and rallied around the widow of Ninoy.

The people are crying for change. Volunteers have bravely come forth in battalions. Even the poorest have offered gestures of support. And the women! They have cast caution to the winds to campaign and lead in the people's crusade. They are determined to prove that people power is mightier than all the men and money of the crumbling dictatorship.

I have crisscrossed the length and breadth of the nation. I have traveled by air, by plane and by helicopter; I have traveled by land.

I have seen the devastation wrought by a policy built on a mountain of lies.

I have seen the broken bodies of men, women, and children buried under promises of peace and progress. I have heard the anguished voices of the victims of injustice answered only by hypocritical pledges of retribution.

I have been kissed by the poorest of the poor, and have felt the warmth of their tears on my cheeks. I have been emboldened by the eager embrace of throngs determined to put an end to this regime.

I have heard them shout that I must win. I have been electrified by their every cry for freedom, and inspired by their every clasp of hope.

I cannot shut my ears to them. I cannot turn my back on them.

PABLO A. TEOCO, JR., student

A few days before the elections, when the atmosphere was filled with tension, my friends called me up for a meeting at the Shoemart Center in Quezon City. They told me that they would bring "important papers." These turned out to be campaign leaflets carrying anti-Marcos articles. They got these materials from a member of the ALMA (Association of Lawyers for Mrs. Aquino). Upon our arrival, we immediately and secretly distributed the leaflets. I was surprised by the overwhelming response of the crowd. They accepted them with enthusiasm. In fact, most of them asked for more copies. Some expressed deep apprehension and warned us: "You might be caught." Little did we know that the guards had been alerted about this. One of them approached us and confiscated the materials. We had to explain that we had every right to distribute them. People were watching but could hardly do anything. They just had to wait and see. The security guard, irked by the shoppers' cold stares and murmurs, was forced to return our leaflets on condition that we vacate the premises. Instead of heeding his advice, we continued to distribute the remaining copies and then went to see a movie.

CORAZON C. AQUINO
(From a speech delivered on 4 February 1986)

When the organizers asked me where I wanted to hold the final rally, I told them: "Luneta." One organizer looked at me and asked: "Do you think we can fill up Luneta?" I answered: "Who were the first to be awakened when Ninoy was killed? Weren't the people of Manila the first to awaken?

They were the ones who stood up and said that they were ready to fight." So I am grateful to all of you. I did not make a mistake when I chose Luneta for the final rally. I know that you love me.

Tonight, I want to share with you what I feel in my heart. I am overwhelmed by happiness. I am sure that we will win the elections.

During the one and a half months of campaigning in almost all the provinces of our nation, before all kinds of people and groups, I saw, I witnessed, I felt that we have won. Freedom is as close as the coming dawn. And not only Cory and Doy will win. All of us, the whole Filipino nation, will win.

Now, about courage: From Ninoy's arrest and incarceration to his assassination, I was able to bear all the Lord's heavy trials. If I had been less courageous perhaps I wouldn't be facing you now. I was able to face the trials in my life. I will be able to face the challenges of our nation's presidency.

We have nothing to fear. We only have to fight the darkness that envelops our nation. The road to recovery is not going to be easy or quick. All of us will have to make sacrifices than I myself am prepared to offer.

Let us join hands and, together, let us help one another so that we can rebuild from the ruins Mr. Marcos has left us.

On February 7, our liberation will begin. There are three emotions that are intense and contagious. The first emotion is love. If this emotion were not intense and contagious, we wouldn't have this many people on earth. The second is fear. Mr. Marcos knows that this emotion is really contagious, thus he terrorizes endlessly. I think that he cannot terrorize us anymore. The third is courage. We must infect each other with courage and strength of will, on February 7 and, if necessary, on the days to follow. I recall the lyrics of a song: "Fear is all in the mind." My courage and strength will come from Ninoy and from all of you. And I am so grateful if I am able to help you become more courageous and strong-willed. Opportunities like this are rare in the history of nations.

We must stand up against Mr. Marcos. We must all commit ourselves. We have an opportunity to create history. We have to decide now. We have nothing to lose but the chains that have bound us for so long. We must be able to tell our children when we grow old, when we talk about these historic times, that we did what we had to do, we responded to the call of the times, we faced the challenge to fight for our future. We staked our lives for a noble cause—a free tomorrow.

GRACIA M. CARIÑO

Cory! everyone calls her by her nickname. And yet she is a princess. If there is a Filipino princess, she is one. (The same breed as that lady we saw in the demonstration, the lady in her London Fog raincoat and Christian Dior umbrella and a folding chair to sit upon while she waited in the rain for the rally to begin.) If you look at Cory's bio-data, she stayed here long enough for grade school, then she was shipped to the US— Ravenhill and Notre Dame for her high school and Mount St. Vincent for college. I know the caliber only of Mount St. Vincent, but the rest must have been good convent schools, too. Filipino aristocracy has a way of knowing the best schools in the US and Europe at that time.

Last Thursday, I listened to her speech before a packed room of Rotarians. Her American accent was never more obvious—but it is a clean precise accent, very convent school. Providence has shaped her and given her this fine education because she is to be a leader of her people. Did those nuns realize that the little Asian girl they were teaching would one day galvanize her whole country to hope again? I believe in God's providence: see how well prepared Cory is for this mantle of leadership.

Ever since she was thrown into public life by the assassination of her husband, I have listened to every major speech she gave. Correction: every major remark of thanks and appreciation in the recent two plus years. But this time, she actually makes speeches. She has such power and authority, while remaining low-key and even monotonous at times. It is as if overnight she had been transformed—I know she has changed.

There is a tangible strength to her and it is seen in the way she walks, the way she talks. No more the martyr-widow, no more the private person forced to hide her grief and pain. She is herself now—strong, authoritative with the strength and the authority that the people themselves have given her.

It is not possible to be unmoved. I told you about the Rotarians. They filled the main ballroom of the Manila Hotel, about three thousand people, all seated on velvet-covered chairs and around a formal lunch service. It was announced that there were more guests than

Rotarians. I too was a last-minute guest.

My friend Madge was living in the Manila Hotel and I took a package to her. As I crossed the lobby, I saw this seemingly endless stream of people and TV technicians entering and making for the ballroom. I followed the crowd and learned that Cory was to be the guest speaker. I asked how much is a ticket but was told that I could not buy one if I am not a Rotarian. However, I could go in for free if I were a guest, I was told. I wondered out loud if I could find a Rotarian friend and the man selling tickets said he was sure I would find one if I just stood around long enough.

I went to the ballroom door and stood by it. In one minute, out came our family doctor. I collared him and asked him if he was a Rotarian and he was. I asked him if I could be his guest and he said Yes.

Taking my hand he led me into the ballroom, by then thickening with people. He installed me at a table and found me a velvet chair to sit on. (People were stealing velvet chairs from the lunch tables, so that they could sit but not have to eat.)

For a while, I felt very uneasy among those well-dressed Rotarians. (Our doctor immediately left. He was in the presidential table with Cory.) But I remembered that I had a string of pearls in my purse, so I whipped that out and put it around my throat and felt instantly in place.

Cory's arrival was announced shortly. You won't believe it, but the whole ballroom with its elegantly dressed crowd erupted in cheers, calling her name, jumping and dancing. I could not see anything because people stood up, some of them right on the velvet chairs. I kept decorously to my seat, clapping and calling: "Cory, Cory, Cory!" too. Then I looked around and saw Jaime Zobel de Ayala—standing on top of a velvet chair, too. He is nearly six feet tall, but that did not matter. He wanted to see and so he stood on the chair and cheered and cheered and cheered.

Off went my shoes and I stood on the chair and cheered and cheered, too. Cory entered to rhumba music: "La Paloma Blanca." People were dancing in the aisle ahead of her, in whatever inches there were to spare. Beside me was an old Rotarian, probably in his eighties, evidently retired. He was holding on to my delicate velvet chair so I would not fall while I stomped and cheered and swayed to the rhumba. Once in a while, I looked down at him to show my appreciation and, in that joyous melee, I realized

that he was weeping. Tears were streaming down his old cheeks—tears of joy, tears of jubilation.

Cory had a fighting speech that afternoon and men were reduced to tears. The guy to my right, when she was particularly powerful, said with pride: "Will do."

I had many long thoughts during that lunchtime speech. Among them: Cory is fighting in place of all those elegantly dressed men. They were cheering for her and weeping for her, but she is doing all the fighting for them.

CORAZON C. AQUINO
(From a statement issued on 5 February 1986)

While I have done everything humanly possible to bring back power to our oppressed people, there comes a point when God's power has to intervene.

We cannot win this election without God's help. I have no cheating experience. I have no "salvaging" experience. I have no experience in arresting and terrorizing people.

After we have made a vow to be vigilant and to sacrifice even our lives to dismantle the Marcos regime, we can only pray.

We already have our people's overwhelming support. And prayer is all we need right now.

Young girl captures a balloon bearing campaign stickers for Ferdinand Marcos running for President and Arturo Tolentino running for Vice President in the snap elections set for February 7, 1986 — one year ahead of schedule due, it was widely believed, to US government pressure on Marcos to institute reforms. Confident that Marcos would get a new mandate and that the opposition could not get enough support during the 60-day campaign, the ruling party, KBL, moved men and well-oiled political machines throughout the archipelago.

Ferdinand Marcos speaks at a campaign meeting in Iloilo, right. Banking on lengthy experience in political campaigns and maneuvers and using his clout as incumbent president, Marcos wooed votes in major cities and provinces despite the handicap of evident ill health. He was always accompanied by Mrs. Marcos who initiated the entertainment numbers by singing, above. On her own, she went out to places where Marcos did not go and delivered the campaign speeches in his behalf.

Overleaf: Even before the official campaign period began, a groundswell of support rose for Cory Aquino as candidate for President. This is a rally in Quezon City in Metro Manila, the district where Cory Aquino has lived for many years.

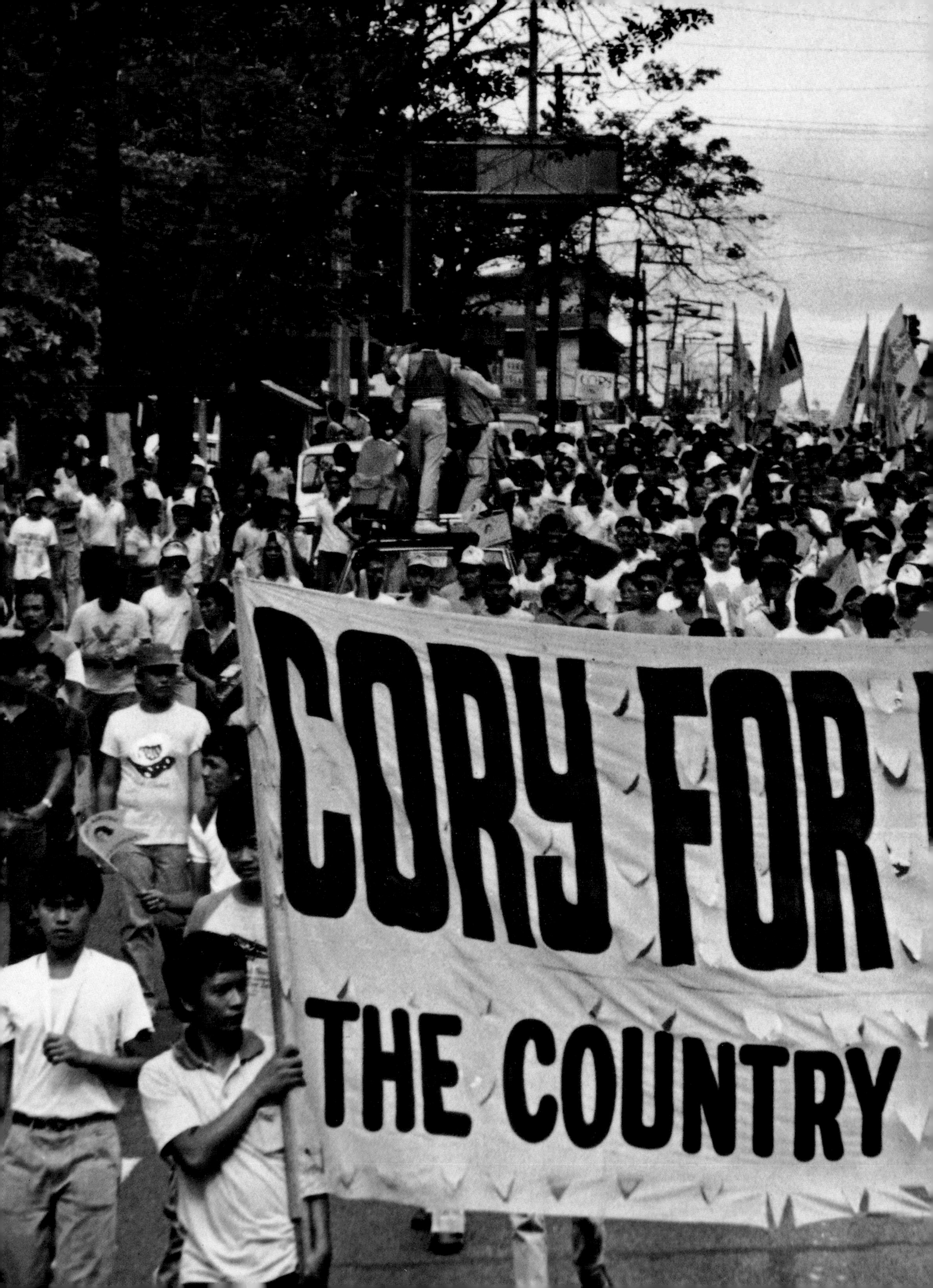
CORY FOR
THE COUNTRY

A little girl's ecstatic·face as she is engulfed in a crowd of people flashing the L sign of support for Cory Aquino captures the exuberance of the campaign, left. This was in Cebu City where Cory Aquino got one of the biggest crowds ever to gather for any political campaign. The same exuberance marks her progress in Iloilo, above. Beside her is Salvador Laurel, candidate for Vice President.

Campaigning for votes among the people of the Cordilleras in northern Luzon, Cory Aquino and Celia Laurel try some steps of the mountaineers' festival dance, above. They wear the traditional wrap-around overskirt of the mountaineers. The setting is in high contrast to the campaign on Ayala Avenue, the country's main business and financial center, but the avalanche of support was identical, left. Overleaf: Cory Aquino speaks to well-wishers from her van as she winds up the campaign in Metro Manila by visiting her alma mater, St. Scholastica's College, and other schools.

IV The Election and Ballot Watch, 1986

Scenario

FRANCISCO S. TATAD

About a thousand foreign correspondents, an official delegation of American observers named by President Reagan, and another group of observers from other countries made sure that the February elections in the Philippines would make the news headlines.

What had begun as a political fever was clearly now an epidemic. "Cory! Cory!" resounded all over the land. She had clearly become the voters' choice. The only question was "Will her votes be counted?" After nearly 60 days on the campaign trail, she still did not have the organization to translate crowds into votes. NAMFREL was there, but its duty was simply to police the elections. The Catholic bishops, who supported NAMFREL, had issued pastoral letters, and offered Masses and novenas for clean and honest elections, but no one knew how much that would help. Aquino would get the votes, but the count would go to Marcos.

The Left seemed to have no doubt about it. Neither did diplomats and correspondents. This, NAMFREL had to prevent. It was a herculean task. Still resentful of NAMFREL's performance in the 1984 elections, the COMELEC had renewed the citizens' arm accreditation only in response to intense public clamor and with great reluctance. Even so, it had imposed unrealistic conditions before allowing it to conduct a "quick count."

Vote-buying, strong-arm tactics, and other forms of naked electoral violations marked the voting, not only in remote areas controlled by political warlords, but in the very heart of Manila, before the eyes of news correspondents and foreign observers. The situation became worse as the nation waited for the NAMFREL count. Volunteers risked life and limb to protect the ballot. Keeping round-the-clock vigil, they formed human chains, tied themselves to ballot boxes and tried to ward off lawless elements out to create mischief.

A full and open conflict developed when NAMFREL's unofficial tally started showing Aquino ahead, while a media count organized by pro-Marcos newspapers and the COMELEC count showed the opposite. Marcos himself led the verbal assault, denouncing NAMFREL as partisan, foreign-funded, and out to cheat him of his votes.

This got inflamed when President Reagan, in his very first statement on the elections, discounted the gravity of the frauds and tended to embrace Marcos. At this time, in the plaza of San Jose, Antique, masked men had just assassinated the 43-year-old Evelio Javier, one of the more promising opposition leaders in the Visayas. Javier was a good friend of Ninoy Aquino. He had been the governor of his province at 29; had studied at Harvard, and because of Ninoy's assassination, had come home to run in the 1984 *Batasan* elections, only to lose to a Marcos henchman in a bloody contest in which seven of his followers were fatally ambushed.

Javier's death sent up a flare in the dark and lit a new fire on the path of Aquino's supporters at a time when they had begun to wonder whether they could force Marcos out of Malacañang. In Manila, as in his home province, Antique, and elsewhere, his name—like Ninoy's—became an instant rallying cry, and thousands filed past his casket to pay their last respects. It was August, 1983, all over again.

Reagan had to send Ambassador Philip Habib to Manila to look at the situation. The *Batasan* had begun the official canvass of election returns. But on the eve of the *Batasan* proceedings, a group of young computer workers staged a dramatic walkout from the COMELEC to protest the deliberate posting of erroneous returns to show Marcos ahead.

The walkout discredited the COMELEC count altogether. But it had no effect on the *Batasan*, which went on to show Marcos winning despite the generally questionable electoral returns. By the time Habib came, the canvassing was over, and Marcos and his running mate had been proclaimed winners. With Marcos sandbagged inside Malacañang and Aquino unwilling to consider any compromise, mediation had become impossible.

On·February 13, the Catholic Bishops Conference of the Philippines (CBCP), in an unprecedented statement, described the elections as unprecedented in their fraudulence, said the government had no moral basis, and called on the faithful to resist evil by peaceful and nonviolent means. On February 16, before a crowd of one million at Manila's Rizal Park, Mrs. Aquino launched a boycott of "crony establishments."

Before the event was over, Reagan's statement came on Radio Veritas saying that the evidence tended to show that massive frauds had been committed in the February 7 elections by the party in power.

The tide had turned.

Voices

VICENTE PATERNO, NAMFREL Chairman for Metro Manila

From the first week of January '86 onward, I was no longer attending to my business. I devoted my time to NAMFREL work. I was not too worried about the little time we had for preparation. I was relying on the fact that NAMFREL had an organization in 1984 and it would not be too difficult getting together the core group back again.

The Marcos Administration gave us trouble through COMELEC. The COMELEC was clearly trying to prevent us from getting organized. They were creating all kinds of roadblocks, particularly for the Operations Quick Count (OQC). They concentrated on that. They were also delaying the implementation of the accreditation of election registrars. They had agreed—on December 24, 1985—to accredit NAMFREL as the citizens' arm. But they put up very stringent conditions so that if we did something that the COMELEC did not order us to do, we could be disaccredited.

The OQC was something they particularly resisted because the OQC was the main achievement of NAMFREL in 1984. Their main tactic—which we did not anticipate—was the scrambling of the voters' lists. This caused, in our own estimate, at least 15 per cent of voters in Metro Manila to be disfranchised. That was about 600,000 people. In Metro Manila and other places where the opposition seemed to be strong, there was a lot of disfranchisement. Voters' lists were scrambled so that people, who were probably going to vote for Cory, could not vote.

Before the elections, I had a difficult time in the COMELEC, trying to get the OQC documented and agreed upon. It was really most difficult. The memorandum which specified what the procedures would be for the OQC for Metro Manila was not signed until seven o'clock on the day before the elections. And on that afternoon,

they had sent out instructions to the telegraph companies, which changed the procedures which had been set up earlier.

We had designed a form which we called the "precinct tally form," so that the telegraphs could be sent in the set order—the number of the precinct, the name of the municipality, the number of votes, etc. RCPI knew how to send that particular telegram. But on February 6, COMELEC said that RCPI could not be used, except in 368 municipalities, and that we had to use PT&T for the others. We had not made arrangements with PT&T and with the Bureau of Telecommunications. COMELEC tried to slow us down and made it difficult for us to send the messages. They wanted to confuse our provincial chapters. In Metro Manila, they wanted us to bring the precinct tally sheets to the election registrars so that these could be verified and authenticated. But in a number of places in Metro Manila, they did not start to verify until around ten to eleven in the evening. However, they made a miscalculation because after ten in the evening, when the election registrars were not verifying, some of the NAMFREL chapter chairmen called me, asking if it would be all right to bypass them and send it straight to me.

CECILIA MUÑOZ PALMA, opposition leader

I published an ad in the *Philippine Daily Inquirer*, appealing for volunteers to help on Election Day. That ad appeared for only one day, but I received letters even from Davao. In that ad, I was asking for help here in Quezon City. I also said that in all places in the country there should be organizations that will help protect the ballot. We needed volunteers for that.

About 400 or more came to this house for our first meeting. We were able to organize the Quezon City Polling Center councils. This group would take care of the food for the inspectors and watchers, including the KBL watchers. They would make sure that there were candles and flashlights available, just in case. They would recruit watchers for particular polling centers, since each knew the residents of his area. There was a division of labor. As Chairman, I handled the needs of all polling centers all over Quezon City.

ERIC ENRIQUEZ, student

On Election Day, I was taking pictures for NAMFREL. At 10:00 a.m., we received a tip that vote-buying was going on just two blocks away from the polling center. When we got there, we saw people lining up in front of an apartment, at 82 Luskot Street in Quezon City. I wanted to take pictures without attracting too much attention. I noticed a video shop in front of the apartment. I walked in with one of my cameras and a zoom lens and asked if I could take pictures from their garage. The owner agreed. A kid opened the garage gate—just a little, enough for me to take pictures.

Through my lens, I saw people line up in front of the screen door of the apartment. There was a hole on the door and through that same door, someone was handing out carbon paper or hundred-peso bills. I was able to take three pictures with my zoom lens. After that, the main door closed. Someone saw me.

I went back to the polling center and told my friends what had happened. After about 15 minutes, we got another tip that it was going on again. I guess I was a bit overconfident when I got back there. My friends could not keep up and we were separated. When I got there, a man slipped out of the apartment and boarded a jeep.

Since the jeep was moving slowly, I was able to run in front of it and take pictures. He saw me and covered his face. His companion reached out and punched me in the face. Then the jeep sped away.

I went back to the polling center and told them everything. It caused an uproar. NAMFREL and UNIDO people wanted to protect me. There were tips that goons wanted to get my camera. Then, we heard news that the vote-buying was going on again. This time, the people prevented me from going back. Instead, the UNIDO lawyer helped me file a complaint. After that, everyone advised me to go home. I didn't listen, of course. I met my photographer friend from the *Inquirer* and gave him the negatives.

RODOLFO CALING

On Election Day, I thought I would not be able to vote because I could not find my name in the voters' list. "How can that happen?" I asked. "I am a newly registered voter," I told them and even showed them my registration papers. I tried to be patient and let the others vote. There was no reason to delay others—I could wait. So I waited. I did not leave my precinct. I stayed there the whole day. Finally, a minute before closing time, the COMELEC representative, probably convinced by my determination, wrote my name in the voters' list.

CAROLYN O. ARGUILLAS, journalist

Jigs Rentillo had only about a week to live. He wanted only one thing: to vote on Election Day—and to vote for the leadership of Cory Aquino.

Jigs, 49, single, had terminal cancer. He begged his doctors at the St. John Hospital in Toril, Davao City, to keep him alive until February 7, so that he could vote.

His sister, Sol Parro, tried to dissuade him, but Jigs refused to listen. At his bedside, he kept his voter's affidavit in a yellow t-shirt that had the words: "If Ninoy's death does not rouse us, what will?"

Jigs got his wish. He was carried on a stretcher to voting center no. 735 in the Juan de la Cruz Elementary School in Toril. All fell silent as Jigs—weak and emaciated—made his thumb-mark on the ballot, which was filled up by his nurse, Heidi Lebumfacil.

In the hospital, Jigs had practiced writing "Cory Aquino" and "Doy Laurel" for his ballot. But in the voting center, he was gently told that his handwriting was not legible enough and could therefore invalidate his ballot. His thumbmark was enough of an effort.

Jigs' doctor, Dr. Romanito Pilay, said that he was steadily slipping but rallied momentarily when he heard that Cory was leading in Davao.

FRANCISCO RODRIGO (SOC), opposition leader

It was the dirtiest election ever, full of vote-buying and terrorism. All of Tarlac was terrorized. Mrs. Aurora Aquino and I went there two weeks before the elections. I spoke to former Secretary Feliciano in Concepcion. He said that he was afraid Cory would lose even in Ninoy's hometown.

Ruling party goons were terrorizing the barrios. They did not threaten the voters. They made threats against the voters' children. They told Cory supporters that they knew where they lived and where their children went to school and what time they left the house. A man might be willing to die for the cause, but he is not ready to risk the lives of his children.

BENJAMIN RIEZA, NAMFREL volunteer

I was a NAMFREL volunteer assigned to an

elementary school in Marikina. I was responsible for three precincts in that school. I was going from one precinct to another, checking the tallying of the votes. At 3:20 p.m., Aquino was leading in all the precincts. After a while, gunshots were heard. I took cover. People were running everywhere in panic. I saw the armed men poking their weapons at a NAMFREL volunteer, and telling everybody to go outside. I didn't budge from my position, I just hid my NAMFREL vest and I.D. Soon afterwards, a group of teen-agers, about 15-17 years old, wearing red and blue striped t-shirts, entered. They were armed with handguns. They told everybody that if they would not leave, they were going to shoot on sight. This was further punctuated by a series of gunshots.

A masked man soon appeared, carrying a hand grenade, and threatening to throw it. One woman, who turned out to be the wife of one of the goons, began to cry. She pleaded with her husband not to do this thing. The man just told his wife to go home and keep out of the matter. He said they needed money, so he accepted the job. I took the opportunity to run away. I saw some of the goons kicking media people around, and destroying their equipment. I ran for cover in the NAMFREL booth and locked the door. I was there with six other people. We had to leave the place, because some of the goons saw us and threatened to blow up the booth if we didn't go out. We took shelter in the nearby church.

VIC OLAGUERA, NAMFREL volunteer

At three in the afternoon, voting was closed and we started the prescribed process of checking the ballot stubs, and the number of ballots cast against the list of voters who were able to vote. It took us about an hour to do that. Just when we were about to start counting, there was gunfire from an automatic rifle. After a few seconds, another burst. And then panic. Pandemonium. People were rushing out of the polling center. We stayed at our post, too shocked to move. Two goons came in, brandishing knives. One snatched the ballots on the table. The UNIDO watcher grabbed the ballot box. One of the goons pointed a knife at his throat and told him to put it down. I was not too scared. Maybe it was the adrenalin. The goons ordered us out of the building. I wanted to stay to find out what they were going to do. But my wife started to scream. So I grabbed her, overturned some chairs to

prevent pursuit, and dashed outside. I went back twenty minutes later, and helped the Board of Election Inspectors file a report because obviously we could not proceed with the counting. They took all the ballots, the tally sheets, the voters' list... even the handbag of the chairperson of the Board of Election Inspectors. Not all the precincts in our polling area were terrorized. At the precinct where my houseboy was assigned, they were able to close the door. But the members of Board of Election Inspectors were so scared, they decided not to continue the count. One third of the precincts were subjected to similar treatment. The NAMFREL head of the area decided to withdraw all the volunteers. Some bravely stayed and went on with the counting. But only about half succeeded in counting all the votes. So we made the move to invalidate the votes in that area.

DANTE P. ARSENIO, NAMFREL volunteer

I was assigned to watch the voting in a polling place in Malabon. We caught a teacher switching ballots at around midday. The news immediately spread to the crowd outside the polling place. They got angry and demanded: "Get that teacher out here right now so that we can get at her."

The teacher continued working until all the ballots had been counted. She was the last of the teachers to finish. She stalled because she knew there was a vengeful crowd waiting outside for her. We would not let her go until the clamoring for her stopped. Even then, we had to escort her out of the polling place, because the people were trying to get her.

Some councilmen in a Marcos campaign vehicle, complete with banners and posters, drove right up to the polling place, breaking the rule that all campaign vehicles must keep a 50-meter distance from the polling places. The foreign correspondents in the area saw the vehicle and started photographing it. Thinking nothing of being photographed by foreigners, the councilmen got down from the vehicle and even posed for them.

VICENTE PATERNO, NAMFREL chairman for Metro Manila

The operations center of NAMFREL was also the Operations Quick Count center in La Salle, Greenhills. On Election Day, I voted early and got to NAMFREL at about 8:30 in the morning.

We had been set up so that Cris Monsod and I were supposed to take care of the command post. We had to take messages, refer them to the right people or take care of the more important ones.

Around ten in the morning, I told Cris that I wanted to go to Makati where I heard there was trouble. Anyway, I said Cris could take care of things at the command post.

When I got to Makati, Isabel Wilson was up in arms. "The elections are a farce," she said. I told her it would be best to go to COMELEC itself and get a Commissioner. I went and talked to COMELEC Commissioners Layosa and Savellano.

Before the elections, we had organized strike forces—about 300 people and 25 jeeps. The idea was to send the strike force, which had a lawyer, a photographer, and at least 12 labor unionists. In two hours, all these strike forces were deployed—there were so many trouble spots in Metro Manila.

After the discussions with COMELEC, I rode in a radio car of our communications group and returned to Makati.

Along the way, we heard a Mayday call: goons with Armalites had come to terrorize a polling center in Guadalupe, Makati. Shots were being fired in the air. So we went straight to Guadalupe Nuevo Elementary School where the trouble was. The goons had left but the place was in turmoil. The coordinator of the area had ordered our NAMFREL volunteers to leave, but some of them did not want to go. They asked me if I really wanted them to leave.

I said that I first had to talk to their coordinator before deciding on anything. But they should make a headcount of those who were willing to stay in the precincts. I felt that if they could not cover at least 10 per cent of the precincts, it would be useless. I went to look for their coordinator but found out that she had already left for the San Antonio Parish Center. The volunteers told me that they had enough men to cover at least 75 per cent of the precincts. And so I countermanded the coordinator's orders and told them to do what they wanted. They stayed.

I went to the San Antonio Parish Center and found out that as a result of the widespread violence in Makati, Isabel Wilson had to call in the volunteers. They held a meeting to decide whether they should continue or just demonstrate against the irregularities of the elections. I told them to think about it because there were still some volunteers, like the ones in Guadalupe Nuevo, who were willing to continue in spite of the obvious dangers.

From there I went to Mandaluyong, which ranked third among the chapters which had suffered the most violence, next only to Makati and Muntinglupa. I went to Isabel Ongpin in the Benguet Building to find out how she and the chapter were. She asked for more strike forces but I said that we had already dispatched all of them.

I went back to La Salle and at about 2:30 p.m., I received a call from our chapter in Muntinglupa. They said that armed goons were roaming around and that five polling centers were in trouble. They asked if they could pull out. I again said that they were in the best position to know and that they should decide for themselves. I only asked that if they should decide to leave, they should do so in an orderly manner and consolidate and regroup. I said that the volunteers who left their polling centers should go to other polling centers and reinforce them. In this way, we could make strategic withdrawals and consolidate our forces.

At that time, it was really a war situation. There was a report, for example, of a man who was stabbed in Malabon. Some areas of Metro Manila were quite peaceful. Quezon City, Manila itself — except for a few cases — Las Piñas and Parañaque were all relatively peaceful. But the south sector — Muntinglupa, Pateros, Taguig — and the north sector — Malabon, Navotas, Caloocan — were problem areas.

We did not anticipate problems of that magnitude. I thought 300 people in 25 strike forces would be enough. And we had fielded 600 nuns — the NAMFREL Marines. We had gotten a list of critical polling places and the NAMFREL Marines had been deployed to these areas. We had a radio communications network. We had made arrangements with Rainbow, Para, and Pugad Lawin so that our radio communications were superior to what we had in 1984.

In 1986 we had the NAMFREL Marines; we had the strike forces; we had probably about 30,000 volunteers. We had an army. We did not think that the fraud would take place on the scale that it did and with such brazenness.

We were also counting on the fact that this election was going to be covered thoroughly by the foreign media. I told the people in Makati: "You are a chosen instrument of divine will in this election because the violence that took place in Makati was seen on television all over the world." I told them in the Thanksgiving Mass of the Makati chapter that their walkout and march to Guadalupe Nuevo, which was led by Joe

Concepcion, was seen on television all over the world and was part of the process of convincing the world that this was a fraudulent election. Nothing that happens is wasted.

The brazenness of what the ruling party did — they beat up people in front of the television cameras — and the brazenness of their accusations — they accused our nuns of cheating and stealing ballot boxes — were things that we did not expect. We expected them to cheat but not to be so blatant about it. For example, the cancellation of classes before the elections was for scrambling of voters' lists and preparing of fake ballots.

During previous elections, flying voters came towards the end of voting and used the names which had not been used yet. During this election, the voting turnout was heavy during the morning. At 7:30, the lines were already very long. It was very sophisticated. They knew what names to vote under. They knew what precincts to go to. The lists were definitely scrambled. Not only were legitimate voters unable to vote but also flying voters got registered. This was done through computers. And that is why they needed the 10 days or so of preparations.

And they learned from 1984. In 1984, they had given money to the voters but the voters did not vote for their candidates. This time they were prepared. They had carbonized paper — sample ballots or calendars — which were placed under the real ballots. They were so sure of this method that they were paying people as low as 20 pesos.

NESTOR G. FABIAN, engineer

On the afternoon of Election Day, I was shocked to hear over the radio that one of our colleagues, a precinct chairman in the next barrio, had been stabbed and rushed to the hospital. But we continued to do our duty. Our enthusiasm and courage did not waver. The following day, I found out that my injured friend needed P8,000 to pay for his hospital bills. We went to the canvassing site and announced over the PA system that our friend, the precinct chairman, needed help. The people responded quickly. In less than five minutes, we collected four thousand pesos.

BERTRAND GAGNAN

My friend in NAMFREL named Rodriguez was in Guadalupe when the goons came in around quarter to three. He got caught in the middle of the hallway. He said to them: "You touch me, and you're gonna get it. I'm the son of Governor Rodriguez of Rizal!" And you could read clearly on his NAMFREL card: "Rodriguez." So, the goons didn't touch him and he was only bluffing. A NAMFREL guy stepped in and said: "My grandfather is gonna hear this." This genius had the same family name. Unfortunately, he didn't scare all of them because one of his friends who was also working for NAMFREL got beaten up.

When I was at the municipal hall, a group of people came in, about 200 of them. They walked all the way to Makati Municipal Hall to bring the ballots. They came walking with candles, carrying the boxes and chanting all the way. When they arrived at the municipal hall, they were singing *Bayan Ko* (My Homeland). It was so beautiful. You had at least four people per box surrounded by two lines of people bunched together. These people with candles were absolutely, absolutely beautiful. I was very touched by it. The people were doing so much, just to preserve this democracy.

VICENTE PATERNO

Emotionally, the high point for me was in Guadalupe Nuevo at around 3:00 p.m. after the second wave of violence. I went there when I heard on the radio that they were asking for ambulances. When I came in, this *barangay* captain of Pinagkaisahan, Elias Tolentino, was coming down from the second floor with a .45 tucked in his waist. He had been the leader of that violence. I was afraid that the volunteers who had come from the San Antonio Parish Center — they were about 600 of them — would do something to him. But they did not. They just booed as he walked away. And I was told that when he reached the gates of the schoolhouse, he took out his .45 and brandished it around, trying to look brave. After the booing, somebody began to sing *Bayan Ko* (My Homeland). And all the volunteers — some had never attended a rally before — joined in the singing. For those people, the revolution began then.

What impressed me most was that those who were beaten up were the most militant and the most vigilant in the vigil and the canvassing. The attempt at intimidation on the part of the KBL and the *barangay* captains elicited a different reaction from what they had thought. They thought that the people would be frightened and go home. But the people were convinced that it was time to make a stand.

In Malabon, Navotas, and Mandaluyong, chapter chairmen were being threatened. My north sector coordinator, Frances Gloria, received death threats but she chose to stick it out. The volunteers from Muntinglupa who were chased and forced to withdraw from the polling centers remained very militant. Attempts at intimidation elicited quite a different reaction from the NAMFREL people. In fact, I felt that Cory's call for boycott was a bit too mild because I knew that the NAMFREL people were ready for something more.

VIC PUYAT, NAMFREL volunteer

Tony Esteban and his family were really involved with NAMFREL. They were assigned to a *barangay* in Makati. The *barangay* captain insisted on entering the polling place, which was contrary to law. So Tony requested him to step out. He stepped out and then he came back. He was gently reminded to step out. He did. When he was asked to leave for the third time, the *barangay* captain started cursing. He came back with goons and they started to beat up Tony, Jr., who had a camera. He was able to take a picture of the *barangay* captain, who was hitting him with a chair. His sisters tried to help. They too were manhandled. Tony tried to take a picture of that, and they hit him in the back. He fell on a table, wrecking it. He grabbed one of the table legs and started swinging at the goons. The goons retreated. The family finished their job, and after they had brought the ballot box to the municipal hall, they went to the hospital for treatment.

I heard this story from another NAMFREL volunteer:

Goons approached them and asked: "Are you with NAMFREL? Beat it!"

They would not leave. They said: "How many are you goons anyway? Ten? Twelve? If I radio for help, 200 will come. So you beat it."

The goons left.

On the evening of Election Day, volunteers were asked to guard the ballot boxes all the way from the polling places to the municipal hall. When they got there, they found out that the ballot boxes were being kept in this half-finished warehouse. Some of them cried; they had risked their lives for these ballot boxes and now they were being kept in this flimsy building. They decided to surround the warehouse and they stayed there for days.

At Pio del Pilar, the goons managed to drive away the NAMFREL and the UNIDO volunteers.

The residents took over. They tied the ballot boxes together with a length of rope, and then carried them in a procession to the municipal hall, chanting and cheering all the way. The volunteers at the municipal hall welcomed them as heroes.

KAA BYINGTON, writer

The Americans don't seem to understand this election. They speak of it in terms of politics, of two-party systems and of partisanship. This is not a political event at all. It is a moral issue, a contest between good and evil. NAMFREL is not partisan toward UNIDO even if COMELEC is partisan toward KBL. NAMFREL is dedicated to preventing fraud. That is its partisanship. There are no shades of gray in this, there are no conservatives or liberals or left or right. It is not a question of who has the better platform or the more experience. There is only one "issue": a clear choice between good and evil. *Vox populi, vox Dei.* The people in the streets believe that with God on their side they cannot lose. They are right.

LULU CASTAÑEDA, wife and mother

This was the awakening of the people. The world realized that there were heroes in the Philippines. Before then, the world thought the Philippines was a country of one tyrant and 50 million cowards. We showed that there are Filipinos who so believe in democracy that they are willing to lay down their lives to protect the ballot.

CORAZON C. AQUINO

The lessons I have learned and taken to heart from these elections are: the simple faith of the common people in democracy, the modesty of their demands, the courage of their convictions. The Filipino people asked me for so little: freedom, dignity, and some reason to believe in government and to hope for a better life. After that, they would take care of themselves and even take care of me. They pressed hard-earned money into my hands for my campaign. They came out in unprecedented numbers to show the rest of the country and the world that they were for me. They voted for me and, as far as they could, tried to get their votes counted. I have seen with my eyes what Ninoy saw with faith: that the Filipino is worth dying for.

The other lessons of this election are those I do not want to learn and will never apply: the lessons of violence, bribery, outright fraud, and that an honest and overwhelming victory is not 100 per cent proof against them. The cause of democracy triumphs at the polls without applying these lessons and it will continue to triumph in the streets in the same spirit of peace and determination.

NINIT PATERNO, boutique owner

When the ballot boxes were being brought to the National Assembly, we were worried about possible tampering. There was a big crowd and we were all anxious. It was dark, and there was not much we could do. All at once, everyone fell on his knees and began to sing the Lord's Prayer. I knew then we were going to win.

GEORGE WINTERNITZ, insurance manager

So many prayers, so many Rosaries were said before Election Day and during elections and in the tense days and nocturnal vigils that followed. During the vigil over the election returns at the municipal hall, we prayed the Rosary. After a few minutes' rest and light talk, we prayed again.

When there was talk of fire engines coming to disperse our vigil, we prayed the Rosary. When they said Metrocom troops were positioning themselves a hundred yards away, ready to come after us—and when a group actually came through the municipal hall's grounds in a Ford Fiera— we prayed. With renewed fervor and dedication, we prayed. This was a prelude of things to come. The fire engines went away, the Metrocom troopers returned to their base, and the tension was relieved. Dawn broke without incident.

DANTE P. ARSENIO

Other NAMFREL volunteers and I escorted the ballot boxes to the Municipal Hall of Malabon and stood vigil over them. One young volunteer was inspecting the entrances to the room containing the ballot boxes. He saw that one door was left open and unguarded. When the chief of police noticed him inspecting this door, he apprehended the boy and took him to the police headquarters. This caused a big commotion in the Hall. A NAMFREL volunteer was pushed aside by this policeman when he tried to stop him from taking his friend away.

Several NAMFREL volunteers, including myself, some priests and seminarians, followed the policeman and the volunteer to the headquarters to demand his release. When we arrived, one seminarian went up to the chief and said: "Let the boy go and take me instead, if you have to detain someone!" They would have come to blows if we did not hold them back. The boy was released.

MICHAEL TRINIDAD, 13 years old

I was keeping vigil at the Makati Municipal Hall with my sister Trixie and other NAMFREL volunteers. On the afternoon of February 8, there was a commotion on the second floor. Four men tried to get hold of the election returns, and the people tried to stop them. A guy in khaki ordered us to disperse and started to hit the arms of those who were in the cordon.

I was hit on the leg. My sister saw this and took pictures of the guy who hit me. They surrounded my sister and put her in a room and closed the door. My cousin and I were left outside. But I screamed and hit the door. I wanted to be with my sister. I wanted to protect her.

So they opened the door and pushed me into the room. They tried to pull my camera away but I fought back—screaming, shouting, kicking. The people who were beating us up were in blue uniforms. The others in the room just stood there like statues. It was as if they did not even care. I was really making a lot of noise, so that the people outside would hear.

Five men brought me to the secretary's room which had no windows. They thought they could prevent my screams from reaching those outside by putting me in that room. But they were wrong. My screams can penetrate anything.

A thin, black guy with a long chin pulled my camera from me as the other four guys hit me with their sticks.

They brought me back to the first room where they were still hitting my sister. I even saw this guy hit her really hard. They already got my camera and were now trying to get hers. But Trixie, who was now crying, would not let them have it. She did not give up the fight. When I saw this, I grabbed my camera back, and said that I was not leaving until they gave me my sister's camera. They pushed me and took my camera again.

All this time, my mom and my aunt, who had just arrived, were downstairs on the first floor. They heard that some children were being held and harassed in a room upstairs. They joined the crowd which was saying: "Let the kids go." They did not know that it was us.

We were cheered on by the people there after we were released. A girl approached my mom asking if her children were okay. My mom did not know what she was talking about. Another person told her that the children involved were young. My mom got even more confused. She said: "That cannot be. My eldest is already a third year pre-med student and my youngest is thirteen and is already big."

My mother only got to know everything when we finally went home at 5:30 in the afternoon.

JOHN CHUA, photographer

There was a lot of cheating on Election Day. I just wanted to sleep. I wanted to believe that it was a bad dream. I wanted no part of it. But when I woke up, things were still the same. I was so depressed. I went crazy. The Wednesday after elections, I told my wife that I had to go out and do something. But she did not want to go. I told her: "You have to make a stand. You have to do something. Let's be part of this. If I do nothing else, at least I can record this."

I went to Mandaluyong and Makati. I think I was able to help in a way. People like the feeling that they are being recorded. They raise their hands in the *Laban* sign and shout. When you press the shutter, you give them the feeling that: "Hey, someone is with us." I think that was my contribution.

MANUEL ESCASA, teacher

After the elections, I heard a call for volunteers to guard the ballots in Makati. I went but found out that people were just milling around. I ran into one of the parents from school and she told me that if I wanted to do something, I could stand by the ballot boxes. I did. But a friend told me that it might be useless because we could have been standing vigil over tampered ballots. It did seem pointless, but I said that at least they would not be tampered with again. The people in Makati wondered if they should allow the counting of ballots to proceed; if they did, they would be granting its legitimacy. So they did not know what to do with the ballots. But all I thought of was that they would not be tampered with anymore. So I kept vigil over them.

FR. FRANCISCO J. ARANETA

Part of the Philippine Christian tradition was the old *bantayan*—the watchtower— on a hill by the seashore. Guards remained there day and night to watch for the approach of pirates that might raid the town. If any showed up on the horizon, the call went out to mobilize the men.

Radio Veritas became the national watchtower. Whoever needed help dialed this fortress of truth and the call for help went out over the air to the thousands of dedicated and determined men and women ready to respond.

Students of comparative government think of democracy in terms of institutions and structures. True, political democracy needs political structure. To set up and maintain such a structure, you need power. You need to be in power.

But I have realized that democracy is not just a matter of institutions and structures. It is, more fundamentally, a matter of heart, will, and spirit.

LINDA KAPUNAN, computer programmer

I went off-duty on Sunday morning, February 9, at around 11:30 a.m. I went home to sleep. I received a call late that afternoon from a friend who also worked at the COMELEC Quick Count. She told me that there were indications of cheating and the other programmers were getting agitated. I got back at about 7:45 p.m. I asked them what was going on. They said: "Linda, there is cheating going on. The figures on the tally board do not match the figures we get on the printout."

One of them, who was in charge of the printouts, glanced at the tally board occasionally to compare figures. If the figure on the board was say, 3 million, the figure we had was only 2 million. They did not think it could be a bug in our program, because only the figures of two regions were affected— Regions 1 and 2. If it had been a bug, the error would have been consistent. This had been going on since midnight of the night before.

At 9:00 a.m. on Sunday, the two sets of figures suddenly matched. So we passed it off as an honest mistake. Then the others noticed there had been foreign visitors around at the time who had been given copies of the printouts. After the foreigners left, the discrepancy began again.

I asked them for proof and they gave me copies of the printouts. I realized then that they really were cheating. I knew I would not stand for this. I asked the group what they wanted to do. Everybody agreed to walk out.

When we left the hall, these foreign journalists were scrambling to get a statement from us. They wanted to know why we were doing this. But we decided not to make any statement, just leave the place and go home and drink our blues away.

There was pandemonium in the corridor. People were all around us clapping. Many were shouting: "It's a miracle!" There was a human barricade around us. We kept hearing: "You are protected, you are protected." We were shocked by the reaction of the people.

It seemed forever before I saw a familiar face. All of us were crying from shock and tension. Finally, I saw my husband, Red, and he led us to where the cars were. We piled in. We realized later that there were eleven of us in one small car. We decided to seek sanctuary in Baclaran church.

At the church, we were asked for our statement. I said we had nothing to say. But after a while, we realized we had to say something.

We decided to write a short statement to give to the public. I was chosen as spokesman because I was the most senior in the group. In the statement, we emphasized that we were non-partisan. We were not organized. We decided to do it when we realized that something wrong was going on. Nobody paid us to do it.

We stayed in the church until most of the people had left. The food donations started pouring in. Somebody sent cash but we refused.

We heard rumors that a high KBL official had issued orders for all of us to be tracked down. We kept hearing Dr. Baraoidan's statements attacking us, casting doubts on our professionalism and our integrity. This hurt us.

We sat down together to discuss everything. We feared for our security and our future. There could be attempts to harm our families. But in the face of these uncertainties, we stood by our decision. Our dignity, our professional integrity, is not negotiable.

SYLVIA MAYUGA, writer

On February 9, 38 computer technicians at the COMELEC Quick Count realized that they were being made party to election fraud.

"This is cheating! I won't stand for it!" said the leader of the group. They took off their clinical smocks, gathered diskettes and printouts for evidence, and walked out.

They huddled in hideouts on the other side of town as sacks of rice, cartons of food, and thousands of pesos poured in from a grateful public. News of liquidation squads combing the city for every one of them came from all directions—and, on the heels of that, there were leaks of something called Operation Everlasting, a master plan for the arrest and murder of opposition leaders, the closure of the troublesome alternative press, and the declaration of martial law, part two.

Linda Kapunan, the senior computer technician who led the walkout, comforted her tearful colleagues with the help of her husband, Lieutenant Colonel Eduardo (Red) Kapunan of the Philippine Air Force, an intelligence officer and, fatefully for everyone, an original member of the Reform the Armed Forces of the Philippines Movement.

RAM, they called themselves, this motley group of gentlemen from all the major military commands bent on restoring dignity and honor to a uniform disgraced by years of martial rule. They had begun to question the counter-insurgency program, the summary executions, the elaborate torture, the spying, surveillance, wire-tapping, disappearances, violent dispersals of peaceful rallies because, like the rest of the nation, they too had been shaken by the murder of Ninoy Aquino. The long shadow of the Ver military faction, the blatant corruption of overstaying generals loyal to Marcos and the confused war against an "enemy" whose commitment to a larger cause had gained their grudging admiration rankled and forced them to look for explanations not found in their military handbooks.

Red Kapunan did not wear the military uniform as he shuttled back and forth from office to hideout those two weeks after the election. Never had so many women cried on his shoulder before. Nothing in his Mindanao training as combat pilot had prepared him to know what to say to this group.

People other than the technicians had been endangered by the walkout. Red Kapunan and the reformists had long been aware of the cold eye cast on them by Marcos and Ver. The Marcos camp, as soon as it recovered from the walkout, lost no time in telling the press that the walkout was a reformist plot and that the technicians were really secret oppositionists.

Red made sure that the Minister of Defense, Juan Ponce Enrile, who was sympathetic to the movement, was the first to know. "I don't want the ministry to get into trouble for this, sir," he said, "but I want you to know that my loyalty will be torn if they hurt Linda. I don't know what I'd do if they hurt Linda."

Enrile gave Red P20,000 to take care of the fugitive computer programmers and RAM surrounded Red with a security cordon. RAM knew that with this totally unplanned event, they were running out of time even faster than they had expected. Already General Ramos had passed on information that the reformists were high on the list of Operation Everlasting. Other sources confirmed this, one of them a RAM in the Presidential Security Command. The arrests, they were told, would begin on February 22.

RICARDO CARDINAL VIDAL, president , Catholic Bishops Conference

We began our meeting by asking each bishop to tell his personal experience or the reports he received from his priests and from laymen about the conduct of the election.

To save time, I divided the group according to regions. After half a day, some of the bishops even exceeded the time set for reporting. The reports showed a general trend. We saw the same pattern. Yet, we were not satisfied. We asked for further consultations with the heads of religious orders and they gave us their opinion. We also consulted with some lay people and with theologians.

We broke off to have a holy hour of prayers and, after we prayed together, we each went off alone — to reflect, think, come to a decision.

We made the statement on February 13. Normally, we assign a committee to draft our statements. The following day, we discussed the draft. It took another half a day to arrive at a consensus. We finished at about half past noon.

We had a discussion again and it had to be re-written because some bishops were not satisfied with it. We ended almost at 3:00 p.m.

It was not an easy job. We deliberated on it. We prayed about it. We reflected on it as bishops.

THE CATHOLIC BISHOPS OF THE PHILIPPINES
(In a statement after the election, 13 February 1986)

The people have spoken. Or have tried to. Despite the obstacles thrown in the way of their speaking freely, we, the bishops, believe that on the basis of our assessment, as pastors, of the recently concluded polls, what they attempted to say is clear enough.

In our considered judgment, the polls were unparalleled in the fraudulence of their conduct. And we condemn especially the following modes of fraudulence and irregularities:

— The systematic disfranchisement of voters. The sheer scrambling of the voters' list made it impossible for a vast number of our people to express their proper preference for candidates.

— The widespread and massive vote-buying. The vote-buyers in their cynical exploiting of the people's poverty and deep, if misguided, sense of *utang na loob* (debt of gratitude) deprived a great many of any real freedom of choice.

— The deliberate tampering of the election returns. The votes of the people, even when already duly expressed and counted, were altered to register choices other than their own.

— Intimidation, harassment, terrorism, and murder. These made naked fear the decisive factor in people not participating in the polls or making their final choice. These and many other irregularities point to a criminal use of power to thwart the sovereign will of the people. Yet, despite these evil acts, we are morally certain the people's real will for change has been truly manifested.

According to moral principles, a government that assumes or retains power through fraudulent means has no moral basis. For such an access to power is tantamount to a forcible seizure and cannot command the allegiance of the citizenry. The most we can say then, about such a government, is that it is a government in possession of power. But admitting that, we hasten to add: Because of *that* very fact, that same government itself has the obligation to right the wrong it is founded on. It must respect the mandate of the people. This is the precondition for any reconciliation.

If such a government does not of itself freely correct the evil it has inflicted on the people, then it is our serious moral obligation as a people to make it do so.

We are not going to effect the change we seek by doing nothing, by sheer apathy. If we did nothing, we would be party to our own destruction as a people. We would be jointly guilty with the perpetrators of the wrong we want righted.

Neither do we advocate a bloody, violent means of righting this wrong. If we did, we would be sanctioning the enormous sin of fratricidal strife. Killing to achieve justice is not within the purview of our Christian vision in our present context.

The way indicated to us now is the way of nonviolent struggle for justice.

This means active resistance of evil by peaceful means — in the manner of Christ. And its one end for now is that the will of the people be done through ways and means proper to the Gospel.

We therefore ask every loyal member of the Church, every community of the faithful, to form their judgment about the February 7 polls. And if in faith they see things as we the bishops do, we must come together and discern what appropriate actions to take that will be according to the mind of Christ. In a creative, imaginative way, under the guidance of Christ's Spirit, let us pray together, reason together, decide together, act together, always to the end that the truth prevail, that the will of the people be fully respected.

These last few days have given us shining examples of the nonviolent struggle for justice we advocate here:

— The thousands of NAMFREL workers and volunteers who risked their very lives to ensure clean and honest elections;

— The COMELEC computer technicians who refused to degrade themselves by participating in election fraud.

— The poll officials — registrars, teachers, government workers — who did their duty without fear or favor.

— The millions of ordinary voters who kept the sanctity of their ballot untarnished, their dignity intact.

— Radio Veritas and fearless press people who spoke and reported the truth at all times.

Men and women of conscience all — we cannot commend them highly enough.

There are thousands of their kind among government officials in the *Batasan,* the military, the COMELEC, among millions of our people who in the face of overwhelming odds voted and acted as their conscience dictated. Are there other men and women of conscience who will stand up like them and courageously confess their Christianity?

Now is the time to speak up. Now is the time to repair the wrong. The wrong was systematically organized. So must its correction be. But as in the election itself, that depends fully on the people; on what they are willing and ready to do. We, the bishops, stand in solidarity with them in the common discernment for the good of the nation. But we insist: Our acting must always be according to the Gospel of Christ, that is, in a peaceful, nonviolent way.

May He, the Lord of justice, the Lord of peace, be with us in our striving for that good. And may the Blessed Virgin Mary, the Queen of Peace, and patroness of our country, assist us in this time of need.

ENRIQUE A. ZALDIVAR, governor of Antique province

Evelio Javier's political life was built upon a dream: "Let freedom ring." With faith and vigor, he pursued that dream in Antique, in every mountainside and every hamlet.

Where there was sloth, he gave work; where there was silence, he gave speech; where there was timidity, he gave courage.

Finally, where there was death, he gave his life.

He knew we were both marked men since 1971 when he and I fought the goons, the guns, and the gold, with him running for the governorship of Antique at the age of 29. His own "goons" were the schoolchildren, his guns were his guts, and his gold was his dream—a dream that someday freedom would ring in our province. He won. The years of his tenure as governor from 1971 to 1980 turned him into a folk hero.

I saw his transformation in those years. He was not a nine-to-five-o'clock governor. You could make house calls on him even at dawn. His organization was his people, he said, and his bailiwick was the faith he induced in them.

He moved freely among people who took him as though he was their own son. He moved recklessly among his enemies.

He went to the farthest mountainside and to every hamlet in the province with no bodyguards, believing he could always manage to outstep the threats against him.

In 1980, he chose not to run for re-election and asked me to run instead. He went to the United States in that year and came back in 1984 to wage his campaign for the National Assembly.

In the evening of the elections of 1984, the Sibalom Bridge Massacre became the crowning glory of the reign of terror in Antique. Evelio's supporters—seven of them—were killed. The tyrants of Antique did their worst, aware as they were of their inevitable defeat at the polls. That carnage, along with the massive fraud and COMELEC chicanery, accounted for Evelio's protest of the *Batasan* polls. By NAMFREL count, Evelio was the runaway winner.

Evelio's election protest is still pending in the Supreme Court, unresolved and undecided.

The people of Antique and I regard him as the duly elected Member of Parliament.

In the months before the 1986 elections, there came to the fore confrontation between good and evil. As the campaign manager of the opposition in Antique, Evelio was keenly aware of these distinctions but he did not choose the safe side.

Only a few days before his death, he said to a friend: "We are sitting ducks here." Someone asked him why he chose to be a sitting duck. He replied: "For Cory and for country."

PRECIOSA JAVIER
(Mrs. Evelio Javier)

It was evening, February 11, when I got the long-distance call from my brother that Evelio had been killed. The boys were doing their homework and I did not want to disturb them. I transferred the phone to the bedroom so that I could call our friends.

We have a kind of support group in Los Angeles: Evelio's family, the Rodriguez, Kalaw, Estrada, and Zaldivar families, my family. When they have news, they pass it to me. When I have news, I pass it to them.

Sometime that week, someone called me and said: "Precious, Cory won in Antique and Evelio is fine." I was very happy. I told everybody: "Cory won in Antique. The elections are over. There will be no more problems." I was wrong.

I told our friends that Evelio had been shot. Every once in a while, I looked out to see if the boys had finished their homework. Since they had not, I went back to the phone.

When I saw that they had finished and were ready to go to sleep, I brought them to the *sala*. I put David on my lap and I said: "Guys, I just got a call. Your father has been shot. He is dead."

They looked at each other: "Dad is dead." Gideon became emotional. David cried—not loudly, not hysterically, just tears. I said: "Let us kneel down and pray for your father. That is what he needs now." We knelt down, held hands and prayed. Whatever came to my mind, I said out loud. Whatever came to their minds, they said out loud, too. It had a calming effect. When we were calm, we sat down and I put David on my lap again. I encouraged them to talk.

Gideon got emotional again, so I said: "Let us kneel down again and pray." We did that several times: talk and pray, pray and talk. David even fell asleep on the sofa.

When Gideon decided that he was going up to sleep, he took David in his arms and brought him to his own bed. That was the first time I ever saw him do that. He was very gentle. He stayed beside the bed and watched until David settled in. I told Gideon: "You really have to take control of yourself. Your Dad's gone. I don't think I can tackle everything by myself. You are the man in this family now." That calmed Gideon down.

FR. FRANCISCO J. ARANETA

I had many political arguments with Evelio. In 1984 I had berated him for running for the *Batasan*. And he gave me an answer so many of my young friends give me: "This is my life. I have to do this. What other way is there to save our country, our people, without bloodshed?"

Evelio, I had always told you: you were a fool. You should have followed my advice. Now you are dead and what have you gained?

But Evelio, I salute you. I envy you. Yours was the foolishness of Christ, who gave his life that all of us might live. You gave your life so that your people, whom you love, might live. So that bloodshed might be avoided for our people, you shed your own blood.

I knew Evelio personally. But how many more, whom I never had the privilege to know, have given their lives for me in these elections? How many more will have to make the same supreme sacrifice?

I am humbled when I hear of busy doctors, lawyers, office clerks, teachers, society matrons, teen-aged boys and girls on Election Day and quite often since then, standing up to goons, sometimes Armalite-armed, and refusing to surrender ballot boxes, election returns, and our rights.

I am humbled and I am awed. What I write about and lecture on, these people do. I word-process democracy. These people live.

PRECIOSA JAVIER

Evelio was very angry over Ninoy's death. Our life changed the very day Ninoy died. First there were the phone calls to Evelio from all over Los Angeles, from as far as the East Coast. People—Filipinos in the US—wanted to talk to Evelio.

Then Evelio left everything—including his job.

After his year at Harvard, Evelio found a job with the state government in Sacramento. Then he joined a group of Filipinos who had a brokerage and Evelio worked in brokerage insurance. I had a job, too. But Evelio was not happy. It was as if he was only doing it as a sort of transition. We worked because we had to survive in the US.

When Ninoy died, Evelio dropped everything. I was upset. I said that life must go on and that he should help me out. I thought he was doing very well in the brokerage business. He said: "No, that is not what I plan to do with my life. I only do that kind of work because we are here but I do not intend to stay here."

I said: "Think of what you are doing. We have to pay the rent." He said: "You can take care of that."

He returned to the Philippines in December 1983. He was very sure that that was what he wanted. I did not stop him, because I saw the demarcation line.

In February 1984, I learned about his decision to run for the *Batasan* in May. He seemed very happy with what he was doing, so I just kept saying Yes. In fact, I campaigned with him. But after the massacre of our campaign workers, I was a nervous wreck. I had to fly back to Los Angeles. I was so depressed.

Evelio often wrote to me during the Cory campaign. He was sure that she was going to win, but he was under no illusions. He knew that he should watch out against fraud and terrorism. He had long, long sections in his letters about that. He knew what kind of fight it would be.

He was not afraid for himself, but he knew he was being hunted. On February 1, I came home from work and found the boys talking to him on the phone. When I spoke to him, he talked about the campaign. He also said he called to say goodbye: "I am leaving for the airport. I'm on my way to Antique." Then he said: "Let me say goodbye to the children again." After he spoke to each one, he said: "Let me say goodbye to your mother again." We talked, then he said: "Let me say goodbye to the children." After the children, he wanted to say goodbye to me again. It seemed endless, his goodbyes, and that was a long-distance call. Normally, he did not talk that way. He never called me just to say he was going to the province.

JAMES DONELAN, S.J.

God has a sense of humor. He lets us think we are doing something for Him, but in the long run we find the opposite is true. Such was the flight to Antique—and to far-off happy days.

Antique is so poor a place that not even PAL flies there. So when Father Nebres, my Provincial, a good friend of the murdered Governor Evelio Javier, asked me if I could borrow a small plane and fly him there for Evelio's funeral, I was happy to do so. Burying the dead is a work of mercy.

We took off for Antique at six o'clock, just as the sun was coming up. Sunrise is a beautiful time to fly, and one realizes then why these shining islands are called the "land of the morning." We climbed on top and set a course of 167 degrees over Mt. Lobo on the Batangas shore. Lake Naujan in Mindoro, then Wasi and the Semirara Islands. At 7:35 a.m. Boracay lay off to the east, like a silver-edged emerald. We landed on the dirt strip at Antique at 8:13 a.m.

As we drove through the town, I was struck by the depressed, poverty-stricken atmosphere: the poor roads, the primitive buildings, even the way the people dressed. No wonder no PAL flight comes here. And, I thought, this is the land and the people for whom Evelio left his comfortable life in America to come back and serve.

When we got to the *poblacion,* Mass had already started and the only two seats vacant faced into the sun. Not being blessed with much natural protection on top, I felt my brains sizzling in the sun as the hours went by.

Up to this point my involvement in the events was merely that of a pilot-chauffeur. Of course I was saddened by the death of a bright idealistic young man and I had already said Mass for him in my chapel at AIM. I knew he was an Atenean through and through, so I was also proud of him—but I didn't recall that we had ever met, and so there was no personal element in my grief. I was just one of the Fathers.

But later in the course of the ceremonies, a young woman in black came up to me, and greeted me warmly. She said how glad she was to see me there and asked if I knew how Evelio loved me and admired my writings. I was quite taken aback. The lady, who, of course, turned out to be Evelio's wife, Precious, told me how Evelio had collected my speeches when he was at Ateneo.

While she was talking, I kept desperately searching my memory for a clue. I simply could not remember Evelio. There was no face to go with the name. Then she talked about one of my speeches that impressed Evelio so much that it became a sort of plan of life for him.

It was about St. Thomas More and a lawyer's conscience. Precious told me that when I gave that speech at the Ateneo Law School convocation, Evelio was president of the law school student council. She told me how she and Evelio at that time were both teaching theology, she at Santo Tomas and he at the Ateneo college under Father Cronin. Then it happened.

When she mentioned Father Cronin's theology department, I remembered his young lay professors. Out of the mists of those far-off happy days, twenty-two years ago, like a photo in a developing tray, there came a face of a handsome young man. I remembered Evelio.

And as Precious told me how Evelio had been so caught up into Thomas More's spirit that he founded a Thomas More Society and had a Thomas More pin made, I thought to myself how appropriate it was that Evelio should have found such meaning in More's life.

And I thought, too, how pertinent and prophetic for Evelio that speech on Thomas More was. I recalled how it contained More's words when he was asked by Cardinal Wolsey to put aside his private conscience for the sake of expediency and how he had replied: "When a statesman deserts his private conscience for public duty, he leads himself and his country by a short road into chaos."

I recalled, too, how the speech ended with the words of the sad Cardinal who himself had deserted his conscience for public duty: "Put aside personal ambition. By that sin the angels fell. Let all the ends thou pursuest be thy God's, thy country's, and the truth. Then if thou fallest, thou fallest a blessed martyr."

And so, true to the script to the last word, Evelio fell a blessed martyr.

Later at the end of the Mass, Precious gave her response. Standing next to her husband's body, she looked so young and so deeply touched by sorrow, much like Cory at Ninoy's death. I expected her to say no more than a few words of thanks and appreciation. Instead she delivered a masterpiece. I wondered if any woman had ever paid such a tribute to the man she loved. I thought of Cleopatra's words about Anthony. "For his bounty, there was no winter in it, an autumn 'twas that grew the more by reaping."

For Precious, her husband's distinguishing quality was his shining idealism. And for her metaphor she had only to look up high over the stage where his coffin lay, where on a yellow banner were written the words:

"The world will be better for this—that one man, torn and covered with scars, still strove with his last ounce of courage to reach the unreachable star."

Jousting with windmills, Precious said, is dangerous. The great vanes can smash you to the ground. But they can also catch you up and throw you to the stars.

Those men who killed Evelio out there, she said, pointing to where he died—thought they were smashing him to the ground. Instead they have cast him among the stars.

"Where he has made the face of heaven so fine
That all the world will fall in love with night."

PRECIOSA JAVIER:

When Evelio was in high school, he wanted to be a priest. He was always bugging his retreat master and saying that he wanted to be a priest, but... During his graduation retreat, the retreat master pinned him down: "So what is stopping you?" Evelio said: "I also want to go into politics." The priest answered: "So then, go into politics and carry your Jesuit formation into politics."

In the beginning, my sons were bewildered by their father's death. They could not sort out their feelings at that time. When we came back, they saw a lot of love for Evelio in Manila and in Antique and somehow they were healed. They have begun to talk about their father and his life.

Gideon came to me one day and said that although he knows that he is in a very good school in Los Angeles, in the honors class, in fact, he thinks that he is getting only information. He now says that he wants an education like what his father had—an education with a goal, a vision, a direction.

GOSPEL READING, FUNERAL MASS FOR EVELIO JAVIER, ATENEO DE MANILA UNIVERSITY

MATTHEW 5:1-12. Seeing the crowds, he went up the hill. There he sat down and was joined by his disciples. Then he began to speak. This is what he taught them:
"Blessed are the poor in spirit;
theirs is the kingdom of heaven.
Blessed are the meek;
they shall inherit the earth.
Blessed are those who mourn;
they shall be comforted.
Blessed are those who hunger and thirst for
what is right;

they shall be satisfied.
Blessed are the merciful;
they shall have mercy shown them.
Blessed are the pure in heart;
they shall see God.
Blessed are the peacemakers;
they shall be called sons of God.
Blessed are those who are persecuted;
theirs is the kingdom of heaven.

Blessed are you when wicked men abuse you and persecute you and speak all kinds of calumny against you all because of me. Rejoice and be glad, for your reward will be great in heaven. This is how they persecuted the prophets before you."

JOSEFINA RODRIGUEZ

After the National Assembly announced that Marcos had won, I did not know what to do anymore. I continued to listen to the radio. I heard a group of blind men go on the air. They said that they were blind but they knew and they could feel. I suddenly felt stronger. After twenty years, we could not be blind to the evils of the regime.

JAIME ONGPIN, opposition leader

To me, it is a very grave miscalculation that Marcos will hop in a helicopter and disappear forever once people start storming the palace gates. I'm not so sure that the Presidential Security Command will not shoot at the Filipino people. A lot of people could be slaughtered. While Cory has said that she is prepared to sacrifice her own life, she is not prepared to ask hundreds of thousands of Filipinos to do the same.

CECILIA MUÑOZ PALMA

We were talking to Cory and she was warning us, saying that it was impossible for Marcos to concede. "Do you really believe Marcos will give up and accept his loss?" We had to rely on the power of the people. This time, the power of the people must be shown. So Cory came out with her call for a boycott. We were to begin it the day after Marcos takes his oath of office. Then we were to start a day of mass action on the 26th of February. There was a meeting of people close to her to decide on what course of action to take. The consensus was that it had to be nonviolent protest and the first medium of action was to boycott. But some thought it was too mild. They wanted a more militant protest such as an announcement of bank strikes, not only for a day but for a week. But she did not follow that and

said to see first how people will respond to this. What she had in mind was to test the capabilities of the people to discipline themselves. I thought it would be easy for them to boycott the crony banks, boycott certain products, boycott Rustan's. If we could see that the people respond to this then we could get ready for a bigger one. That was her point. And the people really showed their support.

CORAZON AQUINO

After the election, I went to the Makati Municipal Hall and to the other places where people were keeping vigil. I also kept saying that I was calling for a rally. Some people must have thought: This woman is mad. She has already lost and she is still calling for a rally. Who in the world would call for a rally if he were in her place? It was a gamble but I wanted to find out if people were still supporting me. When they showed that they were, I said: "Let us go on."

VIC HELLY, S.J.

The *Tagumpay ng Bayan* (People's Victory) rally was a joyous celebration. During the long afternoon as I wandered among the crowd, I did not detect even the slightest trace of hatred or anger. People shouted "Cory-Cory-Cory!" or "Cory-Doy, Cory-Doy, Cory-Doy!" and cars honked their horns in unison with the joyous shouts of the crowds. The rally began with the celebration of the Eucharist. We were six bishops and about 25 priests concelebrating the Mass. When Mrs. Aquino arrived, two million voices raised the cry, "Cory-Cory-Cory!" The affection and trust the people offer Mrs. Aquino is beyond belief.

---

7 February 1986: As the Mother Superior signs the voters' registry, her entire community of nuns waits in line in a precinct in Metro Manila. On the day of the Presidential and Vice Presidential elections, the voters' turn-out was early and hefty. Many voters, however, found themselves disfranchised when their names were arbitrarily dropped from the voters' registry. This prevalent fact was seen, upon further study, to be among the list of frauds accomplished by ruling party computers.

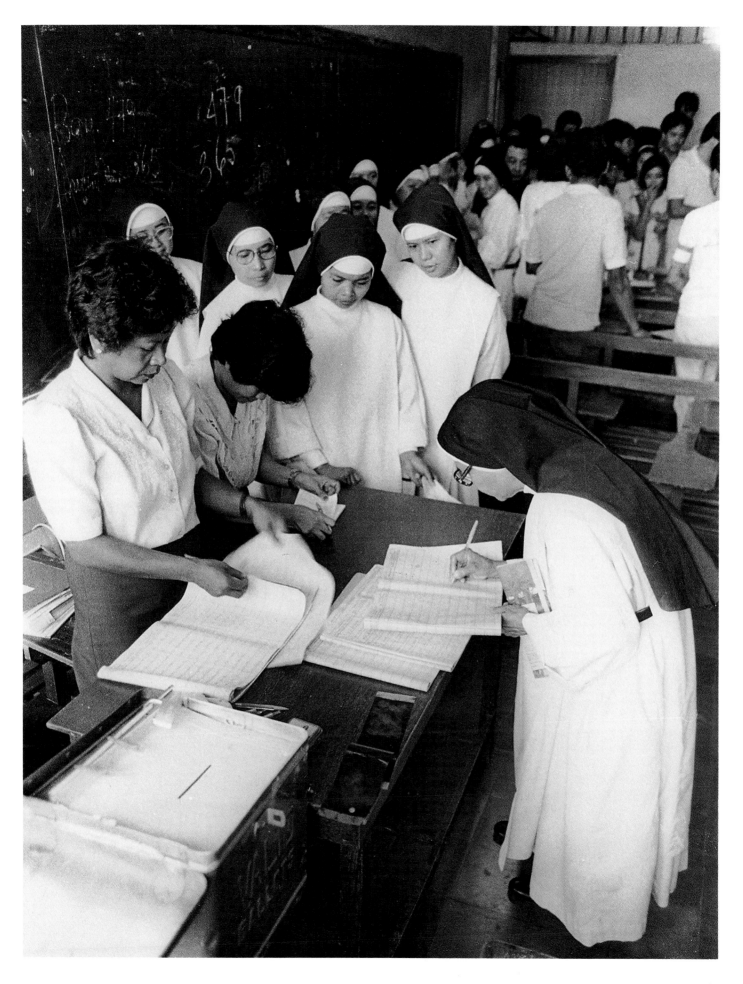

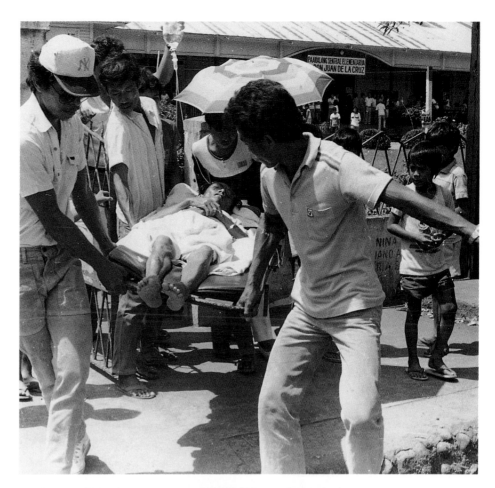

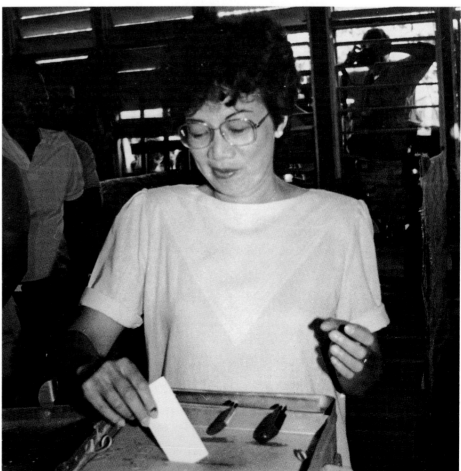

Friends and hospital aides carry Jigs Rentillo from the Davao City precinct where he voted. Knowing that in a few days he would be dead from cancer, Jigs begged his doctors to allow him to vote as "the least and last thing I could do for Cory Aquino", upper right. At about the same time, Cory Aquino casts her vote in Hacienda Luisita, Tarlac, her home province, right. In Iloilo, precinct aides help an old voter, opposite page.

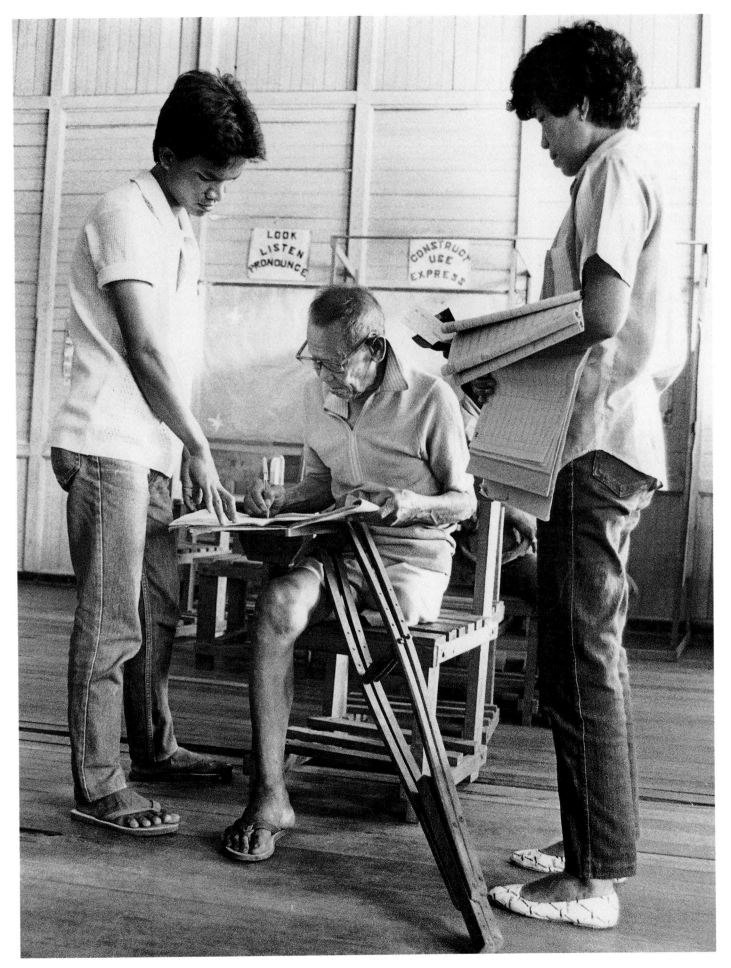

Afraid of ruling party goons who have been known to snatch ballot boxes, to throw them away or to stuff them with favorable manufactured votes, vigilantes form human barricades for boxes being brought from precincts to municipal halls for official tally, above and opposite left. With less manpower, a vigilante simply sits on a ballot box, left.

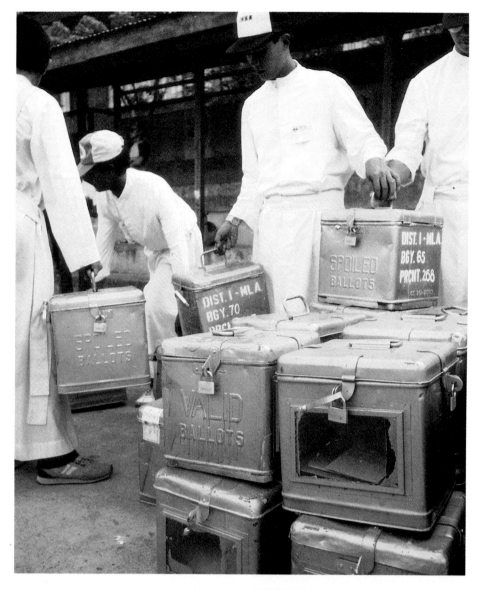

Escort service for ballot boxes were provided by various citizens, among them seminarians who—along with other religious—were called the NAMFREL Marines, upper left. A tight cordon of cheerful escorts surround two ballot boxes on the way to city hall, left. A precinct official lifts

the lid of a ballot box to show concerned vigilantes that its padlock was in place, above. They then escorted her to the municipal hall where the ballot box was deposited for official tally: a scene that took place in many places in Metro Manila late on election day.

NAMFREL OPERA
NATIONAL TAL
MARCOS AQUINO PRECINCTS COUNTED TOLENTINO E
(PER CENT OF REGION)

1,604,795 2,064,
425,283 56,
96,021 7,
11,652 389,
375,281 283,
90,952 88,
42,211 185,
163,759 244,
116,505 3
5,218 3,572
83,768 119,
146,222 168
44,351
15,095

% OF TOTA
DAT

Aide writes early voting results on the board in the NAMFREL national headquarters, above. Watching the results come in are two venerable leaders of the opposition, Don Chino Roces and former Senator Lorenzo Tañada, right. NAMFREL head Jose Concepcion visits the Pasay City hall to check the vote count, opposite page.

Tabulators, aides, journalists, political leaders—either concerned or curious—fill the cavernous gym which was the national headquarters of the NAMFREL during its period of counting votes, left and above. The NAMFREL results consistently showed a lead by Cory Aquino and Salvador Laurel as president and vice president, but the Commission on Election Count showed otherwise.

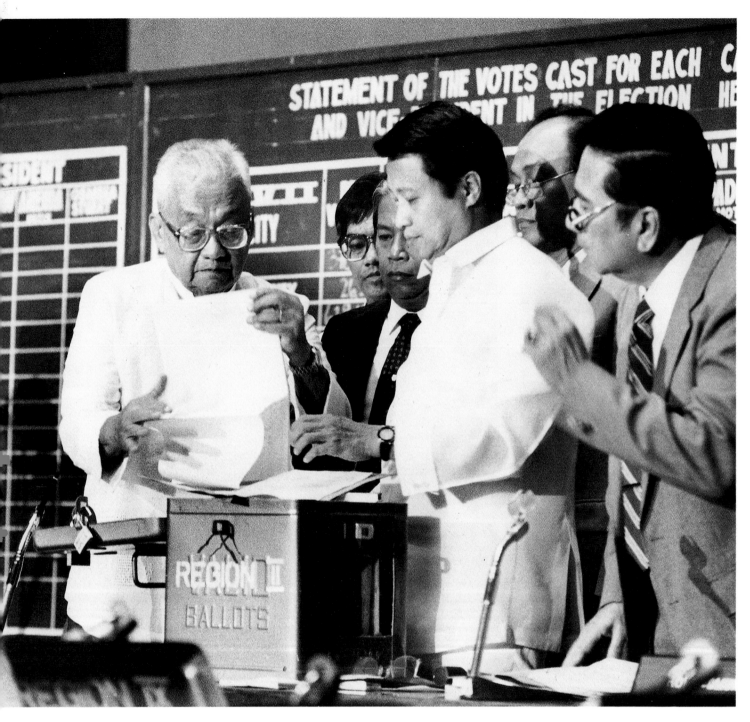

STATEMENT OF THE VOTES CAST FOR EACH C
AND VICE-PRESIDENT IN THE ELECTION

REGION III
BALLOTS

Assemblymen of the Marcos-dominated parliament study the tally sheets of national results, above. According to election regulations, the parliament had to confirm the results and declare the winner. With determined speed, leaving no time nor room for the opposition to question the validity of submitted results, the parliament declared Marcos the winner amid protests from citizens in vigil, right.

A workman paints on the digits for a large outdoor display of election results in Metro Manila, left. So high was the interest in the results that displays were set up in prominent places and the radio was on nearly all the time in offices and homes.

The Lord detests liars

PROV. 12:22

PEOPLE POWER

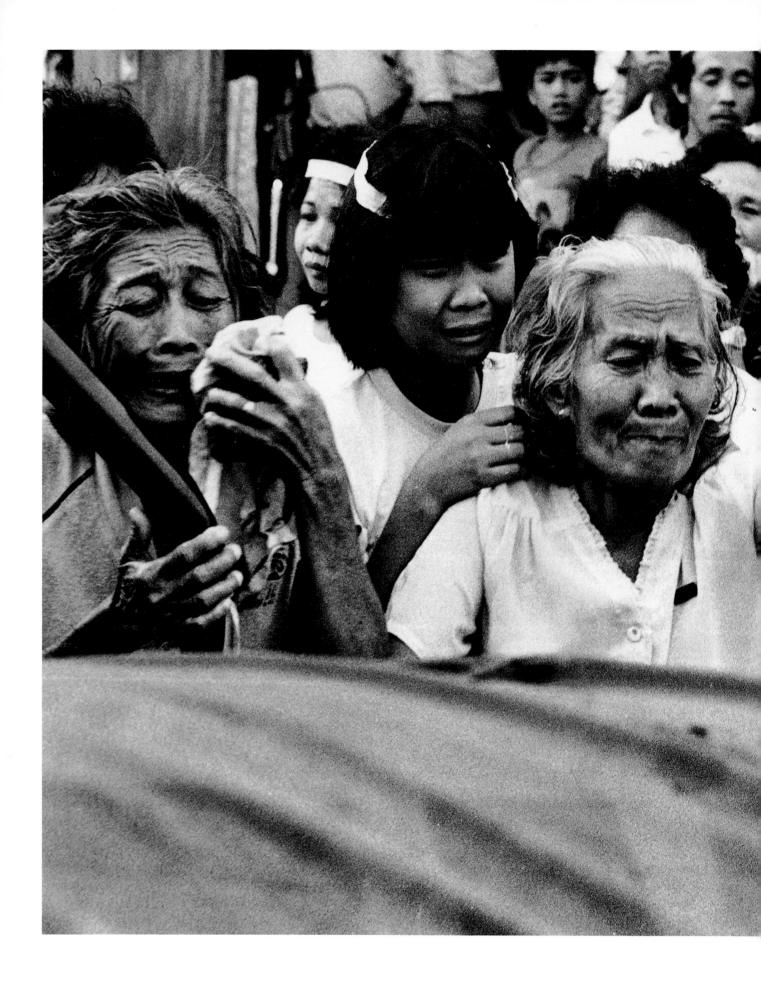

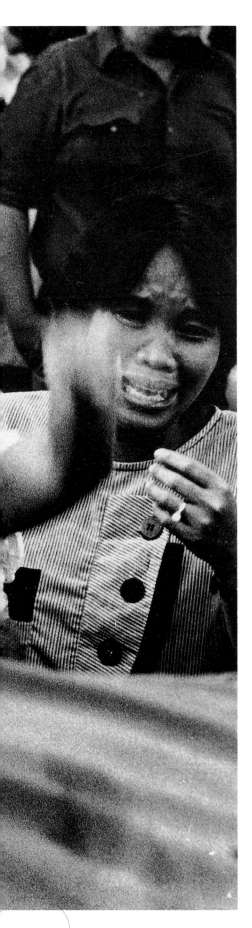

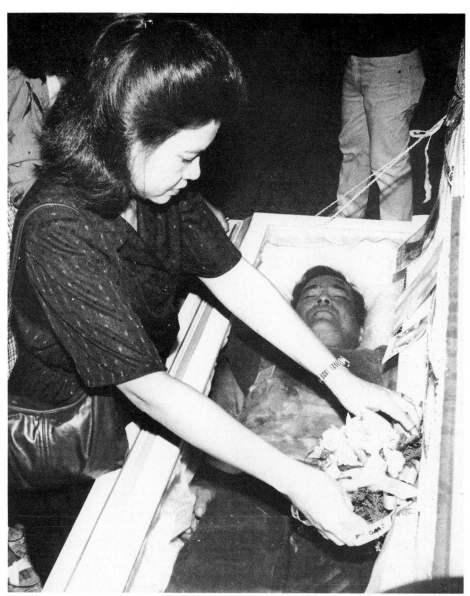

Preciosa Javier pins a corsage on the casket of her slain husband, Evelio Javier, the campaign manager for Cory Aquino in Antique province, above. Four days after the election when he delivered Antique's votes to Cory, Javier was shot to death by men riding a military jeep. A friend of Ninoy Aquino, Javier was governor of Antique at age 29. So promising was he that Marcos' ruling party asked him to join their roster, whereupon he chose instead to go to Harvard and study under a grant. While in the US, he learned that Aquino was assassinated and he immediately came home to Antique to continue the struggle for democracy. He ran for parliament in 1984 but his opponent wrested the seat from him, a matter that was under protest when Javier was killed. For all this, the women of Antique mourn, left.

Cory Aquino listens to Preciosa Javier as they keep vigil in the Ateneo chapel where the wake for Evelio Javier was held, above. The two boys are Javier's sons, David and Gideon. Although Javier was killed in Antique, his body was brought to Manila and carried in procession throughout the main streets, reminiscent of Ninoy Aquino's funeral more than two years before, right. It was after a Requiem Mass for Javier in the campus of the Ateneo de Manila —a Mass in which Cory Aquino was present—wherein many people heard for the first time the statement of the Catholic Bishops of the Philippines saying that the recently ended elections were marked with unprecedented fraud and violence. Overleaf: Another funeral turns into a protest demonstration as cause-oriented groups unfurl their flags during the march through major Metro Manila streets in mourning for Evelio Javier. His death was a bright flare that lit up the muddle of electoral fraud and deceit. After the initial horror at the manner of his death, mourning for him raised courage and determination among Cory Aquino's supporters.

Scenario
22 FEBRUARY 1986

FRANCISCO S. TATAD

Proclaimed by the *Batasan* but rejected by everybody else, Marcos was determined to tough it out. The bishops had spoken, Reagan had spoken, the European community had spoken, Japan, Australia, New Zealand, ASEAN had spoken—all without any demonstrable effect. Aquino's boycott of so-called "crony" establishments had caused a slight drop in the sales of beer and ice cream, and prompted some affected newspapers to editorially protest their innocence. But that was all.

Marcos told the nation he would not vacate. He appeared in no danger of being forced out. Having threatened to meet force with force, he now left no doubt that he would use the Armed Forces to enforce his "mandate." But no foreign government was willing to recognize that mandate. The only exception was the Soviet Union whose new ambassador chose this particularly awkward time to present his credentials and congratulate Marcos. But the Soviets explained later that they had not taken sides in the conflict.

In the afternoon of February 22, a Saturday, the usual playing of "Onward Christian Soldiers" on Radio Veritas was interrupted by an emergency news conference called by Defense Minister Juan Ponce Enrile and Armed Forces Vice Chief of Staff Lieutenant General Fidel Ramos at Enrile's Camp Aguinaldo headquarters. They had withdrawn their allegiance from their longtime president and commander-in-chief, and barricaded themselves inside the Ministry of National Defense, after learning that Marcos had ordered their arrest along with military reformists.

Enrile said they would hold their positions until they all got killed. He telephoned US Ambassador Stephen Bosworth, and the latter assured him he would closely monitor developments. At the same time, elements of the US Seventh Fleet stood by in Philippine waters.

In the evening, Marcos appeared on TV to announce that a coup d'etat intended to be staged by military reformists after midnight had been aborted. He presented some alleged leaders of the coup, and implicated Enrile and Ramos. He asked them to "stop this stupidity" and surrender to General Ver's forces. The coup allegations were laughed off by the reformists.

As uncertainty deepened, Ricardo Cardinal Vidal, Archbishop of Cebu and CBCP president, and Jaime Cardinal Sin, the well-known Archbishop of Manila, publicly offered to mediate. Although no concrete steps were taken, their message over Radio Veritas expressed the hope that both sides would avoid violence. But even before the prelates could speak, Ninoy Aquino's younger brother Agapito had already called on the cause-oriented groups to gather around the camp to provide Enrile and Ramos street support. Cardinal Sin followed by asking the people to send food and to go out into the streets and block any movement of hostile troops. Within the hour, thousands of men, women, and children ringed the gates of the military camps. It was a festive crowd.

By now, Ramos had moved back to his constabulary headquarters in Camp Crame just across Epifanio de los Santos Avenue (EDSA), leaving Enrile with more foreign correspondents than troops.

It was an anxious moment. Would Marcos order an attack? Fevered contact between the Marcos loyalists and the rebel forces produced an agreement that the rebels would not attack Malacañang and that Ver would avoid any troop movements. Thus the evening passed without incident.

By Sunday morning, the crowd had swollen around the two camps. In the afternoon, Enrile went over to Camp Crame to join Ramos. All of Manila and the immediate environs had by then started pouring onto EDSA to support the rebel forces.

Men, women, and children descended on EDSA from all directions, bringing with them provisions not for combat but for a family picnic. They came with their radios, food, and drinks and camped on the concrete highway with their families and friends. Radio Veritas had been knocked off the air by saboteurs, so they followed the news through a makeshift radio station. From time to time, someone mounted the roof of a vehicle to make an announcement, or give directions.

"The tanks are coming!" Somebody would shout from the crowd and at once everyone ran in the direction of the advancing tanks. A false alarm. Almost every approach to Crame now lay blocked with stalled cars and buses, fallen trees, debris or street diggings. But it was the human barricade, swelling by the minute, that provided the biggest barrier to any possible advance of loyalist forces.

Priests and nuns, who had not worn their religious habits in years, stood resplendent in their cassocks and the prescribed attire of their respective congregations. With rosary beads in their hands, and often leading men and women in prayer, they formed "the first line of defense." Citizen volunteer groups provided the field communications support, reporting the movement of tanks to the rebel command which in turn relayed it to the crowd.

The first tanks appeared on Ortigas Avenue less than a kilometer away from Crame. A crowd—mostly women—rushed to turn them back by threatening to lie down on the road if they advanced. This pre-determined the overall result.

After that, men, women, and children turned them back with their smiles, an offer of food and drink, and words of fraternal advice. At one point, some soldiers tried to use tear gas on the crowd. But the wind suddenly changed course. The soldiers turned back.

From the air, pilots ordered to strafe Crame could see nothing of their target except a massive crowd of people forming a huge cross. So while Marcos continued to warn the rebels that his forces were waiting to run over the rebel camp, various elements of the army, air force, and navy were defecting one by one.

On Monday morning, Bosworth telephoned Marcos to convey Reagan's warning not to use heavy weapons on the rebels. It was shortly before Marcos was to go on a live TV news conference, to announce an ultimatum to the rebels. When he finally spoke, he said something else. Ver reminded him that the fighter planes were airborne and waiting for orders, that the troops were poised to strike. Marcos surprised Ver by saying they were not to attack, nor to use any heavy weapons unless the rebels attacked government buildings and installations. There was an unusual exchange between Marcos and his loyal chief of staff. Moments later, the news conference blinked off the air. Marcos, who had dominated the media for 20 years, had been cut off: the government TV channel had fallen into the hands of the rebels.

With the rebels in control of all communications, of the air, the sea, and most of the ground forces, the army's armored divisions and the Marines, loyal to Marcos to the very end, lay immobilized. This caused more defections from the ranks. At the end of the day, only about 20 per cent of the Armed Forces remained loyal to Marcos.

On Tuesday morning, February 25, Corazon Aquino and Salvador Laurel formally took power as President and Vice President respectively of the new government. Aquino was sworn in by the Senior Associate Justice (later to be named Chief Justice) of the Supreme Court Claudio Teehankee, and Laurel by Justice Vicente Abad Santos in simple rites at Club Filipino in Greenhills, a few minutes away from Camp Crame. Her first act was to name Laurel as her prime minister-designate, Ponce Enrile as defense minister and Ramos as the new chief of staff, after promoting him to the rank of full general.

At exactly the same time, Marcos was on the telephone asking Sen. Paul Laxalt in the US about the latest word from the White House. Laxalt advised him to step down. He expressed disappointment. Imelda Marcos broke down upon hearing this. But having scheduled the inauguration that morning, Marcos took his oath as President before the Supreme Court Chief Justice in the presence of a loyalist crowd that filled the Palace's main reception hall. Not a single foreign diplomat was present. Polite applause greeted the oath. Channel 9, which the Marcos family controlled, tried to do a live coverage of the event, but was promptly knocked off the air.

By evening, it was all over. While thousands massed beyond the famous Mendiola Bridge, the scene of many past encounters between students and riot police, US helicopters landed inside the Palace grounds under the cover of darkness. Within minutes, the Marcos family fled to Clark Air Force Base on the first leg of their flight to the United States.

The men and tanks that had for days stood in front of Malacañang, ready to fight and die for Marcos, melted away as soon as the word was out. Instantly, a tumult of voices and feet rent the air. The people surged past the Palace gates, ran up from building to building, cheering, shouting, dancing! Horns honked through the night, every corner of the city lit up, the streets filled with frenzied merrymaking. "A miracle!" "Our prayers have been heard!" "The hand of God has prevailed!" "The people have won!"

A long night had ended. It was the break of a new dawn.

Voices

AMADO L. LACUESTA, JR., screenwriter
Saturday Evening:

It is about 7:30 p.m.

We are on our way home to Loyola Heights in Quezon City from Makati. Lolly and I are discussing one of my film projects while the car radio is tuned to Radio Veritas—as all our radios at home have been since before Election Day.

Suddenly, we are listening to a replay of a news conference that Minister Enrile and General Ramos had earlier at Camp Aguinaldo.

We hear Enrile confirm that Marcos cheated in Region 2, and that he thinks Marcos did not really win. He goes on to say he and his people are prepared to make a stand until they are all killed, right there in Aguinaldo.

Lolly and I cannot believe what we are hearing.

Then Ramos says he is withdrawing his support for Marcos, saying Marcos has made the Armed Forces subservient to him instead of to the people. Next, a report that two helicopters have landed at Aguinaldo, disgorging sacks of arms and armed civilians. An interview with Colonel Roilo Golez, the Postmaster General, follows. He announces his resignation from the government and casts his lot with Enrile and Ramos as one of the first defectors.

When we finally realize what is happening, we shout with joy inside the car. Triumphantly, I exclaim that Marcos is finished, we have won. But after the initial thrill, a dreaded thought chills me and I try to suppress it: civil war. Lolly trembles with fear, uncertainty.

We rush home, eager to monitor the unfolding events.

As we approach our gate, our next-door neighbors—the young husband is an army colonel attached indirectly to Enrile's staff but on inactive status—are just coming out to join a neighborhood Rosary rally for peace. They confirm the infant rebellion but know little more than we do.

As I park the car, I shout to my eldest son, Sarge, to turn on the living-room radio. I also turn on the radio in the bedroom. The news conference is being replayed again in two installments.

The first part of the conference worries me. In answer to a reporter's question, Enrile seems to couch his words too carefully, avoiding any clear commitment to Cory Aquino. But when the same question is asked again later, he says he believes in his heart that Cory won. I am relieved. Still, I hide a trace of apprehension from Lolly. The history of military coups and juntas in Latin America and South Asia is all too real and recent.

I tell Sarge to prepare cassette tapes. I want to tape Marcos' resignation speech which I am sure must come soon. It will make a nice companion piece to my tape of the declaration of martial law fourteen years ago, which I still keep. We are all excited, even my two-year-old daughter, Andi, who keeps flashing the *Laban* sign.

Over Radio Veritas, Enrile and Ramos appeal for "people power," the first time the phrase really makes an impact on me. Not sure yet what Enrile and Ramos really mean, I am skeptical. Only when Cardinal Sin makes the same appeal later do I feel a little better. Surely, if they are openly asking for civilian support and if the Cardinal himself is asking us to support them, things must be on the level.

But knowing Cory is in Cebu, we worry anyway, especially after Enrile discloses a military "hit list" of opposition leaders. I say a silent prayer for her safety. I know Lolly is doing the same thing.

Veritas also calls for more people to gather at its Fairview station. The idea of just what "people power" is expected to do is still not crystal clear.

I ask Lolly if she wants to go to Aguinaldo. She hesitates, says it's up to me. I decide to wait and see. The idea that a rebellion is really taking place still has not settled. I want to think it cannot be happening. Not here, not in the Philippines. Close to midnight, Marcos asks Enrile and Ramos to "stop this stupidity." He assures them his tanks and helicopter gunships can overwhelm them anytime he chooses. He stresses his desire to avoid bloodshed.

I tell Lolly he is bluffing. If he really has the upper hand, he will not waste time threatening. But deep inside, I am afraid he is right.

In bed, I turn off the table radio and clamp my second son's headphone-radio over my head instead. It's quite uncomfortable lying down with it, but I do not want to miss anything although Ver has reportedly agreed to hold off his troops for the night.

I fantasize that, come morning, everything will be all right: the AFP will have come over to Enrile and Ramos painlessly and Marcos will have resigned. I even try to imagine Marcos as he announces his resignation. But I am afraid.

JUAN PONCE ENRILE, Minister of National Defense

Perhaps it was not really human will that was directing the whole episode. On Saturday morning, February 22, I was in a coffee shop with some friends. We knew something would happen sooner or later—and it indeed began to happen.

There was a phone call for me from Minister Ongpin. He said that his entire security group had been arrested the night before. I knew what the arrest meant: almost all of those men were identified with the Ministry of National Defense.

I went home for lunch and talked to my wife, then I read. At about 3:30 p.m., three of my men arrived: Colonel Gregorio Honasan, Colonel Eduardo Kapunan, my intelligence officer, and Major Noe Wong. They said that we were about to be arrested. I knew that it would come to this, sooner or later.

Unknown and contrary to the impression of many, I knew that President Marcos could not be driven from the seat of power unless a plan was devised which must include force.

Over a long period of time, we had to devise this plan, as long as some four years before February 22 itself. Why were we making plans? We did not want to supplant him nor to install ourselves as the power in the land. We made plans because we knew the design of the military chiefs around him.

I knew about this design; I do not know if General Ramos knew about it, too. The design was: if the President dies, a group of generals close to him would withhold the information from the public. Then they would arrest men like me and General Ramos and all other persons whom they considered obstacles to the accomplishment of their objectives. After the arrests, they would then announce the demise of President Marcos and install Mrs. Marcos as the leader of the nation and the wielder of power. According to this design, after six months or a year, they would remove her from the seat of power. A military dictatorship would then be installed in our hapless land.

This information came to me by accident, through a person who was very close to General Ver. I do not know for what reason that information came to me. I can only surmise that it was probably the way of God that I should get the information so that a plan could be made to save our people from the bitterness of tyranny.

We had been planning for four years — but the plan that was put into execution from February 22 onwards was very different from the original plan we made. It became a bloodless encounter with history—for which I can only thank God.

CRISTINA PONCE ENRILE (Mrs. Juan Ponce Enrile)

I was taken aback, but I did not ask questions. There was no time. Besides, I have always respected his decisions. I always think that he knows more than I know.

LT. GEN. FIDEL V. RAMOS, Deputy Chief of Staff

On Saturday afternoon, I was at home because I had to attend to Cory's Crusaders. They were my neighbors and friends who threatened to picket our house with placards saying: "Ramos, Resign!" or "Investigate the Antique Murder." I asked their leader to please settle for a dialogue instead of having a picket. I said that I would make myself available to them. We agreed on a dialogue about issues on their mind.

At 4:00 p.m., one of our good friends, Betty Belmonte, called up my wife, Ming. She said: "Ming, Johnny is about to be arrested, if he has not been already arrested by now." My wife passed the information on to me. I said: "Maybe I will be next. But first, I have to attend to Cory's Crusaders."

We started the dialogue at 4:00 p.m. Very soon, Minister Enrile was on the phone. He said very, very quickly: "Eddie, I think the time has come. Are you with me?" I said: "Yes, sir, I am with you all the way. But please put down the phone. This is not a clear phone." I added: "I will join you, sir, but I will still have to dialogue with some people right here." I went on with the dialogue with Cory's Crusaders and I think we resolved some issues.

Before long, there was another phone call and I knew right away who it was. I said to him again: "Sir, I will join you as soon as possible." I had to say goodbye to my neighbors and left my wife in charge of them. I went to the Ministry of National Defense. I think it was the hand of the Lord which propelled me to join Minister Enrile and decide that really the time had come.

PETE REYES, photographer

We arrived at 4:00 p.m. for the news conference. But it took a long time before Enrile talked to us. The atmosphere in the room was tense. We felt that something was up. Before Enrile arrived, we heard a helicopter land. We thought that the chopper was bringing Enrile in, but we found out that it was carrying Armalites and ammunition.

We were all nervous as we went up to the place for the news conference. We noticed that the soldiers were in complete combat gear, with canteens and knapsacks. We also saw boxes of K-ration. They looked as if they were ready for war.

Enrile said that President Marcos threatened to have Camp Aguinaldo raided and that the only way to stop such an attack would be to ask for the help of the people. When he was on the phone, it seemed like he was about to cry. Enrile was obviously nervous. He was the underdog. He must have felt that the end was near. It was war.

RICARDO CARDINAL VIDAL, president, Catholic Bishops' Conference of the Philippines

Somebody called me up in San Miguel and said: "We are on the eve of a coup d'etat." I heard on the radio that there was something hatching. What was I to do now?

After the Enrile-Ramos news conference, I received another telephone call: "What is the answer of CBCP (Catholic Bishops' Conference of the Philippines) to this present situation that is developing?" I called up Cardinal Sin and said: "We are the only two now who can talk and you are my vice president. I'd like to consult you on what we shall do."

He told me that he was going to make a statement of his own as the Archbishop of Manila. I was to make the statement on behalf of the bishops of the Philippines. That's why my statement could never be taken as partisan. It was spontaneous. I asked the people to remain calm because we had already said in our statement that whatever happens, our response will always be the peaceful and nonviolent means to confront evil.

This was my statement: "I heard about the latest happenings and I understand that the situation is not so good. I would like to appeal to the people not to use violence to solve our problems. If possible, let us not give each side a chance or an opportunity to use force. If possible, let us have a peaceful dialogue. If they want a mediator, they are free to choose any one. I just

hope that no Filipino blood will be spilled. So I appeal, once again, let us not use violence. Let us use a peaceful and orderly solution. If any one should feel that I can be of some help to them as president of the Catholic Bishops' Conference of the Philippines, I will be very willing to help for the sake of peace in our land."

JAIME CARDINAL SIN, Archbishop of Manila

On Saturday afternoon, as I was about to go to Ateneo for the ordination of two Jesuits, Cristina Ponce Enrile called me, crying: "Cardinal, help us!"

Then Juan Ponce Enrile called: "Cardinal, I will be dead within one hour," he said. And he seemed to be trembling. "I don't want to die," he added. "But if it is possible, do something. I'd still like to live. I already heard the order to smash us." He was almost crying. Then Fidel Ramos, who is a Protestant, told me that he embraced the image of Our Lady of Fatima. "Dear Lady," he had said, "I know that you are miraculous." And he told me: "Cardinal, help us by calling the people to support us."

"All right, Fidel," I said, "Just wait. In fifteen minutes, your place will be filled with people." I immediately called the contemplative sisters. There are three communities—the Carmelites in Gilmore, the Pink Sisters in Hemady, and the Poor Clares. I called them one by one: "Prioress, right now get out from your cells and go to the chapel and pray with outstretched arms before the Blessed Sacrament. And fast until I tell you to stop. We are in battle and, like Moses, you have to stretch out your arms." I said I will tell them why later.

I called Radio Veritas immediately. This was my statement: "I want you to pray because it is only through prayer that we can resolve this problem. I am deeply concerned about the situation of General Ramos and Minister Enrile. I am calling on our people to support our two good friends at the camp. Go to Camp Aguinaldo and show your solidarity with them in this crucial period. Our two good friends have shown their idealism. I would be very happy if you would help them. I wish that bloodshed will be avoided. Pray to Our Lady that we will be able to solve our problems peacefully. I am sorry to disturb you at this late hour, but it is precisely at a time like this that we most need your support for our two good friends."

CECILIA MUÑOZ PALMA, opposition leader

When Sonny Belmonte called me on Saturday afternoon to say that Enrile was under house arrest, I told him not to believe the rumors. However, at 6:00 p.m. I got a call from San Francisco, California. It was Steve Psinakis. He said: "I got the news that Enrile and Ramos are holed up in Camp Aguinaldo." I said that I did not know anything about it. Steve said: "You better warn Cory. This might be true. You yourself had better go into hiding."

If they were really being held, I thought that it meant Marcos was beginning to control the military and would really arrest some people. Not long after, the news came from Veritas that Enrile and Ramos were in Camp Aguinaldo. Nothing was said about their being under arrest. Instead, they were making statements against Marcos. They were rebelling.

Then Betty Belmonte called me. She said that Enrile was asking for help and was wondering if I would support them. At almost the same time, I received another call from Steve Psinakis, saying that I should be careful because it might all be just a ploy.

I believed that Enrile and Ramos were sincere. I heard them say that they were against the results of the election and that they were taking over Camp Aguinaldo. So I called Radio Veritas and expressed my support for them. We have always believed that whatever action the civilians must undertake in this fight against Mr. Marcos, they would need the cooperation of the military.

I already knew that it was a case of rebellion. I meant my statement to be considered as that of a co-conspirator.

After a few minutes, Butz Aquino called me. He said: "Justice, is it true that we are supporting Enrile and Ramos?" I told him: "We must support them, but you have to be careful. You might be arrested." He replied: "Oh, it doesn't matter if it is only a question of being arrested." So he went out there with a group and started the whole thing. Cardinal Sin also made an appeal, so the people multiplied.

AGAPITO AQUINO (BUTZ), opposition leader
(Over Radio Veritas, February 22, 1986)

I am here at Camp Aguinaldo. I have just spoken to Minister Enrile. He and his men are bracing themselves against an attack. We are here to try and prevent bloodshed. We are going to work for a peaceful solution.

I am calling on all concerned citizens, especially my friends in ATOM, BANDILA, and FSDM, to meet me at Isetann in Cubao. There we will decide on the best course of action.
(Later in the evening)

We are here at Isetann and we will march to Crame and Aguinaldo. I spoke to Minister Enrile. He and his men are ready to fight if they are attacked. If they are attacked by Malacañang, we will support them.

We will give them moral support. We will surround the camps and protect them with our bodies. We will do this because Enrile and Ramos wish to follow the will of the people. They have declared that this regime no longer has the support of the people and yet it insists on holding on to power.

Anyone who respects the will of the people deserves our help. At this moment, we are still conferring. I call on all our countrymen to join us and increase our number so that we can prevent a bloody confrontation.

AURORA A. AQUINO, mother of Agapito Aquino (Butz)

I asked Butz: "Is there a spare life that you keep at home? Why are you at every happening? You are always the first one out." At EDSA, he was the first to call for people.

CESAR B. UMALI, Jr.

It was around 10:00 p.m. when I heard Butz Aquino over Radio Veritas asking for civilian volunteers to proceed immediately to Camps Crame and Aguinaldo. "What?" I asked myself. "What can civilians do, other than die, amid a firefight between two groups of professional soldiers? Will the volunteers be issued guns to fight side by side with the rebels?" I was probably more afraid to heed Butz Aquino's call than puzzled by his exhortation. I never imagined that the Marcos antidote called people power had already been unleashed. I went to sleep, extremely agitated by my own thoughts.

FR. FRANCISCO J. ARANETA

When I heard of the revolt, I went to load up on gasoline (just in case). I gave the attendants the news, and warned them to avoid Camp Crame or Camp Aguinaldo when going home. By the book, it was the sensible thing to do.

Hours later, I groaned when I heard Butz Aquino sounding off his call for volunteers to join him in Cubao and from there to march off to support the soldiers at Crame and Aguinaldo. "There goes that fool," I thought to myself. By the time that the Cardinal made his appeal, it was good that I was fast asleep, otherwise I would have been guilty of thinking that my dear superior had lost his mind, too.

Who gave Butz and the Cardinal such imprudent ideas? I have a strong suspicion that it was the Holy Spirit.

MARGARITA COJUANGCO, opposition leader

I couldn't believe it at first. But when the phone rang, it was General Ramos. He was looking for Peping, my husband, who was with Cory in Cebu.

He spoke to me instead. He asked me to help mobilize people. So I did, realizing that the revolution was for real. I called whoever I could and we gathered cars and people and stayed until about four a.m. in Camp Crame that first night.

DYFM, Radyo Bombo (Iloilo City)

The phone rang. The technician on board, Ernesto Nieles, casually picked it up. He was facing the announcer's booth where he could see the station manager and the anchorman discussing on the air the post-election developments. There was a glass wall between them.

"Hurry, get me into Boss RA's program," said the caller. (RA is how all the station personnel refer to anchorman Rico Arcones.) "It's critical. Ramos and Enrile resigned. It's war. They are now holed up at Camp Aguinaldo with only their bodyguards." It was a report from DYFM's reporter, Jenil Demorito, in Makati.

Nieles hurriedly wrote down: "Enrile and Ramos resigned." He knocked on the glass wall to attract the attention of the anchorman on the other side.

Arcones glared at him. He did not like to be disturbed when he was on the air. Most of all, he did not like people to bang on the glass wall to get his attention. The technician knew this but he banged anyway, until Arcones saw what he had written: "Enrile and Ramos resigned."

Arcones got the message and thought instinctively that whatever may happen, it would be crucial to the nation. He switched on the mike and said: "Friends, we are very sorry to interrupt this discussion. There has been a disturbing development in Manila." He then aired the news from their Makati reporter, Jenil Demorito. And that was how the rest of the network in the Visayas and Mindanao learned of the Enrile-Ramos breakaway.

VIC HELLY, S.J.

Perhaps four hours after Enrile and Ramos announced their breakaway, Cardinal Sin appealed to Manileños to go to the camps in large numbers "to express our solidarity with our two good friends there." Within an hour and a half about 40,000 of us were clogging EDSA. It was a joyous crowd. The atmosphere was that of a Philippine fiesta.

VIRGENCITA G. JAWID

When we heard the voice of Cardinal Sin calling us to help our friends, Enrile and Ramos, I felt that somebody up there was pushing me to go. Someone was pushing us to go and extend our help to our fellow Filipinos who had no other motive but to end the tyranny of 20 years. I felt someone's hand guiding the Filipino people to make sure they do what was right.

JIMMY VICENTE

Shortly after midnight, barely eight hours after Defense Minister Juan Ponce Enrile and Lieutenant General Fidel V. Ramos defied President Marcos, Jaime Cardinal Sin broadcast an appeal to the Filipino people.

All of Metro Manila, and possibly the whole country, was tuned in to Radio Veritas at the time, and the response was immediate and electric.

"Let's go," my wife said immediately. She is responsive to issues like these, more so if they are raised by a prince of the Church.

I was much slower in responding to the idea because it was midnight, and ours was to be a strictly two-man journey to a new conflict. My wife also did not consider that the issue was between two armed groups. Rubber shoes, flashlights, and a Spanish fan did not really add up to adequate protection.

Not knowing any of the people gathered in front of Camp Aguinaldo, my wife and I decided to just bring our "two-people power" straight to the office of Enrile, also a complete stranger to us.

The camp's side gate on Santolan Road offered an entry through a small window of the sentry box. After asking for some directions, we reached the Ministry of National Defense Building while Enrile was giving his third news conference shortly before three o'clock in the morning.

After the news conference, word reached us and some forty local and foreign correspondents that the Marcos forces would start shelling the building and camp perimeter at four o'clock. The report was relayed to us by a dejected Ramon Tulfo, a *Bulletin Today* columnist who settled in one corner of the spacious social hall on the third floor muttering: "The guy (Marcos) must have taken leave of his senses." Whether the move was crazy or not, the circumstances did not seem to bother many of the newsmen rolling around the premises, sitting and lying down, trying to find the best position that will allow them some much-needed sleep.

Four o'clock came and went, but there was no shelling. The next threat came at dawn, around six o'clock, when the people from the office of Enrile advised everyone to get down to the lobby because of the third floor's vulnerability to shelling. Again, the bombs did not come.

BONG A. LAZO

We found ourselves locked in at Aguinaldo in the first few hours following the Enrile-Ramos newscon, puzzled at why choir practice was still going on at the adjacent evangelical chapel, while combat-ready troopers, diplomats, and journalists gathered at the Ministry of National Defense office. As we tried to catch some uneasy sleep that night, we were confident that there would be neither an air attack nor mortar shelling. Not because Marcos was indecisive, but because we had ample cover from willing foreign mediamen and diplomats within the building, and from a handful of praying nuns on the grounds outside.

ARMIDA SIGUION-REYNA, actress and singer

While we were inching our way to the gate of Camp Aguinaldo, I immediately sensed that I had nothing to fear, that people were grateful for what my brother, Johnny, was doing. "Look, it's Armida," "Thank your brother for us," "Give way to the sister of our new hero," were common utterances. The Santolan gate was locked; people

were pressed against it trying to get a glimpse of what was happening inside. Minutes later, a female soldier came to tell me that they were trying to find a way to let me in. Just then, a military officer took a bullhorn and announced: "Friends, the sister of Minister Juan Ponce Enrile is here with us. She wants to be with her brother. Please move away from the gate so that she can come in." And silently, the people just moved back. I could not believe it.

When I entered Johnny's room and saw him, the gravity of the situation really hit me. I embraced him and could not help the tears.

EULOGIO GONZALES, policeman

We were just waiting for somebody to lead us. We were just waiting to see who would be brave enough to stand up. But even before that we had already wanted to move—we could no longer stomach the circus they had made of the elections and the *Batasan* Proclamation. So when we heard on TV that Enrile and Ramos had decided to turn their back on Marcos, we knew this was what we were waiting for. I immediately reported to Crame because the General had asked for our help. I knew, even then, that we didn't even have enough ammunition to last a whole day. Our greatest weapon was the people around us.

JAIME YULO

My first reaction was: civil war was imminent. I also doubted the sincerity of the revolt. But as Minister Enrile and General Ramos kept castigating Marcos and accusing him of cheating in the snap elections and supporting corrupt but loyal officers, I knew that these two brave men were defiant. I told myself that if these two men with their small band of soldiers could lead a revolt, then the least I could do was to admire their effort.

We still did not know what to do until Cardinal Sin came on the radio to appeal for mass support for the two embattled leaders. After some thoughtful prayer, and after hearing Cardinal Sin, I decided to go.

Since the situation was so uncertain and realizing that a counter-attack could come any minute, I was frankly scared. I brought my son with me, Jonathan, 13 years old, and called some friends to go with me, so that if anything happened to me, someone could inform my wife.

As my son and I reached the intersection near the camp, my fear increased. But I felt I was not alone, because there was a group of about 300 people at the intersection. As we came closer, we saw that there were about 10,000 people at the main gate. Many good friends had answered the call and were there.

The people had barricaded all the entrances to the main gate with all kinds of vehicles. Many were praying the Rosary, some in groups, some just standing alone. As we walked around, what struck me was that the people came from all walks of life—teenagers in jeans and t-shirts, middle-class matrons and their husbands, the poor people, including the peddlers. There were entire families.

The crowd truly represented a cross-section of the people, the rich and the poor, the devout and the frivolous, the man on the street and the big-time executives. All were there, probably fearful, resigned to prayer, excited, with only one thought in mind: to help the revolution succeed in each one's small way.

By doing so, these fellow Filipinos became part of history, perhaps in many ways, just like the street people of Paris in the French Revolution or perhaps more aptly the famous Minutemen of Concord in the American Revolution who spontaneously answered the call to arms. Thus all the Filipinos who were there that night marched into history to join the illustrious company of freedom fighters of other famous revolutions.

CONSUELO LOVERIA, government employee

When I heard the appeal for people power over the radio, all I could think of was: What can I do to help? I am too old to even walk across Camp Crame or Aguinaldo. However, we found out that there were many Marcos loyalist soldiers roaming around the vicinity of our house. They were apparently headed for Malacañang.

We talked to one of the soldiers, and he told us that they did not have food. We gave him coffee and bread and he told us that there were many other loyalist soldiers in that area. They had three tanks.

I told myself that maybe, I could convince them not to be oppressive to the Filipinos keeping vigil. I contacted the Mothers' Club, our organization, and asked the members to collect food from the neighbors and bring them to the soldiers. I called more people so that we could persuade the soldiers not to hurt anybody.

We told them that we were all Filipinos and that we shouldn't be fighting each other. We told them not to follow the command of their officers because they were loyal to only one man, Marcos. What they should be following instead is the command of the people who were keeping vigil in Crame. They told us they couldn't do anything, because they were trained to follow orders. Soon, the rest of our neighbors came, and we kept vigil there for the next three nights.

HERMINIO ASTORGA, former Vice Mayor of Manila

After the appeal of the Cardinal, Radio Veritas announced that there were hundreds of people at the Luneta who wanted to proceed to Camps Aguinaldo and Crame, but they had no transportation. I asked Radio Veritas to inform the Luneta group that I would be on my way to pick them up. Just like that: instant decision, no questions asked. (It took me sometime to reflect that, perhaps, it was the Holy Spirit who made me act the way I did.) Without finishing my dinner, I told my wife: "Let's go." I asked one of my sons to drive the Hi-Ace and another son to drive the Fiera. We reached Luneta in less than 15 minutes.

I was aghast to see the enormous crowd waiting for us. We asked ourselves: "How do we accommodate this whole crowd into our Hi-Ace and Fiera?" I decided to call my residence to send additional vehicles. After I made the phone call, several privately owned cars stopped by and the owners told me: "You can use our cars. We can bring them to Camp Aguinaldo." I could not believe what was happening. As if this were not enough, Dr. Jose Manansan, Dean of the Asian Institute of Tourism at UP, arrived with his Fiera. He told me: "You can use my Fiera for these people." We readily accepted his offer. Then a big open truck came. The driver promptly offered his truck and in no time at all, he was off with a sizeable crowd. Other utility vehicles arrived and they also offered help. Again, we hurriedly filled them with people.

Despite the steady arrival and dispatch of vehicles, many people were still waiting to be taken to EDSA. I saw three taxicabs waiting. I asked the drivers to take the rest of the people at my expense. When I asked them how much it would cost, their answer took me by surprise. "You don't have to pay," they said. "Fill up our cabs and we will take everybody to EDSA for free."

After we filled the three taxicabs and they left, another set of taxicabs arrived. The drivers said that they too were offering free rides. I felt a sudden chill and my hair stood on end. "A miracle is happening," I told my wife. "God, what is this miracle that you are doing here?"

At last we were able to take care of the big crowd from Luneta. On our way to EDSA, I told my wife: "How well God did it."

GEORGE WINTERNITZ, insurance manager

On Saturday evening, our civic action group was listening to Bishop Bacani, who was interrupted by the news that government troops were reportedly massing against Minister Enrile and General Ramos. While our group leaders discussed our appropriate moves and while the Bishop was on the phone trying to contact Cardinal Sin, our group of about seventy persons spontaneously prayed the Rosary.

VIC HELLY, S.J.

I noticed some men from the crowd passing a small table to a man atop the guardhouse. Puzzling. But the puzzle soon solved itself. The men below passed up a five-foot statue of Our Lady of Fatima. Their companion on top of the guardhouse mounted the statue on the table and set candles and flowers at its base. The group began a chain Rosary for a peaceful solution to our problems.

CRISTINA PONCE ENRILE

What many people can't believe is Johnny's total devotion to Our Lady of Fatima. Every night before he goes to bed, he prays to her. He tells me: "She has never let me down."

TERESA C. PARDO, wife and mother

"Please stay at home because it's dangerous. You have to think of the children," my husband said.

I got angry. Precisely it was for the children that I was going to risk life and limb — so that they could hope for a better future. I had to be where the action was. My younger children were safe with a trusted nursemaid. I had encouraged the older kids to go and join the crowd. It was Cardinal Sin, no less, who had exhorted people to come out to defend the military and to pray. How could I now not practice what I preach?

For a second I sat down on the sofa; I was immobile and close to tears. I heard on the radio that people were being urged to man the barricades and that they were arriving even from the provinces. Here I was in White Plains, just a stone's throw from the barricades, and I was being kept in the house.

The decision did not take long to make. I was going out there to do my share. This was the relevance I had been searching for: to be able to express my faith in God, who is sometimes so near and yet often so far away. He was here, right now, asking me to prove myself by going out to be counted.

I couldn't stay put in my comfortable home while thousands from the depressed areas were doing their share to fight for me.

With towels and lemon juice to lessen the sting of tear gas, I walked out into the early dawn alone, out of the house into the street. I walked out of grace—from my marriage, so I thought at the time—into independence and into freedom.

22 FEBRUARY 1986: Soldiers rush weapons into the Ministry of National Defense in Camp Aguinaldo, Quezon City. Similar action took place across the street in Camp Crame, headquarters of the Philippine Constabulary and the Integrated National Police (INP). The arms were in support of Defense Minister Juan Ponce Enrile and Vice Chief of Staff Gen. Fidel Ramos who that afternoon broke away from the Marcos regime. After calling for support from their comrades and consolidating their positions, Enrile and Ramos spoke to the press, overleaf. They said they were not out to seize power but rather, to return it to the people in the person of Cory Aquino, whom they recognized as the rightfully elected president. At the time of the press conference, Ramos and Enrile had less than 500 men, no air, armor nor artillery support; they were no match to the as yet uncommitted 250,000-strong Armed Forces. They were counting only on a small core of reformists in the military service. Outside, the people listened to the broadcast and were stunned and fearful of civil war.

On the phone, Enrile and Ramos speak to friends and relatives who vowed to support them, above. Much of the first phase of the uprising was, in fact, conducted over these phones. Marcos himself attempted to speak to Enrile who refused. A deal, however, was made between the rebels and General Fabian Ver, Marcos' closest military ally: the rebels (rather audaciously) agreed not to move on the Presidential palace and Ver also agreed not to attack. General Ramos confers with some of his core group, right. Many of these men were reformist junior officers who had, for some time, been agitating against abuses by sectors of the armed forces close to Marcos. While the officers bristled with weapons, their anti-aircraft and anti-tank capability was severely limited and a determined offensive by Ver's troops could have finished them at this point.

Apprehensive but resolved seminarians lead the BANDILA group, a moderate coalition, above. They were among the first to fill out the human barricades around Crame. Also among the first to arrive that night was Nora Aunor, the Philippines' foremost film and TV star, right. She had campaigned openly for the Marcos-Tolentino ticket and many of her fans were disappointed. When she went to the barricades on the first night to show her solidarity, she was booed for the first time in her 20-year career during which she received the wild public acclaim given to Cory Aquino. The effect on Nora Aunor was devastating. Weeping brokenly, she was led away by close friends. Meanwhile, the first trickle of food for the rebels arrive, opposite page. Donors were responding to Minister Enrile who said earlier that, although they were ready to die for the country, they had no food for their troops.

23 FEBRUARY 1986

Voices

AMADO L. LACUESTA, JR., screenwriter
Sunday, Dawn:

It is still dark outside. I have been slipping in and out of sleep. It has been like this since the eve of the election.

June Keithley puts General Ramos on. His voice is bright, confident, as he talks about having the support of military units all over the country. They have promised to disobey illegal orders — e.g., to fire on unarmed civilians — and to continue their watchfulness against NPA attempts to exploit the situation.

I quickly turn on the bedroom radio and nudge my wife, Lolly, awake. We are both silent and hopeful. With the rate of military defections being reported by Ramos, it can only be a matter of time.

At about 6 a.m., I sense that Frankie Batacan, the anchorman, is not his usual bantering, good-humored self. Shortly afterward, Orly Punzalan announces that Veritas' shortwave and medium wave transmitters have been destroyed by armed, yellow-shirted goons about an hour earlier. Now, Veritas is using its emergency transmitter. If Veritas goes, how will people know what is going on? How will Enrile and Ramos manage?

We shiver, and it is not only from the morning cold.

ANTONIO MAPA, shipping executive

At daybreak, inside the Ministry of National Defense, we witnessed a very touching ceremony. Two priests blessed a visibly moved Minister Enrile to fortify him in the mission he had embarked upon.

CRISTINA PONCE ENRILE (Mrs. Juan Ponce Enrile)

During the first day, it was as if I were floating. My mind was empty. I did not take any medication. God has His way and He made me numb. The day passed like eternity.

Without God's blessings and guidance, all this would not be happening.

GRACIA M. CARIÑO, wife and mother

On Sunday morning, it all powerfully came to me that Minister Enrile and General Ramos might really be altruistic in what they were doing. I recalled that a little over a month before, Minister Enrile's mother — Petra Furuganan — had died. She was of humble origin and means, I understand. Minister Enrile gave her full honors at her wake and burial.

At about the same time, perhaps just a few weeks after, the father of General Ramos died. He was Ambassador Narciso Ramos, who had served in the government as Secretary of Foreign Affairs.

I was struck by the picture I saw of General Ramos during the wake. He was wearing his uniform, dignified and crisp as always, but he was weeping. He was weeping at the death of his father. I was very moved by that and it was the image I recalled — along with Minister Enrile giving his mother a grand burial — which drew me to their cause that Sunday morning.

I am firmly convinced that when a good parent dies, God uses the fact of death as an occasion for a barrage of graces on the bereaved sons and daughters. I believe that one of those graces is always a powerful reminder of what the good parent has taught, the values of a good life, the example of honesty and high-mindedness. Death has a way of clarifying these values — and that is a grace of God.

I thought that the deaths of Petra Furuganan and Narciso Ramos were, for Minister Enrile and General Ramos, occasions for deep examination of conscience and then for the strength to move according to convictions and according to the virtues of honesty and selflessness that good parents always teach.

AMADO L. LACUESTA, JR.
Sunday Morning:

When the papers come, the headlines are grim: "Enrile, Ramos: We will die fighting."

Further down, the Russian embassy denies having sent official congratulations to Marcos. We whoop in derision.

It is eggs, sausages, and Veritas for breakfast.

There are now more than thirty thousand at EDSA. Enrile and Ramos continue to call for more people to act as a buffer, an insurance against bloody confrontation between their and Marcos' troops. The truth no one seems to want to say out loud is that without the people, the rebels would be crushed quickly.

A close friend from Davao calls. He wants to know what is happening. I tell him we are winning; it is only a question of time. I ask him what is the situation there. He says it is quiet. I take heart. Maybe Ramos wasn't bluffing.

Meanwhile, the rebels harden their stance vis-a-vis Marcos: The bottom line, says Enrile, is for Marcos to step down. He also observes that it is now the people who are protecting the military instead of the other way around. Somehow the remark warms the heart.

Before breakfast is over, Lolly and I decide. She instructs the cook to prepare sandwiches and the Coleman jug. She wears a bright yellow shirt.

I put on sneakers and a yellow Cory visor. I turn down my son Sarge's plea to go out with his friends. These are dangerous times, I say, wishing it were not true. We tell everyone to stay tuned to Veritas.

COLONEL GREGORIO HONASAN (GRINGO), chief security officer of Minister Enrile

Marcos did not order his troops to attack immediately—because he was not sure. He and General Ver had a fortress in Malacañang and they were not sure of how many, where, and who we were. So he built a wall, a perimeter. This is usually what somebody who is not confident of his knowledge of the enemy would do.

JAIME CARDINAL SIN, Archbishop of Manila

Cory Aquino spoke to me on Sunday morning. She said: "We have a big problem. There is a third force."

I told her: "No. I am sure they are staging this because they want you to be the President. Go there and thank them. Without this, you could be demonstrating every day and you will still not be President. But now, you will be. You can see the hand of God. This is the answer to our prayers."

FREDDIE AGUILAR, singer

I was in Lemery, Batangas, for a concert when the revolution began. I learned about it only on Sunday morning at breakfast, just the news that Enrile and Ramos had resigned. I wanted to know why and, on the way home, kept asking for newspapers from venders. We couldn't find a single newspaper out in the streets that morning in the Batangas and Laguna towns we passed. Moreover, our car had no radio. It was only when we got to Makati that I saw a newspaper, read it, and realized that what was happening was far bigger than I thought. When I saw the front page, I said: "Finally what I have been waiting for has come."

I told the driver to go straight to Camp Aguinaldo and he thought I was crazy. When we couldn't go through EDSA, we turned to Shaw Boulevard and I thought then that maybe we should go and see Cardinal Sin. He was not in. I went to Cinema Audio to see Jose Mari Gonzales. He wasn't in either. His son, Michael, told me that the Radio Veritas transmitter had been wrecked and that the Fairview station was next. I told the driver that we should immediately head for Veritas.

Since my home was along the way, I decided to stop by so that my mother would not worry. My wife was not home. I was told that she was doing some panic-buying, but she arrived within ten minutes. I had a hurried lunch and then I went with my brother to Veritas.

ERNESTO R. PASCUAL

We arrived about 9:00 a.m. at Camp Crame, where there were about 5,000 people at the front gate. After a few minutes, we saw General Ramos inside the camp walking towards the gate. He was proudly waving a Philippine flag. I clapped and waved like I've never done before. I lifted my two daughters, Pamela and Patricia, to see General Ramos. I told them: "Look at General Ramos and remember this day — it will always be one of the greatest days of your life."

LIEUTENANT COLONEL PURIFICACION, professor, Philippine Military Academy

The point which turned the balance in favor of the military reformists was people power. It was the first time in history that so many civilians went to protect the military, and this gesture of oneness and cooperation is something to remember.

For the military itself, the crucial thing was the defection of someone with the stature of General Ramos. When he broke away, we knew that the military would see the wisdom of what he did.

COLONEL GREGORIO CAGURANGAN, intelligence officer, Philippine Military Academy

On Sunday, the officers were advised by the Philippine Military Academy Superintendent General Zumel to keep the cadets together for as long as possible.

We speculated that the cadets would be taking sides and, in the back of my mind, I knew which side they would take.

When the reformist movement was being started awhile back, I had some apprehensions that it might be used as a political tool. I really did not know what to do. However, when my classmate, Colonel Jake Malajacan, came out and said he would rather die than let the people die in his place, that changed my mind and my whole attitude towards the reformists. I said: "This is really it."

MARIA FE P. PALLER

Several young soldiers stood guard inside Gate 3 of Camp Crame. One soldier was really perspiring. His lips were parched and his jaws were taut. Suddenly, a withered old man broke from the crowd to offer the soldier a cold drink. Several bystanders took the cue from the old man and offered the soldier cigarettes. The soldier shook his head and smiled weakly. In a moment, he bowed his head. He did not want them to see that he had begun to cry.

A reminder of who is in charge

AMADO L. LACUESTA, JR.
Sunday Afternoon:

Shortly after lunch, word gets around that Enrile is coming out of Aguinaldo. These are historic men and moments, and I mean to see and experience everything I possibly can. I quickly help cordon off a path through the press of humanity. I have ulterior motives: with Lolly's Instamatic, I mean to get a picture of Enrile for posterity.

When the passage from Aguinaldo to Crame finally takes place, I never even glimpse Enrile. Not among the vehicles, not even in the thick knot of fatigue-clad, grim-faced soldiers bristling with deadly firearms as they hurry into Crame. The twenty or so vehicles that pass us — mostly jeeps and cars — are unimpressive. Each carries only one or two battle-alert soldiers. The crowd cheers them and I let myself be carried along, clapping some of them on the shoulders as they pass. But they seem so few.

Before I know it, the passage is over. I hear Enrile has decided to consolidate his group with Ramos' at Crame because Aguinaldo is too big to defend. Though I don't remember ever having been into Crame, I have played the Aguinaldo golf links a few times some years back, and I agree.

COLONEL GREGORIO HONASAN (GRINGO)

I was very scared as we walked toward Camp Crame. But when we reached the first row of people, they started wiping our brows, giving us food, and thanking us. I knew then that we had won. All my fears disappeared. The worst scenario, for me, was not that we would have been bombed but that the people might turn against us.

ANTONIO MAPA, shipping executive

Enrile's short march was emotional, reminiscent of fighting men being sent off to battle and even to possible death. In the years of Marcos' rule, I had developed a deep contempt for people in his government and especially for those in the armed forces who made his regime possible.

But, as Enrile crossed over to Crame, we shook the hands of his troops, wished them well, and told them we were praying for them. Many soldiers wept and hugged us. Perhaps they realized all the more that they were finally fighting for the right cause when they saw the huge throng that waited outside the gates and greeted them already as heroes when they crossed the street. Together and safe inside Camp Crame, Minister Enrile and General Ramos won the opening round of the battle.

ALICIA YAEL HONASAN, sister of Col. Gregorio Honasan (From her diary, dated February 23, 1986)

The last time I had this kind of migraine was when Daddy died. Dear Lord, please let it not be an omen.

It has been the kind of security nightmare that seems to happen only in the movies. Yesterday afternoon, the whole family was called together because Enrile was resigning. At 8:00 p.m., Greg's name was announced on TV as the head of a presidential assassination plot. It became an absolutely sleepless night for Jane (Greg's wife) and their kids. Mom stayed with the boys in Marikina and we were assigned to this hellhole. Until now, we have no idea how long the reformists are going to stay holed up in Aguinaldo.

Last night I asked Jane if idealism is a disease that runs in the family. Maybe all of us are bound to do something really insane at some point in our lives. If I weren't as sick as everyone else, I would probably just condemn the whole thing and write it off as a lost cause and start wondering what to wear to the funerals. Or, to be more morbid, think of how we would get out alive if Gregory gets blown to bits.

Fortunately — or unfortunately — I am not immune to this family virus. Mom's got it. She still manages to pray with an unearthly kind of smile on her face. Jane's got it. She is still able to talk about what will happen when it is all over. Me? I am so tired I could sleep forever. I know this is going to end right.

I have matured enough not to attempt to bribe God with promises of gratitude if He would keep Greg safe and alive. For me now, it is only a matter of asking Him to let it turn out as He wants it. That conviction helps me to believe that the good will win, even here, even now. That is why I am not crying yet.

I winced in frustration when Greg kept me from rallies and from campaigning for Cory. For some brief sickening moments, I actually thought he believed in this pseudo-government he served. For a moment, I thought he didn't really care what happened to this country and to all the people. Funny how he turned out to be the one in the family who loves the country the most. He is ready to give up Jane, the kids, everything. I'd never be able to do that even if I went to rallies all my life.

They have to win, but this ammunition belt and these cold bullets pressing on my side seem to be saying: don't be too sure. My head is killing me.

YOLANDA LACUESTA

I used to hate the military and the police, but on Sunday I found myself preparing sandwiches for them. I heard over the radio that they needed food. I had to squeeze through a crowd just to bring food to the soldiers. I remembered all the times when I cursed them during rallies and was amazed that now I walked so far and worked so hard for them.

AMADO L. LACUESTA, JR.

We park along White Plains Road, about two blocks away from EDSA. Dozens of vehicles already line both sides of the road and the island. We begin to sense some of the excitement as we walk towards EDSA. A group of religious and lay people mill under a loose makeshift awning just outside a secondary gate into Aguinaldo. A large banner identifies their cause. Another restless group is organizing itself across the road in front of a gate into Corinthian Gardens.

When I first see the barricade of sandbags across EDSA near White Plains road, I do not know whether to cheer or laugh. It is barely thigh-high and looks puny, as though it couldn't stop a pushcart. But the young people astride it, waving their banners and laughing and cheering and flashing the L-sign, do not seem worried. One of them brandishes a home-made placard: "Subok sa Krisis, takot kay Mrs." (Tried in Crises, Afraid of Mrs.) I point it out to Lolly and we laugh, flashing the L-sign back at them. Their enthusiasm is catching.

All around us, people are coming and going in every direction. Everyone seems to know why he is there and where he is going. A cheer gathers momentum. People applaud a truck loaded with empty sacks — presumably to be used for sandbags — as it passes on its way to Ortigas.

More people, vehicles, laughter, cheers. I shake my head. This isn't revolution. It's fiesta, only more fun. Towards the main gates of Aguinaldo and Crame, the festive crowds thicken. Vehicles are parked everywhere. The island and sidewalks are littered with mats, cardboard sheets, even makeshift cooking stands where people must have kept vigil last night.

Far away at the corner of Santolan Road, a huge red and black flag spans the southbound lane of EDSA. It must be at least eight feet high and twenty feet long. Judging by the colors, it must be the standard of a radical anti-Marcos group. Beyond it, the controlled riot of people extends to the pedestrian overpass about half a kilometer farther away.

Besides people, it is a riot of flags at EDSA. The dominant color is bright yellow, but sinister reds or combinations of red and black also abound, along with a sprinkling of white and other colors and combinations. The word "anarchy" comes to mind, but I prefer to be more positive and think "people power" instead. Still, it arouses more hope than conviction.

Lolly retreats to the curb and sits down to rest. I tell her that if anything happens we are to meet at the car, and I wander off toward the Crame gate.

In the middle of the highway, someone is calling out names. Someone produces yet another flag and to enthusiastic cheers, the volunteer members of an impromptu civilian Charlie Company — dressed in an assortment of styles and colors — march off to their assigned post at one of Aguinaldo's side gates. The next volunteer group being formed is named Delta Force, to the good-natured bantering of the crowd. The attempt at military-style organization makes sense, but it somehow sounds desperate.

I run into friends and acquaintances I haven't seen in months, even years. One, an executive of a telephone company, is with his wife and son. Another, the president of his own bank, is with his son and two daughters. A third, a senior executive of the investment bank I used to work with, has an expensive camera. I remember deciding not to bring my own camera. I would be concerned more with taking photographs and protecting my equipment than participating in — in whatever. Thus, I have brought only Lolly's Instamatic.

Even then, we decline to take each other's picture. It seems petty, even sacrilegious, to be concerned with souvenir I-was-there snapshots at a time like this.

The crowd is getting thicker still by the minute. There must be, between the overpass at Farmers Market and Ortigas Avenue, about a hundred thousand now, perhaps more — men, women, and children of all ages and classes. And doggedly plying their trade among the people are the ubiquitous venders of newspapers, cigarettes, candies, boiled corn, green mangoes, and Cory souvenirs.

I am amused and impressed by their hardy enterprise.

I work my way to the Crame main gate. The archway and middle concrete awning are crammed with flags and people. No one seems to be afraid they might give way. On the side pillars, about eight feet off the ground, combat-ready soldiers with yellow-ribboned Armalites are crowded by curious civilians. The sight startles and stirs something in me.

JOHN CHUA

The Filipino wants a festive sort of civil disobedience. He is willing to die but he wants to have a little fun along the way. We are not as serious as the Latin Americans. How many would have stayed at the barricades if it had begun to rain? The Filipino wants to enjoy himself too. So people went there with some comforts. I saw this guy who brought his camper which was fully carpeted. He had brought a cooler and he was watching TV.

AMADO L. LACUESTA, JR.

The first sobering hint that the revolution is real and potentially dangerous comes over loudspeakers deployed in front of Crame: truckloads of combat-ready troops and police elements under General Lim are approaching from the north.

For a moment, the crowds stir uncertainly. My banker friend calls his children together and they hurry off toward Ortigas, away from the approaching troops. I locate Lolly and we stand there anxiously, undecided. Then, what was a worried murmur swells and becomes a cheer, a call to arms. And suddenly, the general movement is toward the Cubao barricade where battle may finally — though hopefully not — be joined. My heart warms, my hand tightens on Lolly's shoulder, and we drink from the wave of reckless patriotism that sweeps over the excited thousands.

A short time later, the loudspeakers report that the troops, the police, and the human barricade are at a stalemate. Ramos is on the phone with General Lim, who reportedly keeps saying "Yes, sir." The crowd cheers. How can we not win?

But Veritas has more sobering news: More truckloads of troops and a large assortment of tanks and armored personnel carriers are on their way from Guadalupe. Overhead, a lone military helicopter keeps circling high. I am afraid it is Marcos', reconnoitering or providing cover for his army.

We follow, at our own pace, the fresh surge toward Ortigas.

The next report locates the troops and armor dangerously close, on Ortigas Avenue near EDSA, not even two kilometers away. I wonder if Crame is now within tank-cannon range.

Then: They may also approach through Green Meadows, by the Mormon Church near the White Plains gate, from the east this time. From there, it is only a step and half to White Plains subdivision, which is right behind Camp Aguinaldo. Or they can turn left into White Plains Road and on to EDSA to attack either Aguinaldo or Crame, or both, frontally.

Lolly and I turn left into White Plains to — what?

As NAMFREL volunteers, we helped monitor a precinct count, helped bring the ballot box and election returns to Quezon City Hall. We were part of the gung-ho motorcade that escorted the certificates of canvass to the Batasan.

But this is different. This could be war. Though unspoken, the word hangs heavy in the air. And Veritas is full of ominous updates: so many trucks, so many APC's (even the jargon is becoming ominously familiar), so many Marines. For a moment, I even want to think that perhaps, more years of Marcos might not be as bad as civil war, but the mere thought infuriates me.

Halfway to where I vaguely expect to see my first tanks up close, Lolly stops to rest her feet. While she sits on the curb reading newspaper extras, I decide to see what's going on at EDSA and Ortigas.

About six or seven passenger buses are parked across the wide intersection to barricade it. They are all empty but their roofs are crowded with cheering, waving people. Thousands more are milling around the buses. Everyone seems to be looking toward the far left corner, where a carnival used to be. Occasionally, they chant "Co-ree! Co-ree!"

RICARDO CO

To make the barricade we pushed trucks, buses, cars, and even a trailer. I didn't realize that a task like this would not be heavy if we helped each other. We didn't even feel tired.

JOSE DE LA TORRE

In Pasig, water is sold by the container because it does not flow from the tap, the people who sold water brought their water tanks to Crame. They even brought ice. That was their contribution.

JUAN FLAVIER

It was very touching for me to see and feel the good will and camaraderie that the people extended to one another, even to complete strangers. While walking toward the barricades, I saw an old woman stop a young man who was on his way home—to offer him some water. "Here, my son, have a drink to refresh yourself," I heard her say. "I am too old to help you stop the soldiers, but the least I can do is help you regain your strength so you can rejoin your companions in the front line soon. I will continue to pray for all of you," she added. Then I noticed that she was handing the young man the glass of water with her left hand, she was counting off "Hail Marys" on the rosary that she held tightly in her right.

This good will and camaraderie—which one seldom saw before in the metropolis, where even next-door neighbors are sometimes strangers to one another—were also expressed in the way that people who were just arriving to take their place in the barricades cheerfully waved at those who were leaving to take a rest. It was as if the new arrivals were telling the "veterans": "Thanks for being here ahead of us, pals. Go and rest. We will hold the fort until you get back!"

PATTY C. RIVERA, economist

There were some women on board a bus going to Baclaran. They were pleading to the people in the barricades to please let the bus go through. They said that their relatives did not know where they were. But the boys who had boarded the bus were also pleading with them to please join the barricades. "We're all in this together," they pleaded to the women. The bus driver could not go back or forward. The press of humanity did not let him.

VIC HELLY, S.J.

A platform had been erected in the middle of EDSA and comedians were entertaining the crowds. The entertainment was suddenly broken off for an announcement: "Government tanks are on their way to attack the camps. It is necessary for a large crowd to meet the tanks and to immobilize them." A large segment of the crowd nearest Ortigas turned and went off to stop the tanks. When we arrived at what we were made to understand was to be the first line of defense against the tanks, we stopped.

A low wall of sandbags stretched across ED SA. (Not really a wall; only one bag high.) A man was giving instructions over the PA system mounted on top of a station wagon: "Listen carefully. Pray to God that you will not have to follow these instructions, but just in case, they are important. When the tanks come, if they start firing into the crowds — I hope it will not happen — but if it does, then . . ." I felt a little queasy at the moment. I looked at the people standing on the sandbags. They were young people in their late teens, early twenties, with their entire lives stretched out before them. Young men and women stolidly looking down EDSA, a view which in a few minutes might become the barrel of a machine gun mounted on a tank. Behind them, backing them up, were all sorts of people, a young mother with a baby in her arms and another in her womb, families with toddlers, pre-teens, teenagers. Men and women of all ages. I saw one doctor there who was beyond seventy. They looked a little disturbed and uncomfortable with the instructions. I saw no one leave. I saw no one yield to fear. Instead, many people prayed.

LULU T. CASTAÑEDA, wife and mother

When we were alerted to meet the tanks, I was very self-conscious about two things: my hat and the person beside me.

I was wearing a Christian Dior hat because it was drizzling and I looked so bourgeoise. I wanted to take it off but my daughter Leia stopped me. She said: "Don't, Mommy. You'll get sick. You always catch a cold when you get wet in the rain." I told her: "What are you worried about? We are going to die. I have no time to catch a cold."

We were told to link arms. I looked at the faces of the people around me and especially at the man to my right who was holding on tightly to my arm. My big concern was: I am going to die with this man and I don't know his name. I wanted to ask his name, but then did not want him to think I was fresh. I did not ask his name. As utter strangers, we faced what seemed like imminent death together.

I did say the act of contrition — truly and heartily. And I said the Hail Mary, especially the part which goes: "pray for us now and at the hour of our death." That seemed the same at that moment: "now...the hour of our death." I really knew then what that means to ask the Blessed Mother to be with me — will all of us — at the hour of our death.

My deepest concern was for my daughter because she is so young, only 17. I looked at her with pain and said: She's only 17 and she is going to die. Then I also thought: But if she dies for the country, then it is a good way to die. I think a lot of people were there for the same reason.

AMADO L. LACUESTA, JR.

My curiosity leads me on. Soon I am on Ortigas, looking at my first APC although I initially think it is a tank. Its engine is off as it squats there, surrounded by the people. Even whitwashed walls enclosing a vacant corner lot are lined with agitated people. The vacant lot is crowded with what must be tanks although only their tops and red pennants are visible. It reminds me vaguely of a war movie. My heart starts to beat a little harder.

I squeeze through the crowd on the traffic island and suddenly I am standing on the edge of a sea of kneeling people. They are praying. A pious-faced matron in white is leading the Rosary, face lifted to heaven, praying in a loud, pleading tone. Around her, the crowd on its knees is mostly men and some young women. An Afro-haired mestizo is holding his rosary up before his chest, near a middle-aged man who looks like a long-suffering government clerk. A young woman is weeping as she prays. Someone is holding up a small statue of the Blessed Virgin, similar to dozens I have seen today along EDSA.

My attention is drawn to a tight knot of civilians and camouflage-suited soldiers standing between the kneeling people and the APC, which looks even larger and more menacing. A man breaks away from the group and edges his way out. I recognize him — it is Teofisto Guingona, one of Cory's wise men.

Then someone, a civilian, is grudgingly given a hand by some grim-faced soldiers as he joins them atop the APC. He looks familiar — probably an ex-Atenean I saw during the Mass for Evelio Javier at the Ateneo campus. He looks very serious, very concerned. Someone calls for a megaphone.

Over the uneasy gathering, a military helicopter swoops low, one of several whose deep, dull throbbing as they hover overhead evokes Apocalypse Now.

The soldiers on the APC looks tough and deadly, ammunition strung around their bodies. People in the crowd talk to them with almost desperate kindness, toss packs of cigarettes to

them. But they show no response. They survey the crowd with hard eyes from time to time, but avoid eye contact. They seem even more tense than the people before them. Their discipline is frightening.

Someone says these are Marines just in from Davao and somehow, I feel a disquieting sense of kinship. I want to say I, too, am from Davao, but I don't. The desperate Rosary pauses as the ex-Atenean starts to address us.

He and Guingona have been negotiating with General Tadiar of the Marines. While awaiting Guingona, who has gone to Ramos with a message from Tadiar, he informs us that Tadiar wants the crowd to let his armor through. The crowd turns ugly, boos, mutters angrily. He pleads for attention. Now, the General climbs up beside him, helped by his unsmiling Marines.

The General looks short, slightly stocky but, like his men, is brown and tough-looking, except that he is in combat fatigues. He takes the megaphone to address the crowd, fixing them with a baleful look when they hiss. I help quiet the crowd, afraid of trying this man's patience.

"I have my orders," he says. He explains (in the tone of one who is not used to having to explain what he wants) that he only wants to move his unit behind Aguinaldo, a simple request. He does not wish to harm anyone.

The ex-Atenean tells him, and us, that it is our decision. He reminds us that we are here because we want to prevent bloody confrontation. If the General's men and armor reach the back of Aguinaldo, they will come face to face with Enrile's and Ramos' men. Who knows what might ensue then?

The prospect wrenches angry, urgent "No's" from the crowd. Suddenly, I am no longer just curious. I, too, shout "No!"

From atop distant buses and the whitewashed walls, the people begin to chant defiantly: "Coree!" Tadiar grimaces. The soldiers atop and before the APC hold their Armalites at the ready. I wonder if the safeties are off.

"I have my orders!" This time it's a threat. Darkness is less than an hour away, the general says. Who knows what might happen when darkness falls? Let us pass now in safety.

Butz Aquino arrives, clambers up unbidden, and takes the megaphone away. Tadiar looks piqued. Aquino plays to the crowd. He repeats what people power is all about — to prevent bloodshed. We are asked again whether we will let the

Marines through. The response is unanimous, loud, defiant: "No!"

The General shrugs, says something to his soldiers. The soldiers prod Aquino, the ex-Atenean, and an intrepid Japanese journalist off the APC. Suddenly, the APC's engine coughs to life, spews black smoke.

Cries of surprise, of anguish. The Rosary starts again, more urgently this time. Panic sweeps over us all. Unthinking, I drop to my knees.

The APC's engine revs up again, spews black smoke again. In the back of my mind, I think of Lolly and our children — Sarge, Kite, Rock, and Andi. Tears rush to my eyes, unbidden; my chest heaves mightily, unbidden; a sob wrenches out of my throat, unbidden. Looking up, I see only the General and his Marines, disciplined, hard-eyed.

I am angry. I am hurt. I am desperate, not knowing exactly why. I only know those men in combat gear are Filipinos. I only know this should not be happening. But there is nothing else now, not here in the path of this huge mountain of ugly metal looming over us.

L for Laban: the fight goes on

I shout and raise my hands, daring them: "Go on, kill us!" I am only dimly aware of angry booing and hissing, from the thousands on the streets, walls, and buses, of cameras clicking, motor-winders whirring furiously.

The metal mountain jerks forward. Defiant, nervous shouts all around. The praying voices rise another key. I wonder what it is like to be crushed under tons of metal.

The metal mountain jerks forward again. But no one stirs except the excited journalists jockeying for better angles. Then the engine stops. There is an astounding split second of silence. The crowd erupts into wild cheers and applause.

General Tadiar looks at us, turns and shakes his head. He disappears somewhere to the rear. His soldiers look around uneasily, unwilling still to concede eye contact.

For the first time, I notice the men around me. They are ordinary men. Some are in sneakers. Most are in t-shirts, some expensive, some cheap. The one next to me is in frayed jeans and rubber slippers, his bare feet unkempt and dirty. Not too many are visibly Cory-people. I feel conspicuous with my yellow plastic Cory-visor and blue headphone-radio around my neck.

For the first time also, I see that at the very front, within arms length of the APC, three nuns are kneeling, praying. They are puny and incongruous, in front of the APC and the soldiers. They look serene.

A cigarette vender squeezes in and out of the tight press of people standing around and plies his trade. I am not certain if I should be amused or dismayed.

Everyone looks up as a military helicopter makes another low sweep. A hundred hands flash the Laban sign defiantly at it. Someone brandishes a crucifix at the helicopter. In spite of myself, I smile. How can such faith fail?

But the confrontation has just begun. One of the Marines atop the APC seems especially belligerent. When someone tosses a pack of cigarettes up at him, a peace offering, he stares balefully at the person. He is booed and hissed. He gathers himself up to his full height, deliberately turns his back on the crowd, and viciously jabs his hand into the air in an obscene gesture. He heads for one of the far hatches, opens it, takes out an Armalite, pointedly lays it on top of the hatch. The gesture is not lost on the crowd. I am afraid of what may come next.

My fear is well-founded.

The soldier now walks back to the near edge

of the APC. Arrogantly, he turns his back on us, signals to the invisible driver. The engine comes to life again, coughing black smoke.

"Sit down! Sit down!" we cry out to each other, following our own urging quickly.

The woman in white raises her praying voice again, as do those around her. I link arms with the men on either side of me. Some of us are weeping. Some are also cursing. Perhaps, this time, they will not stop. Perhaps it will be bloody after all. And all this for one man's impulse to hold on to power. The thought stirs me up again and I do not care what happens next.

The APC jerks forward. Men brace themselves against the advancing metal wall, trying to hold it back. Behind them, the nuns stay on their knees, praying. I am about several people behind the nuns, but the APC is so huge it seems to loom even over me.

The soldier continues to signal the APC on. I wonder how many will be crushed before they realize we mean to stay, or before the pile of bodies makes it impossible for the APC to continue.

All around us, the horde of people that stretches far back to the intersection a block away begins to chant angrily. "Co-ree! Co-ree!" as if the name alone and the *laban* sign had the power to stop arrogant men and metal.

We who kneel in the APC's path alternate between defying it with prayers and imploring the taunting crowds to stop lest they goad the soldiers to anger. Let them kill us unprovoked, in cold blood. Let them hear the crunch of bones.

Just as I am ready to hear the first shriek of agony, a miracle — the APC stops, its engine winds down. Cheers and wild applause. We have won again. The soldiers glare down at us. Again, the thousands gathered chant Cory's name.

The APC's engine starts again and my heart sinks. But this time, thank God, it does not intend to try us again. It only wants to turn and join the rest of its unit inside the nearby walls. The General knows he cannot pass this way.

As the APC swivels, the crowd grudgingly makes way, still suspecting its true intent. But it finally heads for a breach in the wall, accompanied by the cheering and chanting of thousands.

I stand up finally. I cannot believe what I have been through. Now my only concern is to find Lolly. It seems hours since I left her. But the crowd is too thick; it takes an effort even just to turn around. No one wants to leave. I wonder if I can get out at all.

Squeezing finally through the wall of people, I meet an acquaintance I have not seen in years, a former bank president who has been watching the confrontation. We swap observations as a couple of military helicopters sweep back and forth overhead. But I am impatient to find Lolly and I break off quickly.

Walking back, I find myself still aghast over what has just happened. Once or twice, I am nearly overcome with emotion over the realization that we are, indeed, teetering on the brink of a civil war, if not in it already. It seems unreal, something that can happen only in Nicaragua or Chile but not here, not in the Philippines. But the Marines and armor we just stopped, the throb of helicopter gunships, the defiant chanting and cheering all over EDSA, they are real.

When I find Lolly, I blurt out what has happened, what I have just been through. She senses that I am still in a kind of daze and understands. We wonder what to do next and I suggest we go home first to rest, then come back. I suddenly feel so tired.

We reach home to find that our next-door neighbor, the young colonel, has gone to join Enrile's group in Crame. Other friends have gathered at their house, apparently to keep his wife company. My heart goes out to her. She must know her husband could be dead by morning.

One of the neighbors asks us to join the neighborhood Rosary that night. We tell him we are going back to EDSA. I suggest we say the Rosary there instead.

JAIME CARDINAL SIN, Archbishop of Manila

I heard about Mrs. Monzon, the owner of Arellano University. She is 81 years old and bedridden. She has to use a wheelchair to go anywhere.

She had herself brought to EDSA and there she met the tanks. With a crucifix in her hand, she said to the soldiers: "Stop. I am an old woman. You can kill me, but you shouldn't kill your fellow Filipinos." The soldier came down and embraced her: "I cannot kill you. You are just like my mother." Mrs. Monzon stayed there on EDSA all night — in her wheelchair.

Do you know what EDSA stands for? It stands for Epifanio de los Santos Avenue. Epifanio de los Santos was the name of a man, but if you translate the entire phrase, "*epifanio de los santos,*" it means the "epiphany of the saints."

CARLOS G. GUIYAB, JR.

I was at Ortigas when the tanks tried to attack on Sunday afternoon. There were a lot of people, but the real heroes were the nuns. They were the frontliners. When the tanks started to move, the nuns did not budge. Other people began to retreat, but the nuns clutched their rosaries and did not move.

They had a very good strategy. The nuns were cool. They instructed us to stay behind them while they talked to the soldiers. They said that nothing could be settled by arguing. "Let's talk to them. Offer them water or cigarettes," they said. They pacified those who were hot-tempered.

The nuns were our leaders.

RICARDO CARDINAL VIDAL, Archbishop of Cebu

I saw the image of Our Lady of the Rosary being brought to EDSA. I was reminded of the battles of Lepanto and of La Naval de Manila, when the Blessed Virgin was at the ramparts.

Future generations will look at what happened in EDSA in the same way that we look back at the battle of Lepanto and the battle of La Naval on Manila Bay. This time, however, the whole world saw and witnessed the devotion to Our Lady which wins battles.

We realize now the role of the Church — to guide, to give courage, and to show direction, but always without forcing anyone. It is up to the people to take the initiative.

GEORGE WINTERNITZ, insurance manager

People prayed the Rosary in front of tanks and stopped them simply by staying put and continuing in prayer. It was as if Our Lady herself, heeding the prayers, worked directly on the officers directing the tanks.

One father of three daughters related how, on Sunday evening, he chanced on all three of his daughters, all in their teens. Quite unexpectedly he saw them there, sitting on the road directly behind a small group of nuns and seminarians, praying the Rosary, two tanks only inches away from the head of the group. They just sat there and prayed the Rosary.

And they finished another Rosary and another and another. In spite of the tough talk of the fidgety and impatient commander of the lead tank: "Let's finish this," the two tanks later quietly withdrew into the dark.

AMADO L. LACUESTA, JR.
Sunday Evening:

After an early dinner, we are ready to go back. I let Sarge come along. What he will learn from this experience will be invaluable.

We prepare for a long haul: a sleeping bag, a buri mat, blankets, pillows, a Coleman jug of cold water, hot coffee, hardboiled eggs, bread, mugs, flashlights, fresh batteries for the headphone-radio, extra t-shirts.

Let Marcos do his worst now.

From Veritas reports, it seems Marcos is preparing to do just that. The Marines and armor we stopped at Ortigas have regrouped somewhere in Libis; another battalion or two are ready to move out of Camp Bonifacio; an artillery force is already operational at the University of Life grounds less than five kilometers southeast of Crame; more troops and armor movements have been reported north near Fairview.

At about 8:30 p.m., we are on our way back to the barricades.

We are quiet in the car. Already, the Veritas signal is weakening, beginning to sound like a clandestine, tenuous shortwave broadcast in a B war movie. Only there are no parallel cut-to-cuts to assure us that somewhere out there , a gung-ho regiment of friendly forces is on its way to succor us and provide an upbeat ending.

At the corner of Katipunan and Santolan, a stirring, surreal sight greets us: A cheering, chanting barricade of people illuminated dramatically by shifting yellow-orange flames of the burning tires, flags waving over them in the smoke-filled night sky. It reminds me vaguely of a painting of a battle-scene from the French revolution. Engrossed, I do not notice on the opposite corner what Lolly would talk about later — Marines massed on the road that winds down to Libis after the corner Caltex station.

We proceed slowly through a gauntlet of citizens waving and exchanging Laban signs with us. Again, the atmosphere is more carnival than revolution. But monitoring Veritas' fading signal that, by rights, should have given out hours ago, I know the day-old revolution is real, and that it is not doing so well in spite of the Veritas people's veneer of lighthearted confidence.

When we get to the White Plains gate at the Mormon Church corner, the road to the right that leads to EDSA is blocked by a loose barricade of rocks, sandbags, and some cars. Hundreds of people are milling about, among them a group of priests and seminarians in white soutanes, knapsacks on their backs. Many others, I learn later, are NAMFREL people and their children.

I park the car in front of a house beside the gate. The grass between the sidewalk and the fence looks like a nice place to bed down on later. Several other cars are already parked on both sides of the road.

Veritas is dead now. Although one or two other stations provide a coverage of what is going on, it is different. They are merely observers of the revolution. Veritas was an active, vital participant.

But Veritas or no Veritas, the revolution goes on. We pick our way through knots of people swapping stories, sitting or lying down on the sidewalk, past another small barricade, to the main barricade a few meters past the Mormon Church. This is one of the likely routes for the Marines who have regrouped in the Libis area. Although they are nowhere in sight, the chill night air is tense with the knowledge that they are poised to march again from only minutes away.

At the main barricade, a group of people pray the Rosary by candlelight before a statue of the Virgin. Outside the group, others are talking in hushed tones or moving around restlessly. The afternoon confrontation with combat troops and regular reports of continuing hostile movements from all directions have changed the prevailing mood from festive to somber. For many, the revolution has finally become real, even though there has yet to be a shot fired or blood spilled.

On the radio, someone reports that food donations continue to flood into Crame. Another relays a request for spoons and forks. Then, a plea for meat — most of the donations appear to be bread and canned food.

After looking the main barricade over, Lolly and I decide to rest for a while, conserve our energy for the more critical midnight-to-morning stretch. On our way back to the car, we marvel at the sight of a late-model Mercedes-Benz parked across the road as part of the secondary barricade. Will this revolution's wonders never cease?

Even with a mat and sleeping bag, the grassy ground and open air threaten to aggravate the cold I already have. Instead, we spend the remaining hours till midnight in the car. Lolly has dozed off. Sarge has run into two high school friends and is talking with them a short distance away. The car radio is on while I try to rest without drowsing off. I learn about a contingent of soldiers landing at MIA. I do not know who they are, where they are from, whose side they're on, and what has happened to them. But the radio doesn't mention them again.

JOHN GWINN, guidance counsellor

We took care of the food distribution station at Gate 4 of Camp Aguinaldo. There were times when I looked out at the hundreds of people waiting in line and wondered how we would feed them all. But when I looked again, our food supply had been replenished and had begun to pile up again.

On Sunday night, the college students of the Ateneo set up a table right on the middle of EDSA. On it were images of Our Lady and two lighted candles. Later in the night after many cars passed by it and also thousands of people — we went to retrieve the table to save the images. When we got there, the candles were still burning and the images were untouched.

Reformist soldier: hope and good cheer

TELLY BERNARDO

At the main gate of Camp Aguinaldo, somebody was putting up a yellow flag, while the soldiers watched indifferently. This was it, I told myself. Make way for me, the take-charge guy. I was about to start issuing orders on how the flag was to be fixed when a van arrived, carrying a statue of the Blessed Virgin. The statue was hoisted and installed on a platform on top of the gate. Before I could issue orders, somebody started leading the Rosary. Oh, no. Somebody else was in control. So much for this take-charge guy!

Minister Enrile (right) and aide: raise high the Marian standard

VIC HELLY, S.J.

During one of the nights at EDSA, between the two camps, a comedian was on the platform in the middle of the street, entertaining the crowd. Loud laughter, hooting and calling, guffaws. Suddenly the comedian began waving his arms in an urgent gesture, appealing for silence. I looked down the avenue and there, out of the darkness beyond, was a lovely apparition. A statue of Our Lady clad in a white satin gown, a sumptuous gold cape falling from the shoulders, and a crown upon her head, came into the light, carried on a cart, pushed by two young men. A silence settled on the crowd as, attended by the people's prayers, the Virgin made her way before them.

AURORA A. AQUINO, mother of Benigno S. Aquino (Ninoy)

From December 1984 to December 1985, the Philippines celebrated Marian Year. We proclaimed it as the year of the Blessed Mother. That was why we had pictures and images of the Blessed Mother everywhere. I think that the Marian year was really a preparation for what happened in February 1986. Our Lady was everywhere in EDSA. I heard a story about one soldier who was in a tank. When he looked out, he saw the image of the Blessed Mother, and he cried.

LULU CASTAÑEDA, wife and mother

At EDSA, while waiting for the tanks, I was thinking: "Did God create me to die here? If He did, then I must be ready. But if He did not, then I am safe. There is nothing to worry about." That was why I was very, very calm.

CESAR B. UMALI, JR.

Sunday evening I was at home reading. The telephone rang. It was my friend Al. He said: "What are you doing at home? I have been in Crame since last night."

Shame ran through me. While my friends and thousands of my countrymen were keeping vigil, I was in the comfort of my home reading.

I thought: I shouldn't let the others do the fighting for me. Revolution, like love, cannot be understood solely through reading.

LOURDES M. AGBULOS, wife and mother

All my sons, seven of them, responded to the call. I stayed home, praying so hard that the rosary beads almost got crushed. I stayed glued to the radio and was awed to hear of the big crowd out there and its heroism. I was bothered by the thought that I was home, safe and comfortable, while others were out there fighting. This was history and I was not part of it.

When my boys came home for some sleep, they said they were going back. I decided that I had to go with them. Guns are repulsive to me, but I thought I would be more repulsive to myself if I remained indifferent.

FREDDIE AGUILAR

In Hobbit House, where I was singing Sunday night, the people were tense and the band didn't want to play anymore. They said that it was more important to go to Crame. There were some foreigners in the audience, including a Japanese journalist, and they decided to go with us to Crame. We took our musical instruments with us.

We went to Gate 2 via Mariposa Street, which was not barricaded. It was a weak spot and if the Marcos loyalists had known they could easily have penetrated Crame through that street. When we got to Gate 2, I was amazed at the size of the crowd. We set up the sound system and it took us until 2:00 a.m. Meanwhile the seminarians were singing and making inspirational readings from the Bible. We were setting up on top of a 6 x 6 truck. We had no lights, so people turned flashlights toward us. One foreign correspondent said: "I have never seen a revolution like this. People are dancing and singing. You see this in the movies, in fiction. This is for real." The TV correspondents had floodlights, which they turned on us, too, as we played rock. We were euphoric. A woman came to me and asked if we could play something else. So I shifted to folk music, relevant music, and we played until morning.

ZACARIAS G. MORALES

My son, Dick (Army Captain Ricardo Morales, PMA Class '77), was one of the four officers presented on TV by Marcos as a coup plotter.

If not for his farewell letter, we in Davao would not have known his motive for doing the very risky thing he did. The letter, which he wrote in Manila on February 17, reached us with much difficulty through couriers on February 27. Here is his letter:

Hello all!

By the time this letter gets to you, things will

Girl and mother: is this really a revolution?

already have happened that shall affect all of us, as people and as Filipinos. This might be my last chance of communicating with you.

I don't want to alarm any of you, but there must be questions in your minds that deserve to be answered. I'll try as best I can.

I have joined a movement that intends to restore pride, self-respect, and democracy to the Filipino and to the Motherland. The initial phase of this movement will demand everything a man has to offer—and I have volunteered for it.

I do not do this out of adventurism or recklessness. I really feel that it is my sworn duty—my destiny—to share in a glorious and honorable moment like this. If we fail, then at least we gave our all. If we succeed, then we shall reap the gratitude of a liberated nation. Everything else that I have been, all that I have done, is focused on this single moment.

Of course, I hope to see the fruits of my efforts, but the possibility of failure is always there.

Should I fail, then remember me with pride and understanding. Please don't disown me—or my memory.

I have lived a good and full life. I have seen the world and experienced its pains and pleasures. My own regret is that I have not served you as much as I should have—or to have children of my own. But then all Filipino children will have a better future should we succeed. Let this be my legacy to them.

Please kiss the little ones for me—Hazel, Dongdon, and Rora. To you all, I send my love and my deep gratitude for looking after me all the while.

Mommy, please don't take this negatively. My final thoughts will be with you.

Please pray for me.

GRACIA M. CARIÑO

It was Father and Son Day in school, the annual sports fest. My sons wanted to know if they should go. Their father was out of town and so did not figure in the decision. I felt that the boys should go; they weren't needed in the rebellion. Their passage would be safe, I thought. The sports fest would take place in a campus far away from the scene of action, if any.

Early in the morning of Sunday, I took them to the bus terminal, and they went off along a route that would have passed down the highway in front of Crame. I did not know until much later that the highway had been closed to traffic and that the boys took a roundabout route to get to the school campus.

I sent them there deliberately. I did not want them home, twiddling with fear. I felt that it would be sporting to say, in the future, that on the first morning of the military rebellion, they went on ahead and played football in the sports fest. Life went on as usual—not for lack of concern, but because—for them and for me—that was the bravest act of faith.

ALBERT G. GRUPE

Whether we liked it or not, we had to be part of the people power around Camp Aguinaldo; our house is right beside one of its walls. In fact, if the battle of Aguinaldo ever took place, we would have had a ringside seat.

Many of the houses around us were evacuated, but the same unseen hand of God who orchestrated the revolution seemed to beckon us to stay. We joined the crowds around Aguinaldo and Crame. Once, after four hours of walking, we returned to our car only to discover that its stereo had been stolen. We had a car alarm but its sound had the familiar "Cory, Cory" cadence. Amidst that sea of people, no one paid attention to it and so the thieves had a lot of time to cut the alarm wire. We were not too upset, though. The problem seemed little compared to the ongoing crisis.

FRANCISCO RODRIGO (SOC)

I was there. My grandchildren went, even if my wife did not want to let them go. I said to her: "Let them. If you stop them, they will never forgive you, because this is history." I got there early Sunday morning. There were still only a few people. The Ateneo contingent came after a while. We heard Mass. Then people started coming out in force.

It was like a picnic. They realized the danger but they did not leave. They even brought their babies. Normally when people hear of a place being teargassed, they run away. Not in EDSA—they rushed toward the place. If there were reports of tanks, they looked for them.

I was amazed by the number of people; there were millions. And these were, by and large, not organized groups. There were a few who were organized—Ateneo, UP—but the majority came on their own to see how they could help out.

That's it, I suppose. People try but it is God who makes everything work.

RENE OCAMPO, S.J.

On Sunday, I walked down Santolan Road all the way to EDSA. I saw all kinds of people. Two people approached me and asked: "Are you a priest?" I was wearing my habit and our habit usually makes it easier for people to talk to us. They told me they heard about the events in Crame over the radio and they felt they had to be part of it. They were not, I think, college students. They seemed to be out-of-school youths. They were rough; they didn't give me the impression of being educated but they wanted to learn: "Could you share your experiences with us?" I could see they were very interested. So we sat together on EDSA and had our very own teach-in.

JOSE QUE, engineer

On the night of February 23, there were soldiers on the corner of Ortigas and EDSA. At about 8 o'clock some of them called on their drivers. Some people stopped them. They said they were just going back to their camp. I warned our leader that they might turn the other way toward Libis or Corinthian Gardens. Two trucks were able to get away. The people pushed a JD Transit bus to stop the third truck. The people sat in front of the third truck. One soldier shouted: "Go on! Run over them!" We saw one car. The owner wasn't there so we lifted it and placed it at the middle of the road.

SAMUEL DUGUILES, student

One of my friends climbed up an advancing tank and pleaded with the soldier: "Please don't kill us. We are only doing this because we want a better future. Our families have been suffering for far too long." The tank slowed down. Finally it had to stop because there were too many people and several buses blocking its way.

RENE A. OCAMPO, S.J.

When I saw a girl trying to talk to a soldier, I was moved. I could see Filipino psychology emerging. Actually, the basic principle there was nonviolence but it was more significant because these people had no formal training in nonviolence. I guess it is really a very deep part of our culture.

The people appealed to the soldier's humanity. I heard the girl ask: "Do you have a girlfriend?" When the soldier didn't answer, she tried other questions along the same line. Later she realized that the soldiers spoke a different dialect. So she asked: "Where are you from? Are you Waray?" Then she called out to the people, asking them if there was anyone who could speak the soldier's dialect. She figured if you spoke to them in their own language you could win them. Later, other people offered the soldiers cigarettes. Little by little, they won the soldiers over.

JAMES B. REUTER, S.J.

One provincial army commander, in the far north, came to Dick Kraft, SVD, at our station DZPA, in Bangued, Abra. He said: "I cannot figure out what is really happening. Tell me." So Dick told him the truth, as best he could. Then the commander received an order from his regional superior: "Take all the men you can afford, and move to Manila. They need help there." The commander checked with Dick Kraft, saying: "What do you think is going to happen?" Dick said: "I think Marcos is finished. We are watching the end of an era."

The commander prayed over this, and then did not move. He did not obey the command of his superior officer.

KAA BYINGTON, writer

One evening, I went to dinner with a couple of seminarians. They had just completed their duties of standing guard over the thirty programmers from COMELEC who, I learned, had been hidden in a retreat house. None of us had a clue that a few hours later, Minister Enrile and General Ramos would make their spectacular stand at Aguinaldo. We ordered noodles, and then tried to find something to drink on the menu that wasn't boycottable.

"What kind of beer do you have?"

"San Miguel only."

"What about soft drinks?"

"Coke and Pepsi."

"Do you have any fruit juices not made by Magnolia?"

"No."

"Just give me water," I finally said.

"You can't have water either," said Willie, one of the seminarians. "NAWASA is crony, too, remember?"

When I heard that Ramos and Enrile had rebelled, I understood immediately. They wanted to get it over with so they could have a San Miguel beer.

Flagbearer at his perch: a highly placed witness

That night, Monina and I listened anxiously to Enrile and Ramos over Radio Veritas. The rest of the Mercado family was hither and yon, all over the city, working at Radio Veritas, or organizing boycotts. Our anxiety began to turn to hope when we heard their assurances that this was not the dreaded military coup, and these two brave men were pledging their lives to the will of the people: "We will stand and die here, if we must." A reporter asked: "Are you prepared for a siege?" and General Ramos answered, rather wistfully, I thought: "No, we don't even have any food."

Now Monina had all along been telling me that the thing I must first understand about Filipinos was that everything depended on food. "The entire Cory movement has been floated on a sea of donated food," she explained. "We can't do a thing unless we are surrounded by food." And she had immediately taken me, on Election Day, straight to Mass at Santo Domingo, and then to the house of a Cory's Crusader chairman, to see the food that had been collected to send over to the UNIDO poll watchers. Have you ever seen three thousand hard boiled eggs, all neatly divided and labelled? I have. Now, upon hearing Ramos, Monina smiled, and said: "See? He's a real Filipino. He said: 'I am prepared to shed my blood for my country, but first send food!' "

The barricades, human and otherwise, went up, and from then on I was either at the barricades or listening to Radio Veritas. When I had time, I wrote down some of the appeals that came over the airwaves. The juxtaposition was often wonderful. Here is one sequence:

"Can someone please pick up cooked rice from number XX Ibarra Street, Makati, and take it to Crame?"

"The Sultan is in Camp Crame and is asking all Muslims in the Manila area to rally to him there."

"There is a report that three six-by-sixes and two APCs full of loyalist troops are nearing Guadalupe Bridge. All nearby vigilantes, please go there at once."

"This is an urgent request. We desperately need aspirin, toothbrushes, and yellow ribbons."

I suppose everyone had his favorite *panawagan* or message on Radio Veritas, and mine was the same as many others. As no one will ever forget, the head of the Marines who were about to attack Aguinaldo and Crame was General Tadiar. The General, in his pictures, looked very tough. Ver's forces were massed to

A walking flag: shield and standard

Seminarian and cross: faith at the ramparts

attack. The people too were massing at EDSA. I was glued to the radio and I heard: "We have an appeal to General Tadiar. General Tadiar, are you listening?" Then another voice came over the air. "Arturo, this is your Uncle Fred speaking. Your Aunt Florence and I and all your cousins are here in Crame. Now, Boy, please listen to me." For whatever reasons, General Tadiar did not attack. At dinner we toasted "Uncle Fred" who called the meanest Marine in town "Boy."

FLOR VICTOR

I saw loyalist troops trying to march toward Camp Crame, only to be stopped by the people. It was afternoon then, and humidity was very high. An old lady offered cold water to a loyalist soldier who refused. The old lady drank the water to show that it was not poisoned or anything. She offered another drink to the same soldier. This time, he accepted it. Then other soldiers asked for water. Everyone started clapping and cheering. It was a significant victory.

JOSE HEBER

There were loyalist soldiers posted inside Camp Aguinaldo. Some of them had already defected in small groups but the other soldiers left behind were still deliberating. Some soldiers, while trying to make their decision, popped their heads over the camp wall. Every time the crowd saw a head pop out, they clapped their hands and flashed *Laban* signs. Others shouted: "Long live the soldier!"

The soldiers who chose to defect climbed over the camp walls and landed straight into the arms of the people. The people lifted them and carried them on their shoulders in victory. People and soldiers were crying in the streets.

GRACIA M. CARIÑO

Briefly, I was on EDSA, not to be part of the barricades but to savor the spirit. As I had gone before to rallies and to Cory's campaign sorties, I needed to go to EDSA to quaff the spirit of the people, to be buoyed by their hope.

I was with my two sons and my best friend. We parked the car on EDSA, just across the construction site of the Asian Development Bank. It was hard finding a parking space. You'd think we were in some show, concert, or shopping arcade, the way both sides of EDSA were occupied with cars.

We walked toward Crame. Right by the Poveda Learning Center was the first barricade, a low wall of rubble, parts of concrete culverts, tires, and some lengths of barbed wire. I looked at this barricade and wept, the first of the tears I shed that afternoon. I wept because, looking at the barricade, I realized that it took much effort and organization to make it. The rubble was piled in the perfect balanced style that the Igorots use to make their no-mortar stone walls. There was evident thinking, planning, and design. There was evident muscle power, too—I cannot imagine how the culverts got there; some of these were filled in with rubble, too.

I knew that Crame was still a good kilometer or two away, but there were barricades one after the other—puny barricades when you think of tanks but real barricades in the sense that they were placed with a lot of hope. They were psychological barricades, more than anything else.

I wondered who planned their positions. It was good thinking to have the barricades far away from the main line of defense. The enemy would be fighting skirmishes along the way and would, we hoped, end up maimed or exhausted before reaching the last line of defense.

The barricade near Poveda Learning Center, although low, required some tricky climbing. We did not want to do it; the rough rubble looked cruel and could easily sprain an ankle. We went to its end on the sidewalk and found two men who had appointed themselves as check-points. They were polite and they said simply: "We need to check your bags. No one should have a gun or a grenade or any explosive." We willingly opened our bags to show the contents to these two apparently unofficial, nonpolice checkers. My friend and I laughed because what the men were doing reminded us of our pet peeve: our bags being checked in five-star hotels.

We ambled on toward Crame. It was not easy going—people were going to and fro in great streams. It was not possible to walk unimpeded for even the shortest distance. My young son said it perfectly: "This is like crossing the street in Quiapo." That was well put, except that we weren't crossing a street, we were going down a street.

At the intersection of Ortigas and EDSA, I saw a shrine to Our Lady atop a van. Her image was on the roof of the driver's cab; there were flowers, and vigil lights burning. With the statue of Our Lady was a crucifix, a breathtaking work of art that was antique and, by its style, apparently the work of a Mexican sculptor. I was amazed and appreciative; the shrine moved me to prayer. I remember thinking then: this is what an icon is for—to move the believer to prayer. I also thought: what great panache to bring this work of art to EDSA! Both the wonder at the beauty of the antique crucifix and the surge of prayer it brought me made me think that I was in a church. Yet it was open air, people were going to and fro, radios were blaring, and sellers of all sorts of edibles were busy. As we progressed down EDSA, I saw that there were other shrines like this first one. None of them moved me as much.

MAXIMO V. SOLIVEN

The people fought and prayed at the barricades. Their banners were yellow, their none-too-secret weapons were serene, white images of the Blessed Virgin. These people came from every walk of life (the poor donated water and bread, the middle class sandwiches and steaming platters of meat, the rich, whatever— nobody munches caviar or *paté de foie gras* at the barricades) but the tension was leavened with fun—and with hope. Their reinforcements continued to stream in from the surrounding provinces. Their cry: Freedom!

I am reminded of the deathless poem by G.K. Chesterton, committed to memory in my youth, but whose title I can no longer recall: Our Lady stood on the standards rent,/ as lonely and as innocent/ as when between white walls she went,/ amid the lilies of Nazareth.

The Marines and other Marcos loyalist troops fired their Armalites in the air or sometimes to kill. But the people and the priests and nuns continued to press forward, imploring them to join people power and the "revolution." Some of them yielded, but words and prayers will not always work. There are no bloodless revolutions. It is not the way of the world.

There is danger in the almost universal surge of joy—which may lull us into believing the war is over.

23 February 1986, early morning: Young men cut down a tropical pine, drag it to the middle of the street and leave it there as a barricade against tanks, above and right. As the news began to spread that Minister Enrile and General Ramos needed citizens' help, people took it upon themselves to create various kinds of optimistic, primarily nonviolent resistance against Marcos forces.

Hoping to prevent Marcos troops and tanks from reaching Minister Enrile and General Ramos, people make barricades using sandbags, a left-over lamp post and even a drainage grill, left and below. Banding themselves into teams, they put these barricades at several points across Epifanio de los Santos. Better known as EDSA, this ten-lane street is flanked in the Cubao area by two military camps: Camp Aguinaldo where Minister Enrile was holding the fort and Camp Crame where General Ramos was in command. The peoples' barricades were set up as far as five to three kilometers away from the camps, the better to deflect Marcos forces.

Across the ten-lane Epifanio de los Santos Avenue (always referred to as EDSA), a group of volunteers make a sandbag barrier from sacks donated by a cement factory, above. Later in the day, people begin to lend themselves as human sandbags, as optimistic deterrent to assault by Marcos forces, as open protest to the Marcos regime, right, upper and lower photographs.

Early in the morning of Sunday in and around Camp Crame, civilian support grew undeniably, while the few rebel soldiers supporting Enrile and Ramos stayed alert, right and below. Inside Crame itself, the day begins with the Mass, left. Outside, the human barricade grows with people who arrive on foot and on wheels, lower left.

Nuns continue to say their Rosary on Sunday morning and the prayer was to become an anchor of the uprising, the endless chain of pleas to Mary, the Mother of God, for her protection, opposite page. Meanwhile, citizens continue to march to EDSA as individuals or as organized groups with their own safety rope, provisions and banners, upper photograph. The children too were in the uprising —such as these boys who made their own stone barricade and this child for whom his mother brought a chicken teepee as shade out of the sun-drenched highway, above and right.

The Ortigas family, owners of vast and important real estate on both sides of EDSA, strolls around on Sunday morning, above. Age did not matter to these two gentlemen who brought their own appurtenances to the barricade: a Capuchin monk with his hat and cloth pouch, an old man with his transistor radio, the perfect companion which gave up-to-date news and vital information to those out on the streets as the civilian buffer zone, upper left and right.

At the gate of the military camp, the image of Our Lady, known as La Naval de Manila, presides as if upon a shrine, above. This image of Mary commemorates five successive naval victories on Philippine waters in 1646, victories of the underdog, namely the Spanish colonial fleet of two commercial galleons against as many as 15 Dutch warships bearing down to wrest the Philippines from the Spanish empire. The defenders entrusted themselves to Our Lady of the Rosary and each time they sailed into battle they recited the Rosary on their knees out on the decks. With the memory of this miracle as assurance, devotees of the Rosary brought the image of La Naval de Manila to the siege of EDSA early Sunday morning.

Food and provisions pour into the military camps, opposite and upper photographs. In improvised kitchens, nuns prepare and cook them for the rebel troops in Camp Crame, above.

23 February 1986, early afternoon: Minister Enrile and General Ramos decided to consolidate forces and to work in the same place, Camp Crame. To do this, Minister Enrile needed to cross the street, which was by then jammed with thousands of citizens. The people first knew of the decision when they saw reformist troops moving out of Camp Aguinaldo in formation. They asked the people to make way and they did. Linking arms, the people create a protective wall for the reformist troops, opposite page, upper and lower photographs. The troops cross a seeming sea of people, above. The experience exhilarates a young reformist, left.

Col. Gregorio Honasan forges ahead to shield Minister Juan Ponce Enrile as they cross the street towards Camp Crame, above. "I was very scared when we started out," said Honasan, the chief security officer assigned to the Minister. "But when we hit the first row of people, they started to wipe our brows, give us food and thank us. I knew then that we had won. All my fears disappeared." At a brisk pace, walking from Camp Aguinaldo to Camp Crame should take less than half an hour. For Minister Enrile and his troops, it took more than an hour to walk among the eager and supportive people, right.

Waiting inside the Crame gate, General Ramos meets Minister Enrile and takes him into the camp, above. They acknowledge the support of the crowd, upper right, opposite page, and then Ramos settles down to his work, right. Asked by a reporter why he was unarmed while Enrile carried an UZI submachine gun, General Ramos replied, "As long as I have my cigar, I am all right." On watch inside Crame, reformist troops hold rosary beads given to them by the people, right, opposite page. Meanwhile, only less than two kilometers away, Marcos loyalist troops were approaching in six tanks, eight jeeps and 13 trucks carrying grenade launchers and machine guns. When crowds stopped the tanks, one of them crushed right through a concrete fence within less than a kilometer to Crame, overleaf.

Commanded by officers loyal to the
Marcos regime, Marines and their war
machines arrive within artillery distance to Camp Crame, the defense
position of reformist troops who were
with Minister Enrile and General
Ramos, upper and lower left, opposite
page. They were waylaid by a crowd of
nearly four thousand people and about
a hundred cars and buses parked in the
middle of this intersection of Ortigas
Avenue and Epifanio de los Santos
Avenue. Marines disembarked from
their tanks, left, but machine guns
remained cocked and aimed at the
crowd. Meanwhile, one of several
helicopter gunships provides air cover
for the Marcos loyalists, above.

Arms linked, men face the tanks as
some of them cry out to the Marines:
"We are all Filipinos. Are you going to
shoot fellow Filipinos?", above. Closer
and closer, the crowd edges to the
tanks and creates a human barricade
against its formidable metal flanks,
upper left, opposite page. His torso crisscrossed with ammunition, a Marine
faces the unarmed phalanx lower left,
opposite page, while another Marine
stands beside a grenade launcher, left.

Hemmed in by thousands of unarmed men and women, the Marines keep their positions on their tanks with machine guns cocked, left. Never for one moment were the tanks left unmanned although the other Marines had disembarked from their military vehicles. The people watch and beg and cry to the Marines—some in anger

and defiance, some in frustration,
some in hope that reason and the
humane spirit will prevail, above.
While a few provocators raised their
voices in curses and insults and while
some hotheads threw stones at the
Marines, cooler voices and wiser men
kept tempers down on each side.

Ten deep in many places, a human wall against a line of seated Marines defines the stalemate, far left. As Marines await orders to attack Crame and as civilians block their way, it is the young people who make the first moves—a child offers some stalks of flowers to a soldier and a young girl moves in with a plea, left and above.

A Marine officer accepts a cut-out heart, as the people continue to cajole the Marcos troops to join them in the popular uprising, above. Earlier, the same officer is bemused and then charmed as he finally accepts a gift of orchids, left.

From a hefty bouquet, a girl gives a daisy to a Marine, above. A matron offers a whole bunch of spring flowers to a Marine resting on his helmet atop an ammunitions box, far left, as another girl gives candies, left. Throughout Sunday afternoon within this large field where the Marines were stopped by people power, overtures of friendship and peace continued and were encouraged by radio announcers who called in yet more people to bring flowers and candies to the soldiers.

The siege of flowers continues and armed with a garden basket spilling over with assorted blooms, a girl goes to each soldier with a peace offering, upper photograph. She is joined by friends, lower photograph. Moved by the attention, a Marine tucks a single orchid into the strap of his bag, right.

Visibly relaxing, the Marines accept cigarettes, upper and lower photographs. In the periphery, people keep a tight watch as their ranks swell with those who heard of the confrontation and wanted to be part of the nonviolent action.

Long past the half-hour deadline he gave the people to move away from the path of the Marines, Brig. Gen. Artemio Tadiar, the commanding officer, confers with leaders of the crowd, above. "I don't want confrontation but I am proud of this," he said as he pointed to his Marines badge.

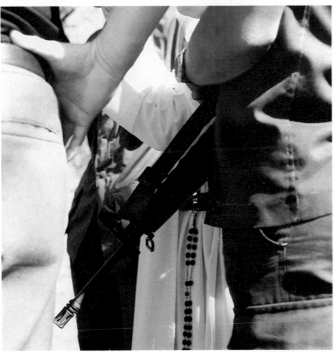

Here and there in the crowd confronting the Marines and their tanks were pockets of prayer, spontaneously created by the people themselves. Kneeling on the road athwart the path of armed soldiers, two nuns say the Rosary, far left. Some individuals in the crowd bear images of the crucified Christ and of the Blessed Virgin Mary as standards of defense and perhaps as a call to the Christian conscience, above. To the believer, the confrontation with tanks was a confrontation between military might and prayer: an insight that is captured in this close-up of a priest's rosary beads contrasting with a gun, left.

Right into a Marine's ear, the nuns pray the Rosary, above. Entire families kneel on the road and pray openly and loudly, with the force of faith in the providence of God and in the reasonableness of men, left and far left.

The fighting spirit came in many guises that Sunday afternoon when people power confronted the tanks. For these four people, it was the serene abandon of sacrifice, as lambs are meek when led to slaughter, as the innocent are at peace when brought to martyrdom, above. For others, like this woman, it was the fervor of prayer, with mind, heart and face raised to God in urgent plea, right.

Puny hands against the hefty metal of tanks: this was people power at its most visible during the confrontation on Sunday afternoon. Once in a while, when overtures of peace, negotiations and prayers were going on, the drivers gunned the engines of their tanks. If it was meant to tease, the people thought otherwise. Each time the tanks roared, they laid their lives on the line. "I discovered that the exhaust of a tank engine was strong, hot and black, like the breath of a vile dragon," said a woman who was close by.

Pulling out of the stalemate late Sunday afternoon, Marines make the L sign of the opposition by way of insuring safe passage through the crowd, left. They did not entirely withdraw but moved away from the crowd to park for the night. In a mixture of curiosity, vigilance and tentative victory, the people follow, above.

24 FEBRUARY 1986

Voices

AMADO L. LACUESTA, JR., screenwriter
Monday, Pre-dawn:

Shortly after midnight, I snap to attention at the latest report: The Marines at Libis are starting to move.

I nudge my wife, Lolly, awake and call Sarge, my son, back to the car. We lock up and head for the main barricade together. All about us, people are moving about briskly now, organizing their groups.

When the radio reports that more people may be needed at Santolan to stop the Marines there, a group of seminarians and priests quickly fall together and head there.

More reports follow of troop movements — from Guadalupe, from Commonwealth Road, from San Juan — and of armor, artillery, and air attacks expected before daybreak. The tension is building. The crowd at the corner of White Plains Road and Katipunan thins out as people head for either the Santolan corner or EDSA.

I latch on to a knot of people who seem as undecided as we are. One of them, a nun, asks if Ting Paterno is coming back. Apparently, he is the leader of this group of NAMFREL volunteers and has gone to find out where people are still needed. No one knows where he is or whether he is coming back. The indecision bothers me and I try to organize the NAMFREL group and some students from San Beda, in case Ting Paterno does not come back.

The students are eager to follow someone, anyone, but the NAMFREL people — nuns and older people mostly — are still anxious about their leader. Somehow we agree to set up a second line of defense at the corner in case the Santolan or the nearer Mormon church barricade fails.

I get someone to position his old Kombi van across the road. I plug the remaining gap with my car. A passenger jeepney is already blocking the other lane. But eventually, and mainly because the prospect of our snap barricade being of any real use seems remote, we all decide instead to march down toward Santolan. So much for my brief career as a revolutionary officer.

Near the guardhouse at the corner of Sarangaya and Katipunan, we find a group of mostly young people with a large flag — Social Democrats (SocDems), Sarge tells me — and others, including, finally, Ting Paterno. We decide to join up with them. There is still uncertainty about what to do until someone driving by from Santolan tells us there are more than enough people there already. Accordingly, we all agree to barricade the Sarangaya corner instead.

From Katipunan Road, Sarangaya winds down to the farthest back street of White Plains Subdivision which leads to a gate connecting White

Plains to another subdivision — Green Meadows, I think — where enemy troops also have been reported to be massing. It is a likely alternate route for the enemy troops to take if they wish to avoid the barricades at the major routes.

When one of the subdivision security guards comes up to the corner in a motorcycle, I suggest posting him near the White Plains/Green Meadows gate so he can spot any troops coming our way and quickly warn us. A teenager from the neighborhood volunteers to go with him, saying a church near the gate offers a better vantage point for spotting troop movements from a distance. I feel like I'm part of a B-war movie again.
It is about 2:00 a.m. and we are still waiting.

Sarge is sitting on a curb, talking earnestly to a young girl. Across the road, the SocDem group is taking it easy, dozing off, impressing me with their cool, casual demeanor. They seem to be in their element. One of them, a young man sitting on the road, is momentarily blinded by a car going out of Sarangaya. He snaps angrily at the driver, berating him for being rude just because he has a car. From his outburst, I sense a deeper resentment, one related somehow to leftist cant about class struggle between the poor and the rich. I wonder how it would be like with the far left running the government.

Wonder of wonders, while fiddling with the headphone radio, I hear what seems to be June Keithley's voice. But having heard Veritas say days ago that another station has been imitating them to mislead people, I am wary. I even communicate my suspicions to a group of nuns at the barricade. Only when I hear "Onward, Christian Soldiers" and "Mambo Magsaysay" do I finally believe it is the real thing.

It is comforting to hear Keithley and Enrile and Ramos again. But the relief is shortlived.

At about 3:00 a.m., Keithley relays confirmed reports of twenty or more truckloads of troops moving toward Aguinaldo from Commonwealth Road, and of tanks and other armored units moving out of Bonifacio.

Afterward, when Ramos makes a long-winded, repetitive appeal to enemy troops to come over to our side, promising them that life will be better, that their future will be brighter, I sense something wrong. I tell Lolly I think Ramos sounds desperate, hoping she will contradict me, but she doesn't. I am afraid the revolution is in serious danger.

At around 4:00 a.m., the situation worsens. I learn that the troops who landed at MIA were ours and that they were surrounded by Marcos loyalist forces before they could even disembark.

Ramos asks Keithley to play the PMA alma mater song for those PMA graduates among the loyalists. Then he makes a personal appeal whose highly emotional content suggests how desperate the situation is: He calls on the enemy officers to remember how he has been their boon companion at jogging, at scuba diving, at athletic competitions; he addresses "Manong Andy" and "Kumpareng Fabian," asking them to remember that it is the blood of brother Filipinos they will be shedding, warning them that the world will know who started the blood bath.

By now also, the often jaunty exchange between Ramos and Keithley at the start of every contact — e.g., "I didn't realize it is morning now, June." — sounds strained. And when Ramos announces the nationalities of the foreign correspondents with them, warning Marcos of the international repercussions if any of them is hurt when Crame is assaulted, I am convinced he is clutching at straws. My heart begins to feel like a dead weight in my chest.

Inside the car which I have moved close to the Sarangaya corner, Lolly and I numbly monitor the deteriorating situation.

At about 5:00 a.m., a report electrifies us all. The Marines are assaulting the Santolan human barricade with tear gas.

From hereon, everything takes on a highly cinematic, surreal quality as I watch with strange detachment.

Events seem to be rushing headlong to certain catastrophe — teargassing at Santolan, armored columns moving down EDSA, a total of about ten enemy battalions advancing from all directions, by Ramos' own reckoning.

Over the radio, June Keithley is relaying instructions from a former member of the US Special Forces, about how to use a bus more effectively as a barricade (flatten its tires, turn it over on its side) and how to handle tear gas (cover the nose, mouth, and exposed skin with wet cloth, hug the ground since tear gas drifts upward, pick up hot tear gas canisters only with padded fingers and immerse them in a bucket of water to neutralize the gas).

Down the road, the SocDems have come alive suddenly. One of them is lecturing his bourgeois comrades, the nuns and the NAMFREL people, about the effects of tear gas: extreme, embarrassing visceral discomfort; burning sensation in the eyes, nose, throat, and on the skin. I remember being gassed slightly years ago on Ayala Avenue and can guess how bad a larger dose must be.

On an impulse, I back the car into a driveway, hoping to keep it safe from passing tanks. Then, we begin soaking our blankets with water from the Coleman jug.

Over the radio, Ramos asks June Keithley to repeat some telephone numbers and to instruct certain friendly forces to call him there for further orders.

I am amused and shocked. The revolution is actually depending on a commercial telephone line, a civilian broadcaster, and a commercial radio station to establish critical contact with its meager forces, all within earshot of anyone with a cheap transistor radio. It is all too much, even for a B-war movie.

With a sinking heart, I tell Lolly and Sarge we will pray the Rosary. They start while I am standing half out of the car, watching the SocDems rally round their flag, their heads, noses, and mouths already covered with handkerchiefs. Everyone else is also preparing for the anticipated Marine advance.

I am ashamed over being torn between joining them and looking after my wife and son. It is becoming really dangerous now. The time of reckoning is nearly at hand.

Over the radio, Keithley tries mightily to keep her composure, but her voice has begun to quaver perceptibly. And when she invites everyone to pray with her in a voice that barely keeps from breaking, I know all is lost. Overcome with anger

Tingting Cojuangco: chic at the barricades

and frustration and a deep sense of betrayal, I pound the steering wheel and sob my heart out. Lolly starts to cry.

Suddenly, I know what I must do, the only thing I can do.

I take off my glasses and stuff them into the glove compartment with the headphone radio. I tell Lolly and Sarge to stay in the car and keep the windows closed. I instruct Sarge to take care of his mother.

They are still praying the Rosary when I leave to join the lost cause. Already, the day is breaking.

JAMES B. REUTER, S.J.

June Keithley, Paolo and Gabe Mercado, and Emer Guigon were on the twelfth floor of the building, where the radio station was, in the center of the city.

June opened with *Bayan Ko* (My Homeland) and with "Mambo Magsaysay," and everyone thought that this was Radio Veritas. Armed men went into the studios of Veritas in Fairview, but found no one broadcasting. They never discovered the source of that broadcast. The people in the streets spoke of "the secret station."

On the twelfth floor, June was really terrified. She said, over the transceiver: "There are only six of us here — three boys and three girls. The place is so tiny! There is only one door! If the military come to that door, with an Armalite, there is no escape! Only the window! And the closest ledge is four stories down!"

One of the boys covered the window with paper, in case a sniper became interested in them. It reminded me of the Marx Brothers. In one of their movies, all four were huddled on the floor of a building, in the middle of a revolution, and a shell went through the window, blowing out the opposite wall. One said, in terror: "Can't we do anything to protect ourselves from those shells?" Groucho stood up, and pulled down the window shade.

The Jesuits, listening to June, could feel the nervousness in her voice. Monina, mother of the Mercado boys, phoned the office and said: "Could I have my sons back? They are in danger!" I had no one left to relieve them, so I was reluctant to let them go. We phoned the Sisters, telling them to assemble in the building, as a protection against the military.

Monina finally went to DZRJ herself. The elevator only goes up to the eighth floor. When she came out of the elevator, on the eighth floor, to her amazement, the corridor was filled with nuns, wall to wall! They were sitting on the stairs, quietly saying the Rosary, led by Ariston Estrada. She had to weave her way up the stairs, through the nuns, and she knew then that her boys were safe.

All that night June Keithley was on the air, cheerful and strong. People's power is a real thing, but it must have leadership. And the leadership comes over the air. The men who smashed the transmitters of Radio Veritas at Malolos were also commissioned to stop June Keithley, but they never found her. It was just an accident of grace. God draws straight with crooked lines.

AN MERCADO, student

My brother Gabe called me at about 1:15 a.m. to tell me that June Keithley was broadcasting again. My brother had been working with Tita June as a Radio Veritas volunteer since the elections. They had spent the early evening looking for a radio station to adopt them since the transmitters of Radio Veritas had been destroyed. Apparently they had found one and Gabe wanted me to call everybody I knew to tell them that the Voice of Truth could be heard on 810 of the AM band. I told him I couldn't call any one at that hour. I also asked him where they were, trying to sound as demanding as possible, as I was sure my mother would be very worried. He said he could not tell me. It was a secret.

JUNE KEITHLEY, radio announcer

I held back for a while. I did not want to be responsible for the lives of these two young boys. If I broadcast, I thought that we would be located immediately because we were near Malacañang. They would be able to get us in less than ten minutes. And if I broadcast for only ten minutes, people might panic and that would create a worse situation.

I called up one of my friends and asked her to get some people together. I decided to wait for them, but in the meantime the boys had set up the radio. I could hear panic: "B1, B1, B8, B9, there's nobody here. Somebody, please air this on radio. We need people in the south gate. The tanks are coming. Who's going to call for help to come? When are we going to air this on radio? Somebody has to do something!"

I kept hearing these appeals. So I said: "We cannot wait. Whether my friends arrive or not, we have to go on the air." We turned on all the switches and I played "Mambo Magsaysay." It was 12:10 a.m. I posted someone at the window and I said: "Keep looking at Malacañang. If you see any tanks coming from that direction, tell me."

I knew that if we did not go on so many people could die. The few lives that were with me in that little tower did not matter as much as the throngs of people out there, as the country itself. It had to be Go.

I looked at Paolo Mercado sitting next to the radio transceiver. He was looking at the crucifix hanging from his necklace. He was turning the crucifix around and around and looking at it. I said to myself: "That poor boy." I wanted to put my arms around him to say we would be all right. But I had no guarantee that we would be. I have a very difficult time lying and saying words just to make things seem better. The pain went right through me, but I had things to do. I had no choice. I said: "Lord, it is all up to you," and I went to work.

After I played "Mambo Magsaysay," I started sending messages to and from General Ramos and Minister Enrile. Within the half hour, my friends arrived — twenty of them — and we really got started.

My husband was out on EDSA when he heard my voice. He didn't know where I was but he got to a phone, called our maid and asked her to give me a message. The maid got to me and she said: "Ma'am, Sir just called. He said you should go home." I said: "I can't go home," and I hung up.

LT. GRACIANO CORPUZ

I sent a tape of the Philippine Military Academy Alma Mater to Radio Bandido. It was important to me that it should be played at that crucial time. The Alma Mater song, to PMAers, is the summary of all our ideals as soldiers.

LYDIA B. BROWN

June kept sending only one message throughout those early hours: "Get out there to help. This is the time to stand up and be counted."

At one point, we played the PMA Alma Mater and immediately there were requests to play songs from the other forces — the air force, the navy. June said that we had only the PMA song on tape in the radio. Later, one of my friends who was inside Camp Crame told me that when some reformists heard the PMA song, they wept.

FERDINAND E. MARCOS
(In a radio broadcast early Monday morning)

I have the power to destroy this rebellion if I feel enough is enough. I am not sick. I am strong.

I will not resign. I will even lead the troops against Enrile and Ramos. I smell gunpowder like an old war horse.

JUNE KEITHLEY

The worst time was when I heard the cries of the people being teargassed and when I learned that the helicopters were coming. I felt so helpless. I was wondering where my husband was. All I knew was that he was out there, but where? At the Crame gate? At the Santolan gate? Had he been gassed?

The darkest hour was before dawn. I kept looking out and praying: "Lord, let the sun come up." It was 5:45 a.m. and it was black as night.

I began to pray on the air: "Lord, you know that there are many people out there. You know what we are going through right now. There are many of us and we are trying to do our duty. We ask you to please guide us, Lord. You teach us to always turn the other cheek. We ask you now to show us in many concrete ways that truly nothing good can come from evil. Show us, Lord, that only good will work in this world. Please take care of all who are out there. Protect them and save them from harm. There are children out there, young girls and boys, parents, brothers and sisters, husbands and wives. Who knows what they may have to face this morning? We add our prayers to the prayers of the people in our country. Lord, I am not very good at this but I just ask you please, in Jesus' name, please save our people."

The sun came up at 6:08 that morning. I know the precise time because I was waiting for it and I was wondering: "What is taking the sun so long?"

WAWEL MERCADO, student

In Libis, sitting there in the half-dark, I could hear singing. There was a group from Tondo and they were singing ballads. I have never heard any of those songs before, but they were very deep, very sad. We all knew that there was danger out there, somewhere. That was why many of us really didn't talk for any length of time. We smiled or chuckled but no one really laughed out loud. The singing, however, went on almost all throughout the night. I was thinking: perhaps singing is ingrained in the Filipino. He sings when he is scared.

POY PANTALEON, wife and mother

That must have been 3:00 a.m. I looked up and saw a procession — young men in cassocks and ordinary people. They were carrying candles and were coming down EDSA toward Ortigas Avenue into which they turned and went up toward the Meralco building. They were saying the Rosary and singing and, at the end of the procession, they were carrying a statue of Our Lady.

FREDDIE AGUILAR

Very early Monday morning, we heard that tanks would attack through Mariposa street. The people started forming barricades and the reformist soldiers cocked their guns. It was scary.

I went up to General Ramos' office to listen to their radio. You heard everything that was happening everywhere: Libis, Aguinaldo, EDSA. I went up to find out where I was needed. I then decided to go to the Santolan gate. At a little past three, we heard the rumble of a motor. We craned our eyes and our ears: it was a garbage truck. Everyone laughed.

Feeling very tired, I went up to the headquarters' waiting room. It was airconditioned and there were comfortable seats. I tried to take a nap but I could hear the radio all the time. It was a VHF radio operated by two kids and from it I could hear reports of Marines forming lines for the attack.

LT. GRACIANO VICTOR

The presence of God was so strong. It seemed as if only one thought ran in our minds and it was this: My God, it is all in your hands.

It seemed at times, inside the Crame headquarters, that people were asleep or staring into space. It was not so. We were thinking. We were praying to God.

FE B. ZAMORA, reporter

At about 4:30 a.m., there was good news. The three tanks sighted earlier turned out to be garbage trucks. General Ramos was amused: "That's symbolic. We have been getting nothing but garbage all these years."

From good news to bad news: June Keithley called to say that someone from Fort Bonifacio reported that "soldiers are massing and are about to leave for Camp Crame." General Ramos dropped his cigar and grabbed the phone. "Now it is clear," he said. "It is Mr. Marcos who is massing troops, not us."

Minister Enrile was dozing in his chair, a baby UZI on his lap. His aide hesitated, but someone wanted to speak to him. A slight nudge was enough and Enrile reached for the phone. "Oh yes, we have public support," he said. "There's an avalanche of nuns here. The people's lives are in the hands of Marcos. If they are attacked, it will be an addition to the sordid record of killing men and women who have no arms, only rosaries."

A soldier came in and informed General Ramos: "The tanks are rolling toward Crame." Ramos' jaws quivered. Enrile smiled: "There are tanks outside. If you want to capture them, better start now."

OLET FERRER, photographer

It was close to dawn that Monday morning but not really dark because the moon was high. I walked down EDSA towards a barricade to see

Masked at the barricades: the reveler's spirit

193

how safe it was because we had heard over the radio that the tanks would come at dawn. I passed so many men sleeping on the traffic island and on the street itself. At the barricade, there was a bonfire. Six nuns were standing around it, talking quietly, keeping watch. But the rest of the people were asleep. I hurried back to my friend and we joined the nuns. For a while, it was just six nuns and ourselves, two men, who were at that barricade, waiting for the dawn and for the tanks.

FLORENCIO S. STA. MARIA

About a hundred meters from the intersection of White Plains Avenue and EDSA, we saw a small group of people huddle around three uniformed soldiers. The three soldiers were all officers of the Air Force, telling the people why they had formed the Reform Movement. As they moved through the crowd people clapped and cheered them on.

I joined a huddle. I overheard one of the officers say they were expecting a dawn attack from Marcos loyalists. I was petrified. I realized that they were probably out on EDSA on observation patrol.

Then I saw something that made me realize the second and perhaps the more important reason the officers had for being out on EDSA. One of the officers put his arm around a lady. You could tell she was trying hard not to cry. She told him: "Oh, Daddy, you should have seen Joey Rufino and Butz Aquino . . . they were crying as they put their bodies in front of the tanks. They were all very brave. We thought they would be run over." She told him more stories and he told her his own stories. It was clear they were trying to boost each other's morale. She was his wife. My heart melted and my knees weakened. I realized the officer came out to bid her farewell.

JOSE V. FRANCISCO

There was an expected attack of armored tanks coming from the direction of Pasig or Makati. Once in a while, people craned their necks, looking east towards Pasig or south towards Makati. But there was no organization. I called some people and suggested that we organize, group together and lock arms when the expected attack came.

We were holding wet handkerchiefs, wet paper napkins, even wet rags, as a defense in case of tear gas attacks.

In the midst of it all, a middle aged man suddenly showed up, pulled his bicycle to the side and from two huge tin cans hanging from the sides of his bike, started giving out breakfast buns.

I asked the man why. He replied that he was supposed to have delivered the bread to the residents of Corinthian Gardens. Finding the entrance to the subdivision blocked and closed in order to prevent the entry of tanks, he decided to give the bread away instead. I tried to give him fifty pesos for his good deed but he refused to accept my offer. He told me: "This is the only help I can give my country."

The man in the bicycle gave out all his bread. The distribution was over in a few minutes. He rode his bike and disappeared into the dark.

FE B. ZAMORA

At 5:10 a.m. tension gripped the room. It was "bad news" again. Colonel Romeo Zulueta, deputy commander of the METROCOM, came in with three aides in tow. "I have verified reports, Sir," he told General Ramos. "The enemy will attack at five." General Ramos checked his watch. "It's past five already. Where are they?" Zulueta replied: "Two battalions in our rear, Horseshoe Village area; two battalions, led by Colonel Rolando Abadilla, deployed in Annapolis Street, Greenhills; two battalions inside Camp Aguinaldo and columns of tanks coming from the direction of Fort Bonifacio." Addressing the reporters, General Ramos heaved a sigh. "Well, this could be it. You may stay or you may not. It's an individual decision now. If there are foreigners here, please inform your embassies now. Are you willing to stay with us all the way?" "Yes! Yes!" they chorused in reply.

An aide dialed for Radio Bandido, and General Ramos made an appeal. "To all Filipino soldiers out there . . . Don't inflict harm on people who have no arms. The blood spilled today will be on Marcos' hands. We offer your friendship. I advise you to turn around and join us. We offer nothing but friendship. Mr. Marcos has assembled an overwhelming force against us. M Marcos has done nothing constructive. We are ready, but please tell the world it is Mr. Marcos who is about to inflict violence and terror, not us."

Turning to the reporters, General Ramos continued: "If they don't respond to our friendly overtures, then we will fight. We have to defend this movement going. It's obviously an overwhelming force, and we don't have enough force to counter them." He ordered his aide to take note of the nationalities present.

The room's silence broke with Cory Aquino's monotone from the radio. But by then, the tension had hit the ceiling. Marks of sweat formed on General Ramos' blue shirt. Enrile lazily crossed his leg. Soldiers nudged each other, fixed their flag patches and ammo belts, shaking off traces of drowsiness. Out of the room they marched.

The tension cracked with good news from June Keithley. "Sir, we have just received this report. Thirty members of the PSC have left their posts to join you." Ramos and Enrile stood up and raised their arms. "Ye-hey!" But the danger remained. "This is a good cause. We will die for it," Enrile quipped, clasping a rosary handed to him by an aide.

U.S. Ambassador Stephen Bosworth was on the phone. Enrile talked to him: "Just for the record, we would like to inform you that Marcos' troops will attack us any moment from now. We are going to make a stand. We are going to fight back to the last man to save freedom in our land." Putting back the phone he turned to the reporters. "Ambassador Bosworth said he will inform his government."

Just as General Ramos was all set to leave the room, an aide informed him an Australian newsman was on the phone. Soldiers had already ringed him, ready for the "evacuation." Grabbing the phone, he answered, stiffly: "We are about to be attacked. Yes, there are two battalions . . . There are also unarmed civilians between us. There are Americans, British, Japanese, Swiss, and other foreign correspondents here . . . They are willing to stay with us . . . Yes, we will fight back . . . Yes, we are willing to lay down our lives." General Ramos' voice rose in anger; his fingers fiddled with his gun. "It is Mr. Marcos who is massing troops . . . Ms. Aquino is safe and she is joining us very soon." He clenched his fist and pounded on the table. "The commanders in all regions have promised to stay behind us. No, this is not what we want . . . This is what Mr. Marcos and Mr. Ver want . . . I cannot answer your questions anymore. We are about to be attacked . . ." His faced flushed. General Ramos muttered: "That S.O.B. is on Marcos' side."

But the reporters were not yet through. Circling General Ramos, one fired a question. But General Ramos had had enough. He ordered all reporters out. "Look, can't you see we are about to be attacked? We are going out on an operation and here you are asking questions?"

LITO BANTAYAN

I was in the second line, right behind the front line of priests and nuns. Behind me there were six more lines of men and women with their arms locked. Our eyes showed disbelief and uncertainty and complete defiance. Time seemed to stand still as we stared at the trucks. Their headlights blinded us.

We couldn't see the soldiers. Then a soldier shouted a warning. His voice sounded more like he was pleading. "Get out of the way," he said, "you will just get hurt." A man from behind me shouted back, "We will not leave." That verbal exchange sealed our fate. We braced ourselves for the assault by locking our arms tighter. A priest began to chant the "Our Father" and immediately everybody joined in.

Suddenly a man wearing a grey bullet proof vest over his black uniform stepped out of the light. He carried tear gas canisters. Before we could finish the Lord's Prayer, he lobbed four tear gas cannisters at us in quick succession.

My eyes hurt. As I ran, my nose and throat began to hurt too. Half blind, I ran, stumbled, ran again, and gasped for breath. All I wanted was fresh air. I ran in darkness — I could only remember where the trucks and the barbed wire barricades were — I ran guided by the voices calling to me: "We have water here, we have water here."

MARIA FE P. PALLER

Everything happened so fast I did not have time to scream. We just scrambled for safety and started running. My eyes were burning and my lips were smarting. Someone fired into the air and I could hear guns being cocked.

My left eye felt really sore. Would I become blind in the left eye? I asked myself. Oh, Mother Mary, please. . . how can I become an actress if I go blind?

We continued to run. A woman came out of her house and offered us water. I washed my face. The burning sensation spread all over my face. Somehow, with a little fresh air, I felt better. I was so grateful I could still see with both eyes.

GEORGE WINTERNITZ

Before dawn, the cry was more desperate: Tanks and tear gas. . . Marines marching against our group. The organizers fixed barricades, grouped our people in organized fashion, repositioned our vehicles, instructed us on how to cope with tear gas, provided buckets of water with *calamansi* (lemons) and rags for our faces. Then a number of vehicles came screaming up the road from the barricade 500 yards to the east, screeched to a halt and, amid slamming of doors, disgorged their passengers yelling: "Help us! Help us! Tear gas! We've been teargassed!" Although it was tense, our group was calm, praying the Rosary.

My mind flashed back to the scene on Saturday evening at the Benedictine Abbey School. "We cannot all go to the war zone," someone said. "Can you organize people who cannot go to pray for those who do?" Immediately someone volunteered to gather up prayer groups who then proceeded to pray the whole night until the full light of Sunday. Another person called friends to ask for prayers. "My children and I are already praying the Rosary," one mother of four said.

Seminarian and soldier: peace to you

"Yes, I will immediately call my friends here and in Quezon City to get them to pray the Rosary too!"

FELICITAS CRUZ, housewife

We were in the barricade in Libis during the dispersal. We felt that we were in a real war. We saw that the nuns and priests were really brave; they were in the frontline. We were in the middle. When the Marines started moving, we ran in different directions. Some of them climbed up the roofs, looking for the enemy. The priests asked them not to hurt or kill anybody but the M-16 rifles were aimed at us.

I overheard one soldier saying that they were trained to kill only those who are armed. They saw that we were unarmed. They didn't know what was happening. They said they came from Mindanao. They were ordered to disperse and attack but they didn't want to attack unarmed people. We were armed with our rosaries, crucifixes, images of Mary, and the prayer song "Our Father."

At first they refused to accept the flowers being offered to them. The nuns approached them, and spoke to them. Then they accepted cigarettes from us. At that time I couldn't understand why I was afraid but at the same time felt brave. I ran away but I turned back. I didn't have anything then but my rosary.

ANTONIO SORDILLA, repairman

I lost my tooth when one captain elbowed me while I was stopping the anti-riot police from entering our ranks in Katipunan Street. I did not run. I told them: "Go on, kill me! Don't you know who's paying you? We're paying our taxes so that you'll have a salary. Now, what are you doing? You're fighting us. Go on. Fight with your fellow soldiers! Go on, kill each other!" We were chanting "*Laban!*" (Fight). We said to ourselves: "Let it be. This happens only once." Fear didn't enter my mind then. I was ready to die for our country. I was concerned about our children. They are growing up. We are educating them for our country, so that they'll be able to run the country in the future. Marcos should step down for them. That was what I was thinking about.

During that time I spent my own money. I was going to and fro, fetching my neighbors in my Ford Fiera. I'll always remember that we didn't run away. We are Filipinos, not strangers nor foreigners — so why should our own soldiers kill us?

LITO BANTAYAN

For the first time, we saw the soldiers, three hundred of them. More were coming out from the smoke behind the truck from where we came. They were slow, and seemed affected by the gas too. They were dousing their faces with water. Armed with shields and rattan sticks, they formed several lines. Those with the guns stood at the back. We were face to face. About a dozen soldiers in black uniforms with bullet proof vests, gas masks, and armalite rifles were roaming around, eyes alert, rifles ready to fire.

There was shouting, shouts of anger and hatred. People at the back of us were arming themselves with stones. A priest tried to pacify some of the people. "Please don't shout. Please don't throw stones." We were praying again, this time louder. Several old priests approached the soldiers to talk to them, but they were shoved away by the soldiers with armalite rifles. A priest went around our line with a cup filled with *calamansi* (lemon) juice, telling us: "Wet your handkerchief with this. Put some in your faces."

A soldier lobbed a tear gas canister in front of our line and then they came rushing towards us. We backed up a few feet but our line did not break. We were more organized, more determined. Suddenly a gust of wind blew the gas away from us into the line of the soldiers. Their line broke! I told the priest beside me: "Father, the breeze is blowing toward them!"

We stood there until the soldiers were able to form a line again. The sergeant had a hard time convincing the soldiers to line up. They were reluctant. Nobody wanted to be in front to form a solid line and they moved ever so slowly. I knew we had won. Even after they drove us away during their last rush forward, I knew we had won. The soldiers were with us and I felt it.

From under their helmets, I could see that they were smiling, they were hitting their shields instead of hitting the people. Even when I stopped running, they went past me. Nobody raised his stick to hit anybody, they were mocking it. Even some of the priests stopped running.

I walked towards Camp Crame, past the lines of soldiers, and nobody bothered me. I was so far back that the tanks were already behind me. Near EDSA the first and second line of soldiers were being embraced and were shaking hands with the people. When I reached EDSA and joined in the singing of the National Anthem, I was close to tears. It was all over, I said to myself. Suddenly I was very tired and weary. I was wet and dirty, but I was very, very happy.

COL. ANTONIO SOTELO, commander, 15th Strike Wing

I woke up at 2:00 a.m., Monday. Immediately I tuned in to Radio Veritas, only to realize that it was gone. But I caught the familiar voice of June Keithley in another station. She was giving a blow-by-blow account of what was going on. It made me sad.

At 3:00 a.m., I got up and asked my wife to make me a nice breakfast. But since I felt like a death row prisoner, the food did not taste good at all to me.

I continued planning the details. I called Sangley and instructed the duty officer to gather the staff at my command post, the wing operation center, so that they could all hear my briefing by radio.

I told the supply officer to send me, by land, another ten M-16s and two boxes of ammo to equip the guards. Of course, it was a fake: we brought all the guns and ammo with us.

In the briefing, I told them to wake up all the pilots and to prepare the aircraft as we may be told to take off early. At this point, the pilots did not know yet their real mission. At 4:00 a.m., I got the call: the guns had cleared the gate. I was happy.

At 4:15 a.m., my son and I bade goodbye to my wife. A brief hug, a kiss, a few words of endearment, the prospect of seeing each other again perhaps only in the next life, last minute instructions, no tears — I did not look back. I got into the staff car and the driver drove off. My first stop was the pilots' quarters. I woke them up. The radio in my car was on; I knew what was happening. It was pretty bad and deteriorating rapidly.

I got to the hangar at around 4:30 a.m. I checked the guns. They were loaded and ready to fire. The rocket tubes were filled. Extra ammo were loaded. My small bag of toilet articles and a few pieces of underwear. Rifles and bullets.

By 5:15 the pilots were all in. I ushered them to the briefing room. I asked if anybody wanted to back out. Nobody did. I strengthened their faith by saying that we would die only once and it was a rare opportunity to die for one's country. The squadron commander said that we had already received our first mission which was for two gunships to be at Bonifacio before 6:00 a.m. to report to the Army's G-3. What a coincidence! I used it as my cover.

I then started my plane at 5:55 a.m. Briefing was finished in ten minutes. The rescue squadron commander was at the briefing for the first time. I was not sure what side he was on so I told him to stay close to me before he went to his parking area which was about 1/2 kilometer from the hangar. This was a precaution. If he were on the other side, we would be gone before the police could get at us.

I called my wife to tell her it was time for them to leave. I told Sangley to call me on the phone as I had confidential info for the staff gathered at the command post. So as not to arouse any suspicion, I talked first to the No. 2 man and asked him a few questions. I then talked to the No. 3 man and asked him a few questions. It was five minutes prior to start engine. I let the other Rescue Squadron Commander go to his unit.

I kept talking to my Squadron Commander at Sangley, to waste time. At 30 seconds prior to start engine I then said: "This is the last time I will talk to you. Your mission is to take off immediately and see me on 119.2 mega cycles or 126.2 mega cycles. If you don't hear from me, land at Clark. Nobody knows these instructions except you."

I put down the phone and ran to the aircraft, shouting: "Start!" On the way I met an officer who came to the hangar. He talked to me but I did not answer. The engines came to life and in a minute or so, we were airborne.

A few seconds later the Number 5 gunship called: "airborne." I had a complete feeling of serenity.

FE B. ZAMORA

Outside the war room, a group of reporters huddled around a small transistor radio. Cardinal Sin was on the air: "May we come to a peaceful solution in our crisis. I will bless the men in uniform but only those who are for peace." As soon as the Cardinal said Amen, a soldier asked the reporters to leave. No one moved. A plane zoomed by, then there was the sound of helicopters. "Here they are! This is it." Photographers scrambled to get into the war room but it was strictly off-limits. Along the three flights of stairs, soldiers stood alert.

FREDDIE AGUILAR, singer

I heard that Malacanang had ordered a full assault by land and by air. That was about 5:00

a.m. I heard that the Marines were teargassing the people in Libis. I was very tense because I could hear everything that was happening. I heard that people were crying in Libis. I did not know what to do. I couldn't move. I heard calls for ambulances and the Red Cross because a lot of people had been hurt. They were also calling on the Crame vigilantes to move to Libis to reinforce the barricades. Then we heard helicopters coming. I said to myself: "This is it." When I looked around I found most of the people had gone. The reporters were not there anymore. There were only four of us left. I did not know if I should run. I just kept on wondering where everybody else had gone. Aside from myself and the two VHF operators, there was only one other person in the room — I think he was a Muslim photographer. He was looking at me. The two operators were not doing anything anymore. We were just staring at each other, probably all just waiting for gunfire. It seemed like eternity. Our lives seemed to be suspended. I just prayed: "My God, if you really want this thing to happen to us, our lives are in your hand. Your will be done."

RAFAEL ONGPIN, student

There is no mistaking the sound of a helicopter. They call them choppers, because that is what they sound like from near or from afar, as they were this time. Everyone on the avenue must have turned idly at the chance to look at something besides tired people, trash, and sandbags.

They were far off at first, a tiny smudge that grew and separated into spots in the pastel stripe between night and day. It took a while before the suspicion surfaced and began to grow. It flashed across our minds suddenly: They're headed this way.

"Oh, are those ours or theirs?" Tito Ting Paterno asked evenly, as if he were discussing sandwiches instead of death machines capable of wholesale massacre. Clambering onto the roof of the jeep, I could make out the lead flight; they were the famous new, fast and expensive Sikorskys. One line from the local press leaped to my memory: "These gunships equipped with rocket pods, 20 mm cannons and 2000-round-per-minute machine guns are primarily intended for use against troop concentrations." Meaning: large crowds of people much like the one I happened to be in just then. I turned to my father and decided not to belabor him with trivial technicalities such as these at the moment. He was gazing at them fixedly.

"Teargas," my father uttered hollowly. "They're firing teargas. Get down from there." I jumped down, and followed his gaze. I saw instantly the source of his confusion. In the early morning fog, the pale beam of the lone headlight on each chopper very much resembled from afar a spray of fine mist. Needless to say, physicists like you or I know that such a mist fired at that altitude and distance a) would billow into clouds instead of streaming straight out, and b) would, if it were indeed teargas, dissipate uselessly long before it could affect us on the ground. I turned to relay to him my latest scientific observations, but he was already rubbing lemon juice all over his face.

There has existed, throughout the history of the Philippine protest movement, a certain resilient belief, probably of ancient Egyptian origin, that the juice of this common fruit is an antidote to teargas. I have never found occasion to prove or disprove this superstition, having always brought a convenient gas mask to rallies likely to be visited by such noxious chemicals. This equipment I brought out now, but it was too late. My father's face was already glowing with herbal protection. He handed me the sticky vial and advised me to do likewise.

"Give that gas mask to the driver—he'll need it more than us." "Good thinking, Batman," I muttered silently, applying the slightly rancid balm to my heretofore quite comfortable, if grizzled, face. Meanwhile, the distant chopping had turned into a clatter. The whole avenue was on their feet staring at the intruders in the distance.

I wonder now how many of those defenseless people knew the peril they were in. Those gunships could have transformed the avenue into a crimson river of spattered viscera, a Mixmaster mush of torn flesh. The soldiers in the camp could have been wiped out, their pitiful small-arms no match for the choppers' heavy belly-armor. General Ramos, Minister Enrile, and the rest of the rebel leaders would have been entombed in their headquarters, shredded into the rubble by vicious rockets. I could only cower behind the jeep, fingering the rosary in my pocket and wishing I could climb in after it. I couldn't recall at that point what exactly the words were that one started the Rosary with. Beside me, my father glanced underneath the jeep, probably wondering if he could get in there, next to the gas tank. It looked too dirty to me.

Inexorably, the clatter was growing into a snarl. They came in low, just above treetop level, their menacing shapes silhouetted in the now china-blue sky. The climbing sun, gaining velo-city, flashed on their tinted windows. They snarled closer, deafening now, and the huddled crowd seemed to be saying with their expressions: *This is it!* And then, with a roar, they were over us. There was a certain pause at that moment, measured by the time it took for the lead ship to touch down — then complete pandemonium broke loose. We were all gamboling toward the Crame walls, through the bars of which the landing field was visible. I was among the first to scramble up the low concrete wall in which the bars were sunk. I may or may not have stepped on someone's head. All I knew was, he tried to bite me.

"Don't touch those bars, son. They're dirty."

"Right, Dad," I said, hastily withdrawing my suddenly black hands and nearly falling over backwards in the process. The choppers were landing everywhere, like bees on a hive. It seemed dangerously crowded, with so many choppers and thousands of people rushing through the grass to meet them.

All of the soldiers were leaping off their helicopters and embracing each other. "Don't do that!" I called out. "It only happens in the movies, not in real life."

I jumped off the six-foot wall which didn't seem so high a moment ago, narrowly avoiding the other prospective Humpty Dumpties overwhelmed by this truly heartwarming scene. I needed sleep.

In the jeep, on the way home, my father said: "Well, that was something you can tell your grandchildren about."

"Yours first," I growled. Boy, I thought, I'll bet those grandchildren are going to find us real boring.

EMMANUEL RIDAD, student

When my brother and I first arrived at Camp Crame yesterday afternoon, a possible bloody confrontation with General Ver's troops was the farthest thing from our minds. We had come to help, answering the call of our soldier friends, Noni and Pete, who had invited us to join them in the camp. They met us at the door of the office of Brigadier General Cruz, the Deputy Chief for Police Matters. They then showed us around, introducing us to other soldiers. Everything seemed normal. Secretaries, still in their office uniforms, were busy typing reports and answering phones. There were not too many soldiers in the vicinity. And the few that were there were simply chatting among themselves. Only the presence of numerous media men hounding the few officers present for the latest developments, pointed to the still unbelievable yet real, abnormal state of affairs.

The somewhat relaxed atmosphere, however, soon took a nosedive as a wave of alarming reports flooded the camp. Tanks and APCs were spotted coming down Ortigas Avenue. General Tadiar and his Marines were reported to be slowly approaching Camp Aguinaldo. A battalion was said to be positioning itself behind Crame. We were surrounded.

Two soldiers carrying brand new Armalites and boxes of ammunition rushed into the room. They began to distribute the guns saying that upon orders, all military personnel were to be issued long arms. My brother and I were also given guns since—as we quickly found out—we were to form part of General Ramos' reserve force.

At around 3:00 a.m., with verified reports of a dawn attack, General Ramos requested all civilians to leave the camp. Many of the civilians, most of them media men, did not want to leave. So instead, their names and their nationalities were just jotted down so as to inform their employers or their embassies of their whereabouts. Preparations were then made to repel the enemy's attack. An officer briefed us on where to position ourselves. My brother and I were placed right behind the front liners. We were in a sense, part of the last line of defense.

We then knelt down to say our prayers. We all shook hands, trying to assure one another that we were all in this together. I embraced my brother. Neither of us said a word. We just stared at each other.

We heard the Sikorsky choppers fly over. It was time to join the others in the building's lobby.

I was nervous. My arms were stiff. My hands were sweating. My lips were very dry. Hearing General Ramos talking with June Keithley over the radio only made me feel worse.

"Load your chambers!" an officer barked.

All guns were now aimed at the helicopters circling above us.

"Iikot lang yan bago tayo banatan!" (They will turn around before hitting us!), the soldier beside me whispered to himself.

With my Armalite aimed at one of the helicopters, I was now ready to die. I was just waiting for the whistling sound of the gunships' missiles and for the building to explode anytime.

But the helicopters did not open fire. Instead, they began to land!

"Don't fire! They're defecting! They're ours!" a jubilant General Ramos shouted.

There was an outburst of joy and happiness among the defenders. Soldiers shouted, cried, and embraced one another. Now it was clear: Colonel Sotelo's command had defected!

CELSO R. PASCUAL

After a while, the group of helicopters tasked to shoot hovered above us. That was the zero hour. As I gazed at my companions, I noticed the presence of Noel Trinidad, the actor-singer, with his family huddled close together in prayer. My thoughts suddenly brought me back home, to my wife and my children. God will provide. After sometime, the helicopters disappeared.

PATRICIA TRINIDAD, student

We were sitting on the roadside at about five in the morning. Dad was kidding, I thought. He put his arms around us, Mom, Joel and myself, and he said: "Okay, we are in this together." When he said that, I thought: "We are going to die."

I began to cry. Mom was crying, too. We were all praying but we were very tense. We thought we would die.

After about twenty minutes, they said that the tanks had defected. People started jumping and hugging each other. Even some men were crying. All of a sudden, we saw four helicopters flying above us. People said: "Wait! Everybody sit down. It's not over yet." The choppers were flying low; they were hovering over us. It really was not over yet.

LT. GRACIANO VICTOR

In the grandstand of Crame, when we went out to meet the helicopters, death was very real to me. I sat there and smiled at Colonel Ciron who was beside me. He smiled back. It was as if we were saying goodbye.

When the helicopters came, I stood up. We all stood up. We were not going to fire—until we were fired at. But at that moment, when I stood up, I was thinking: This is it. Thank you, God, for the life I have had.

I was ready for death.

COL. ANTONIO SOTELO

We circled Camp Crame once; on the second turn, my pilot dropped the wheels, slowed down, and proceeded to land. There was the possibility of gunfire from below but it did not matter. At 6:10 a.m. or thereabouts, all aircraft landed: five gunships, two rescue Sikorsky, one utility BO-105.

Pandemonium broke loose. The rotor blades were still turning but people were swarming all over us. They were shouting and jumping and hugging. Reporters shoved microphones into my face and asked where we came from. I said I was not saying anything until I saw Minister Enrile and General Ramos.

All I wanted to say was: we followed our conscience. I brought along with me sixteen combat-ready pilots of my wing, the 15th Strike Wing. I have not really done much in my life and for once I wanted to make a decision for my country.

AURORA A. AQUINO, mother of Benigno S. Aquino, Jr. (Ninoy)

Father Adorable told me this story. A pilot was flying to EDSA to pulverize Camp Crame, but visibility was poor. There were heavy clouds. He went lower. There was still a haze. He went even lower. When he did, he saw all his relatives below him.

I also heard another story of a pilot who was also sent to bomb and strafe Camp Crame. But he saw many people — a vast crowd of people. At that time, there were not really that many people in the area, but this pilot saw so very many of them that he could not bring himself to strafe nor bomb them. When I heard that, I laughed. I said: "I think Ninoy gathered all the souls in purgatory. I think he herded them all to EDSA. That Ninoy, he can mobilize even the souls in purgatory."

FE B. ZAMORA

From the headquarters, a soldier ran out informing his comrades: "The Marcoses have fled the country! It's on Radio Veritas." His comrades raised their armalites. "We won! We won!" Children and young men scaled the camp's gates. Women shrieked for joy and offered cups of coffee and packs of cigarettes to every one. The headquarters' halls reverberated with the "good tidings."

The war room was still closed but there was joy all over. A captain related what happened: One military officer by the name of Captain Alcantara relayed to Radio Veritas that the Marcoses, aboard limousines, had left the Palace. Another girl also called up June Keithley saying she saw black limousines drive off from Malacanang.

Never, since the start of the siege, was the mood at Camp Crame like this. General Ahorro patted every other soldier's back. "Good work, gentlemen!"

The tumult spread throughout the camp. The gates were opened. Men, women, and children milled in the grounds. Some clambered aboard helicopters for a snapshot. The soldiers obliged.

Amidst it all, General Ramos and Minister Enrile negotiated the three-flight base of the flagpole. "We have won! Thank you. Thank you." Enrile raised his arms. Soldiers abandoned their posts and massed around the duo. Civilians joined them, alternately chanting: "Ra-mos! Ra-mos! John-nee! John-nee!" A devotee raised the image of Our Lady of Fatima. "The people have won," Enrile said. "The enemy is gone."

And what about the tens of thousands of vigilantes outside the camp? General Ramos and Minister Enrile decided it was best to share the glory with them. They drove the short distance to the gate and outside into EDSA as Senator Lorenzo Tanada, the grand old man of the opposition, assisted by student leader Lean Alejandro and feminist Maita Gomez, inched his way in to see the men of the hour.

AMADO L. LACUESTA

By the time a Thanksgiving Mass begins, there must be thousands — perhaps a million — already filling EDSA between Ortigas and Santolan.

Afterwards, the crowd explodes into: "John-nee, John-nee!" and "Ra-mos! Ra-mos!" as the two main heroes of the revolution struggle to climb up the top of a van to address the people. Throughout, someone holds a statue of the Blessed Virgin over them. It has certainly been a strange revolution. I wonder if the Moslem jihads or the Crusades were ever like this.

Ramos jumps happily in the air like a little boy and I lose my heart to him. Again and again, he extols people power profusely, to the pride and delight of the crowd. He evokes no fear in me, only boundless respect and affection. I heartily join in the chant: "Ra-mos! Ra-mos!"

It is a very long walk along Santolan back to White Plains where the car is parked. On the way, we see a large group of soldiers and another of police, I think. Some are seated in a parked military truck. Others are standing in ragged formation against the perimeter wall of Camp Aguinaldo. Still others are sitting on top of the wall. Looking edgy, wary of the passing crowds, and talking among themselves in subdued tones, they are a dramatic departure from the strutting, arrogant men in uniform I have been used to seeing.

I hear a civilian calling for a nun, saying the soldiers want to be accompanied by a nun. I realize with a small shock that these men are defecting. Lolly and I dare to greet some of them, smiling, patting a few on the arm or shoulder, telling them it's finally over. They respond warily, almost grudgingly. I guess they are not yet used to friendly demonstrations from civilians.

GENERAL FIDEL V. RAMOS

Some people have asked me: "General, when you jumped up and down in front of the flagpole at Camp Crame, was that when you learned that Marcos had left Malacanang?" I said: "No, it wasn't. It was because I was happy and light-hearted. I felt that we had a better and freer atmosphere. I was sure that the good Lord is with us."

Don Chino Roces: once more at the barricades

GEORGE WINTERNITZ, insurance manager

Most vivid to me was the image of Our Lady of Fatima, borne on the shoulders of two strong men, following immediately behind Minister Ponce Enrile and General Ramos at Camp Crame. In fact, the statue of Our Lady alone was readily visible; the crowd was so dense that the Minister and the General could not actually be seen at all. You only knew where they were by the cheers of the crowd and the flash of cameras. But Our Lady's image stood out above the heads of the crowd, turning here and there as the men bearing it wound their way through the crowd.

It was as if Our Blessed Mother wanted to be there in person, at once to share the moment with her children and to bring us the message that God was with us, intervening in our moment of history.

It seemed that nearly every group brought an image or statue of Our Lady with them. People set up little portable altars, some atop their automobiles or on the backs of their pick-up trucks. And everywhere people prayed the Rosary. People used to praying it, people who had not prayed it for many years. Young, old, Religious, lay — without distinction, all prayed the Rosary.

CECILIA MUÑOZ PALMA, opposition leader

Because of all the excitement, I felt something heavy on my chest. I asked my husband for his heart medicine and I took two tablets. After awhile, I collapsed and they had to rush me to the hospital. My husband thought I was dead. I was so pale and my blood pressure went really way down.

At the hospital, they said it was an overdose of the medicine. Nonetheless, they kept me for the whole night. On Monday, I heard that Marcos had left. I jumped out of bed and stepped right out of the hospital without clearance. "We have won," I said. "What am I doing in a hospital?"

FREDDIE AGUILAR

Everybody cheered when they heard the report that Marcos and his family had left the country. Colonel Gringo Honasan was so happy and relieved that he started to cry. He said to Minister Enrile: "Sir, we should have done this a long time ago." Other soldiers cried too and said: "At last, everything is over."

We all went out. Minister Enrile and General Ramos spoke to the crowd on EDSA. Then we saw two jet planes flying in circles above us. I thought: "Wait a minute. I didn't hear about jet planes surrendering."

I felt some apprehension. Was it really that easy to make Marcos surrender? I did not think so. I could not really believe that Marcos was gone. Even while Enrile and Ramos spoke, doubt still nagged me. And as we returned to Camp Crame, I kept thinking: "It could not have been that easy."

When I turned on my Walkman, I got Marcos. He was talking. I switched to other stations. It was Marcos. All the stations had Marcos. I told the guy beside me: "Marcos is still here." He said: "No, that is only a tape."

Inside the office, Enrile made efforts to find out if it was really Marcos. He lifted the hotline: it was Marcos on the other end.

Everybody shouted: "Run out there to the people. Tell them to stay out. Marcos is still here." People ran out to EDSA, everywhere, and asked the crowd to remain.

AN MERCADO
(From a diary, dated February 24, 1986)

At 9:20 a.m., my brother and I rushed to the Ateneo to celebrate the departure of Marcos. We wanted to be with our friends who fought hard to end the dictatorship. But we found out that after the barricades they had no energy left to celebrate. They were sprawled on the quadrangle and many of them were asleep. The grassy little hills that once used to stream with ants were strewn with snoring boys. Every car roof was bedecked with a sleeping activist. The Home Base radios were turned off. Only the TV set was on and it was showing Marcos. The personnel were in a daze and they were sure the Marcos conference was phony.

I blinked and tried desperately not to believe what I saw. There were three girls with me and they had been up all night taking care of Home Base. They found it hard to believe what they were seeing.

Then Mang Ed, the janitor, came in; he said that Father Bonoan wanted his TV set back. I wondered if Father Bonoan believed this, too.

I walked out to my brother, who had fallen asleep in the car. I realized that I too had no energy left to celebrate. I did not even have the energy to wake my brother up and tell him that Marcos was still with us. I looked out across the quadrangle of sleeping Ateneans just in time to see the next bus, full of reinforcements, leave for Crame.

GRACIA M. CARINO

At about nine in the morning, my son came in from the barricades at Veritas where he spent the night. He didn't kiss me as is his custom. He sort of leaned on me and said: "We won, Mom!" He was too exhausted to give the phrase any happy ring and I hugged him and said: "Yes, we did." But it seemed to me such an easy victory.

The television set was on and suddenly Marcos was there. He was having a news conference and was showing newspapers to prove that it was taking place really on the same day and that it was on live. He said that contrary to rumors, he had not fled; in fact, he would neither resign nor leave.

I screamed: "Who is playing with our emotions? Who is floating rumors to make us happy, only to plunge us into depression again? How dare anyone play with my feelings?" I could see and hear that Marcos and Ver were having an argument about how to deal with the rebels in Crame, but the throb of my blood pressure seemed to blank out any sharper perception.

All of a sudden, the TV set blinked and the image of Marcos disappeared. My husband yelled: "He's been cut off. They've captured Channel 4." I thought, of course, that he was imagining things. My husband has a quick imagination and it is also often precise, when strategy is concerned.

ROMEO LAVILLA, JR.

At 9:30 a.m., not long after Channel 4 went off the air, we heard sporadic gunfire. We live near Channel 4, so my brother and I rushed out. The way to Channel 4 was swarming with people and cars were blocking the access to the rear gate. There we saw heavily armed soldiers, and from the Philippine flag patch on their left shoulders, we presumed that they were reformists.

At the corner of Mother Ignacia and Scout Albano streets, we saw about fifty to sixty heavily armed soldiers who had white armbands. We presumed that they were Marcos loyalists.

There must have been only about 20 reformists against the 50-plus loyalists. I thought that the reformists could easily be wiped out, but then they had the support of the people.

As the reformists advanced on Channel 4, there was gunfire — first one burst, then another. People shouted encouragements to the reformists. It was at this time when I heard loud prayers. It was from a pick-up truck that was inching its way into the Channel 4 gate. On board was a priest who was saying the Rosary very loudly. He also sang Ave Maria and encouraged the people to pray and sing, too. In the back of the pick-up were statues: one was of the crucified Christ, the other was of the Virgin Mary. From both sides, the soldiers were awed. There was a ceasefire.

Colonel Mariano Santiago, the leader of the reformist troops, accompanied by a priest and several civilians, approached the loyalists for a dialogue. The loyalist commander agreed. During the entire negotiation, the priest in the pick-up continued praying and singing.

PAT. EULOGIO GONZALEZ

The people, more out of curiosity than anything else, formed a circle around Colonel Santiago. They provided a natural protective buffer for the Colonel. They did not really know that they were playing a very important role by simply being there because soldiers will never shoot civilians.

ERNESTO R. PASCUAL

At Channel 4 we milled around just walking and staring at the people. We knew there was danger but we felt confident and brave. My daughter, Patricia, asked her mother: "What are we doing here? Why are we just walking around?" Her mother answered: "We are doing people power, my child."

RICARDO ELIAS, driver

I was at Channel 4 at this time. The reformists had taken over. I noticed some loyalists along Panay Avenue and I sat down and talked to them. I gave them cigarettes and I even tied a yellow ribbon on one of the soldiers I talked to. I talked to another loyalist but he didn't respond. I tried putting a yellow ribbon on his gun. He refused. But what gets me is that when this last soldier walked away, his gun fell and accidentally fired. One of the bullets hit the other loyalist whom I befriended. Until now I cannot forget that soldier.

AN MERCADO, student
(From a diary)

We must remember this time: 1:25 in the afternoon of the 24th of February, 1986. Channel 4 is free and broadcasting for the people.

I cannot believe it. We do not have to see Marcos and be scared that people will believe him. We never have to sit through false news or try to take false news sitting down. We are free from double speak.

We see, at last, the faces behind the comforting voices that brought us courage and hope in the last of the dark days. Maan Hontiveros looks like a true veteran of a revolution. She is unmade-up but she looks good. Even Orly and Fr. Efren look good. They look much better than the carefully made-up puppets that Channel 4 used to have. I think the glow comes from a clear conscience.

DANNY DIMACALI, former *Manila Times* reporter, now in Australia
(From a letter to a friend in Manila)

Harriet, thanks for your lovely letter. I never for once imagined a person from another country telling me I should be proud of my countrymen. But you are so right, Harriet. My mouth was dry and my eyes watery as I watched them make history. You know, I saw a very close friend from my reporting days (his name is Jun Abad) when the rebels took Channel 4 in Quezon City. I jumped up and shouted: "Jun, Jun!" as if he could hear me. At that moment my old reporting instinct was straining at the leash, part of me was saying you are supposed to be out there capturing the color and spirit of this great scene in history. I almost broke down when I realized how impotent I was in front of the TV set, so far away.

KAA BYINGTON, writer

I saw, with my own eyes, all of these dramatic events, but the one thing that meant the most to me was comparatively very humdrum: A logo flashing on a television screen, and a voice saying: "This is Channel 4 serving the people again."

I don't think anyone noticed it, but I cried then. And the reason was that twelve years before I had watched Marines with bayonets take over that very station and arrest the staff. I remember that as the most painful and symbolic event of martial law: the killing of truth with bayonets.

DOLORES DE MANUEL, teacher

As I was leaving home for a second day at the barricades, I heard Minister Enrile on the radio: He wanted women and children to come into the camps, for their safety. It sounded like the echo of a bygone era. How many would take him seriously, I wondered? I certainly didn't intend to, nor did any of my women friends, I felt.

We were fighting not with physical strength but with unarmed courage, and so our women's efforts could certainly count as much as men's.

A scene that showed this conviction coming alive was small compared to events happening around the camps that day. Although it must have been played out elsewhere by thousands of others, being part of it made me proud to be a Filipino — and a woman.

It was 3:00 p.m., at the intersection of Santolan and Katipunan. Our group — some 200 Ateneo college students, teachers and staff, a handful of nuns, Jesuit priests and seminarians, people living nearby — was guarding the Libis area from Marcos loyalist troops already on their way from Camp Capinpin in Tanay, taking the less-guarded backdoor route to the camps. The group was relaxed, considering that we could still smell the tear gas throwing at dawn, and we were fresh from a tense encounter.

An hour before we had confronted the naked steel of fixed bayonets, Armalites ready to fire, and the grim stare of a Marine commander who, when we refused to give way to his truckload of troops, had warned the priest leading us that he was quite used to killing. Seeing that he was ready to do it, we gave way, of course — frustrated, angry, shaken, yet knowing that we hadn't failed, since our aim wasn't to make martyrs but to avoid bloodshed, delay the loyalists, and show them our determined vigilance.

The incident had lasted some twenty frightening minutes. "This can't really be happening!" I thought as I saw the barrel of a rifle appearing over the heads of the massed, crouching crowd. It was outlined against the sky, only a few feet from our faces. But nobody panicked, screamed or ran away. All I heard were appeals to the soldiers for compassion, songs, and prayer to keep up our spirit. For that, at least, we felt we could be proud.

As the group sat on the road after the incident, calming down, preparing for the next encounter, a marshal announced our new formation: women volunteers were needed for the front line of the human barricade, together with a few marshals. This would appeal to the Marines' feelings, we hoped. The tactic had worked in other areas the day before. Come stun them with your beauty, he joked. But the women responded seriously — even while he was speaking, some were standing up and moving forward. Reason told me that only an hour before I had hardly dared to look at the troops — would I really be able to stand face to face with them in the front line?

RICARDO CARDINAL VIDAL

I wanted to return to Cebu, my archdiocese. I had only come to Manila for the meeting of the administrative council of the Catholic Bishops' Conference of the Philippines. I was supposed to be back in Cebu right away because I had a hectic schedule there.

When the revolution broke out, I was concerned about Cebu and I wanted to go home. However, I was asked to stay in Manila because the revolution was a national event and my presence would be needed. As the president of the Bishops' Conference, I was asked to stay. They told me: "You are more needed here in Manila than in Cebu."

I spent the time praying, receiving calls, making contacts. President Marcos spoke to me; he was seeking mediation. I began the effort but

Emblems of faith at the barricades

205

was not able to finish because they had taken sides. Once each had taken a position, it was very difficult to ask them to come together and talk. It was a very difficult time and a very delicate job. I had to remain neutral.

MANUEL G. CASPI, taxi driver

On the afternoon of February 24, 1986, I was driving my taxi near Nichols and Villamor Air Base when I suddenly saw a helicopter drop a bomb on the base. My passenger and I were shocked. We didn't know what was happening. We thought a civil war had begun. My passenger asked me to bring her back to her house in Parañaque. I immediately brought her home. But as soon as we arrived, she ran off without paying the fare.

RAFAEL GUERRERO III

On the afternoon of the same day, we went to the Manila International Airport (MIA) to meet my stepmother. While waiting at the parking lot for the plane to land, we saw three Philippine Air Force helicopters circling above. These helicopters swooped down on the nearby Nichols Air Base and fired on targets below. We later saw black smoke billowing from the ground. We found out later that the attack helicopters belonged to the rebels and had destroyed loyalist gunships.

RAFAELA BALERO, housewife

The events of the revolution brought back memories of World War II, especially to those who had been traumatized by it in their childhood.

We went to Channel 4. When I saw the soldiers coming in truckloads my knees grew weak. I thought: "My God, it's going to be war again, we have nothing to eat, where will we go? Please, God, have mercy. I don't have a husband anymore. Please help us. Please show that you are God."

JAIME CARDINAL SIN

One miracle was the people. They faced danger. They became very courageous. They went where the danger was. Sending our people out was a risk, but it was the only way.

When your faith is strong, even the mountains can be moved. But there were moments when I was disturbed. I was praying:

"God, don't let this happen, please." Never in my life did I pray so much. Every two hours, I called up the radio and said: "Maintain that spirit of love."

I was trying to do my best. I told my auxiliary bishops: "Each of you should be out there for four hours." All of them were there: Bishops Bacani, Reyes, Buhain, and Sobrepeñas. I told them to go to Channel 4, to radio stations, to inspire the people constantly.

JEFFREY ABIERA, Red Cross volunteer

During the People Power Revolution, Red Cross was present in the person of so many Filipinos who volunteered their services.

I was among them in Camp Crame. The Red Cross volunteers there consisted not only of university medical students but also of people who knew first aid. I, for one, came all the way from Laguna. There even was a veteran medic who had served as a medical volunteer in the Korean and Vietnam Wars. It was a very memorable experience, capped by the words of our medic-companion, who said: "I've been in the jungles of Vietnam and in Korea, but I've never seen anything like this before."

As dusk set in, tension began to mount, for an assault from the Marcos loyalists was still imminent. Many didn't listen anymore to the radio to lessen the tension that the reports of trouble areas very near the camp might create.

I was able to get into the Camp by going with a fellow who was supposed to deliver firewood. The Camp Security was so on the alert for infiltrators that my previous attempts to get in had been in vain.

Fortunately, I signed myself up as a Red Cross volunteer and I became involved in doing little odd services for the people, like distributing food and medicines to those in need. The other more experienced ones were in direct medical service.

I saw the great generosity of people who donated a lot of medicines—actually more than what was needed—for the use of the people and the soldiers. However, the paradox of the revolution was that we Red Cross volunteers did not have to deal with serious medical cases. No one was fatally wounded; no blood was shed; it was indeed a triumph of peace and nonviolence.

L. B. FLORES

In front of Polymedic Hospital perpendicular to EDSA, three trucks filled with men in fatigue seated with upraised guns went past the U.P. Los Baños group waiting for their colleagues at the street corner. The trucks were followed by two armored personnel carriers. Some of the soldiers flashed the L-sign, and some yellow ribbons floated prominently among them, in competition with the glitter of ammunition across the soldiers' breasts. The bullets, neatly arranged in ammo belts slung across the soldiers' back, and the guns appeared bigger than any I have seen on TV or in the movies.

These pictures in slow motion passed before us before we could even blink.

Bewildered, the questioning faces of the crowd echoed: "Are these troops ours or theirs?" As if in answer, multitudes—from the direction of Boni Avenue—shouted: "They are not ours! Man the barricades!" As the crowd rushed to seal the street corner at EDSA, the armored carriers advanced toward the crowd. A man swayed a banner in a gesture meant to distract or exorcise the advancing vehicles. Being run over was certainly not on his mind. More people gathered, raising their palms and saying: "Stop!" In this frenzy, some people commandeered a passing truck filled with cooking gas tanks to reinforce the people-sealed corner. The gas truck negotiated the cement island in the middle of the street to cross over to where the armored carriers were. People clambered up the truck as if to match eyeball to eyeball the soldiers atop the armored carriers.

With the immovable crowd blocking the way, the armored carriers tried to maneuver out of the tight street, momentarily endangering the fence at its right.

At this point, the middle aged ladies in the pathway of the armored carriers (in case they chose to bulldoze the fence) began to pray loudly: "Lord, help us. Virgin Mary, help us." Their eyes and hands were raised to the sky. Following their raised hands, I saw helicopters hovering above us.

Anyone who had been there would know that this was a moment that chilled the soul. At this point, shooting could have started—if not from the armored carriers then from the air, hitting the crowd or armored carriers, depending on whose side the helicopters were. But the people stood their ground. Men and women admonished the armored carriers to retreat. At first, the drivers of the armored carriers refused to budge. Non-verbal communication happening at that instant revealed the following in slow motion: The people pressed their bodies against the armor.

Their faces were pleading but they were clothed in nothing but raw courage. In that decisive and tense moment, the soldiers atop the armored carriers pointed their guns of every make at the crowd but their faces betrayed agony. And I knew then, as the crowd, too, must have discerned: the soldiers did not have the heart to pull the trigger on civilians armed only with their convictions. The pact had been sealed. There was a tacit agreement: "We keep this street corner, you retreat." And true enough, the armored carriers rolled back and applause echoed.

The face of that soldier struggling in agony for the decision to shoot or not, in the verge of tears, will forever remain in my memory. I pitied the soldier. Unlike the people who went to the EDSA "battle field" on their own volition and conviction, the soldier came wracked and torn between loyalties to the people (they didn't shoot after all) and to their superiors who could punish them.

DOMINADOR F. GALLARDO

One decisive factor in the people's victory was the liberation of the government's propaganda arm, Channel 4. Cut off from his men in the field, Marcos had no clear idea of what was going on. The reformists on the other hand, had a powerful tool for propaganda which clearly helped soften the resolve of the loyalist forces and buoy the spirit of the people.

I was with my wife when it was taken over. We were part of the volunteer food brigade who distributed food to the people barricading the station, those operating it, and the reformist soldiers who were providing the security. Foodstuff of all sorts, from various donors at one point, formed a mountain-like structure in the station lobby. We even got live chickens! Our group was a mixture of film stars and singers sans makeup and other volunteers. One touching incident I remember was when we gave food to a reformist soldier who said: "Please give some to my brothers in the other side—they're hungry too."

ROFEL G. BRION, teacher

I don't like any of this. I was in EDSA last night and I could have stayed. But I chose the comfort of this bed, in this house where I've been staying since Saturday night because it's safer here than in Cervini. Early this morning, I heard on DZRH that the Libis barricade was being dispersed with teargas and truncheons. The Cervini boarders were there. I'm a dorm prefect and I should be with them. But I couldn't leave the house and unduly worry Berms and Tess—I think they like the fact that their home is my safehouse.

But things are relatively better now—the Ateneans are relatively safe, Channel 4 is now in "our" hands, and in a while we're going to EDSA again. I can write this and not feel guilty about not being with the boarders.

This morning, as the DZRH field announcer frantically reported the dispersal in Libis, the disc jockey started playing Freddie Aguilar's version of *Bayan Ko* (My Homeland). At first, I was annoyed because I felt that the deejay was dramatizing things too much. But I couldn't help but listen to the words (I guess I wanted to forget that I wasn't in Libis): "My Philippines, my homeland/ Land of gold and flowers/ You are blessed with beauty and charm/ But these have drawn strangers to you/ My homeland, you are snared/ You are mired in suffering." And I remembered Babbit, my college friend. He sang it all the time in the dorm. Yes, *Bayan Ko* was a radical song in the early 70s. It was in fact Babbit's favorite song, next to the *Internationale*. The leftists sang *Bayan Ko* when they were not chanting "Down with imperialism, bureaucrat-capitalism, feudalism!" or quoting Mao and Amado Guerrero.

"Birds that fly freely/ Weep when caged./ How can my land so fair/ Not long to be free?" No wonder Babbit and his comrades sang it all the time. It echoed their chants so well. "My cherished Philippines/ Home of my sorrow and tears/ I vow to see you truly free." That was Babbit's fondest dream then—to see his country truly free. That was why he sang *Bayan Ko* all the time, probably even in his sleep.

Babbit loved that song so much that he wanted to write his English term paper on it. We even spent one afternoon arguing about its origin. He said that he had read that it was from Severino Reyes' turn-of-the-century *zarzuela*, "*Walang Sugat*" (Without Wounds). I told him that my high school Pilipino teacher said that it was originally just a poem written by Jose Corazon de Jesus. We searched the library for any book on de Jesus. We found one that said that *Bayan Ko* was written by de Jesus in 1929. A magazine article said that Constancio de Guzman wrote the music for it and incorporated the song into a new version of *Walang Sugat*. But Babbit never got to write the paper. Martial law was declared and he had to stay in Cebu.

Babbit and his comrades sang *Bayan Ko* with an added refrain: "How sweet it is/ To live in one's native land/ If no man is a slave/ Every man is free./ The country now held captive/ Tomorrow will overcome/ The East will turn red/ With the purity of freedom." Maybe that is why the moderates did not sing *Bayan Ko* in the early 70s. The leftists made it completely theirs with the line, "The East will turn red."

But now, the moderates have claimed *Bayan Ko*. Since Ninoy's death, it has been sung in practically every rally. We even sing it after the Mass sometimes. And Freddie Aguilar has written his own refrain: "If we come together/ This will come true./ Our country will be free,/ And we will savor justice./ Evil will not rule/ If we do not let it./ Let us all be one,/ Let us do battle/ With the reigning darkness."

I don't know when Freddie wrote these lines. But this is what's happening now—in this thing people have started calling a "revolution." Maybe the DZRH deejay did the right thing after all. I hope that Babbit, wherever he is today, heard what I heard. And remembered what I remembered.

This thing isn't over yet, this revolution. And people will keep on singing *Bayan Ko* in EDSA.

I think Berms and Tess are ready. We have to go to EDSA.

MAXIMO V. SOLIVEN

The youth of the land learned a lesson in civics and citizenship from the barrel of the gun and the tip of the bayonet that could never be picked up in the classroom. I can only salute them with admiration and wonder.

They come from all sectors of society — from the public schools and the elite schools, from the slums and from the posh villages. They came as Filipinos and they won their spurs in that face-off which won us liberty.

Take the contingent of 200 boys and girls from the Ateneo University who manned the Santolan-Libis front last Monday.

At 2 p.m., a jeepload and a truckload of Philippine Marines screeched to a halt in front of their human barricade. The Marines demanded to pass to assault Camp Crame. The kids — of high school and college age — shook their heads and refused to budge. They pleaded with the soldiers to go back, or else join the revolution. After a stand-off of almost half an hour, the Marine officer in charge lost patience.

He gave the order, "Fix bayonets", as the horrified priests and nuns, and the kids who had linked arms, listened. Then he instructed his men: "When you advance, don't think of anything. Just thrust your way through." Then they started marching forward in lock-step, their sharp bayonets glistening.

At the last minute, the priests ordered the students to give way — and the Marines pushed their way through. Many students fell to the ground or hugged each other, sobbing in anger and frustration. But they had stood their ground, until it was impossible for unarmed and human flesh to resist bayonets. These kids will grow up, knowing how dearly won and how important freedom is.

CARLOS C. YAMUT

Almost every hour General Ramos went on the air to make a personal appeal to fellow soldiers. From time to time, announcements of defections were read on Radio Veritas. People applauded the most for the officers and cadets of the Philippine Military Academy, who declared support for the reformists.

COLONEL GREGORIO CAGURANGAN,
intelligence officer, Philippine Military Academy

On Monday, we finally decided to choose sides. We called all the PMA officers and cadet representatives but even before that, the cadets had already polled the whole corps: 91 per cent for Ramos and Enrile, 8 per cent for Ver.

It was a choice between Ver and Ramos. Marcos and Aquino were only incidental. The bottom line was who would lead the armed forces.

FIRST SERGEANT SERAFIN A. DE AUSTRIA, PAF

On February 24, I received a phone call from Headquarters Air Reserve Division directing all military personnel to draw firearms and ammunition at the unit armory and proceed to the conference room for briefing. The Division Commander, Colonel Pablo Doble, told us that we were going on a very delicate mission and those who were afraid to die could stay behind. We boarded four military jeeps, two staff cars, and some other vehicles, and went to the AFP Logistics Command where there was an ongoing confrontation between civilians and loyalists. It was only then that the officer in our group, the Lieutenant Colonel Fernando, said that we were going to Camp Crame to defect. There were

soldiers in full battle gear deployed around the building. Upon seeing us, the people became apprehensive.

When the people saw us alighting from the jeeps, they immediately began blocking our way. We were able to convince them that we were with them. After this, they shouted with jubilation; some kissed us, the others embraced and shook hands with us. Hundreds of people escorted us to Camp Crame. We were ordered to report to the defection center. Inside the camp there was tension; there were rumors that the camp would be attacked by fighter planes and tanks. Worse, there were rumors of reformist forces attacking Villamor Air Base where my family was staying. But I was able to get them safely to Crame.

SISTER SHEILA LUCEY, SSC

Last Monday on EDSA, some exuberant person released about twenty doves. They streaked across the sky, trailing yellow streamers attached to their legs. Perhaps they could be a symbol of what we hope will come to our people: peace, accompanied by joy, and always the saving grace of good humor and the spirit of celebration.

ALFONSO R. FLORES, vender

On Monday afternoon, my family joined our neighbors. They had organized a trip to Camp Crame. A ten-wheeler truck waited for us at the corner of Blumentritt and Cavite Streets. There were so many of us we could hardly fit into the truck.

On our way to Crame, a lot of people cheered us on. Some said we were heroes without medals while others said we would never come back alive. They said they were staying to clean the chapel so that it would be ready for our wake.

CORAZON C. AQUINO

The people of EDSA amazed me. They faced death. It was a different thing altogether from rallies or political meetings. Life was on the line in EDSA.

That was why I was so angry when my security did not want me to go to EDSA. I told them: "No way can I not be in EDSA." I had announced it on radio. My security was probably getting ulcers because I would not listen to them. I said: "Look, this is all my doing." They argued: "It is our duty to protect you." Finally I said: "If you do not take me there, I am going by myself." I went to EDSA on Monday afternoon.

24 February 1986, before dawn: In the darkest hours of Monday, people in the Libis area barricades pray, above and upper left. They had just gotten word that batallions of Marcos troops were coming up from the darkened cliffs behind their position, a position of defense for Camps Crame and Aguinaldo. Only a few hours earlier,

June Keithley began broadcasting from a secret radio station to take the place of Radio Veritas, which went off the air when its transmitters were wrecked by armed men. With only two young volunteers actually with her—Paolo Mercado, 15 and his brother Gabe, 13—and a technician, June began the broadcasts which bouyed the spirits of the people under threat, left. She was getting information from a network of young people situated all over the city, with one of them inside Crame itself—as well as from General Ramos. Later June's friends joined her in full force to keep the underground broadcast going. At the height of the tear gas attack, June played the National Anthem to fire the people's fervor. "I don't remember praying as hard as I did during those long dark hours," said June. She was on the air for 12 hours.

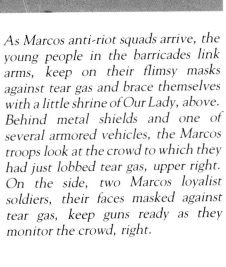

As Marcos anti-riot squads arrive, the young people in the barricades link arms, keep on their flimsy masks against tear gas and brace themselves with a little shrine of Our Lady, above. Behind metal shields and one of several armored vehicles, the Marcos troops look at the crowd to which they had just lobbed tear gas, upper right. On the side, two Marcos loyalist soldiers, their faces masked against tear gas, keep guns ready as they monitor the crowd, right.

As the sun rose on Monday morning, the crowd at Crame heard a distant snarling in the sky. They had been warned of an air attack by Marcos forces. Overhead, they suddenly see the menacing helicopter gunships, upper and lower left. Guns are cocked inside the camp; outside, the people in the crowd realized that there was hardly any place to hide. Many prayed

aloud, others stared in silence at the choppers. Terror swept through them silently, like a cold hand at the back of each neck with the knowledge that this could be the end. But the helicopters did not fire. They landed one by one inside Crame amid instant jubilation, above. The world seemed to be yelling at once and the joy wiped all the terror away.

A hug and a handshake at the same time welcome a defecting helicopter pilot into Crame, the rebels' camp, above. He was one of 16 combat-ready pilots brought by Colonel Antonio Sotelo, commander of the 15th Strike Wing, right. Their defection turned the tide in favor of the rebel forces. "We followed our conscience," said Colonel Sotelo. "I think I have not really done much in my life," he said. "For once, I wanted to make a decision for my country." The helicopter pilots went to work right away. On Monday

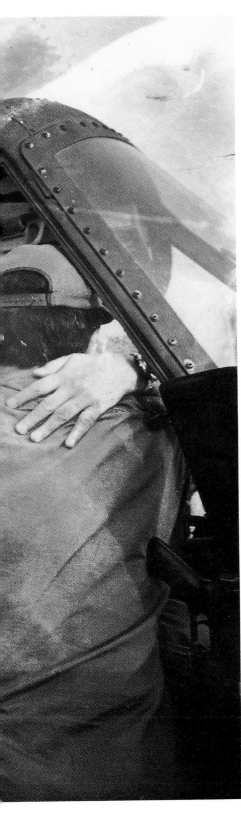

alone, they fired at various points around Malacañang as a warning, destroyed the three presidential helicopters in Villamor air base and provided air cover to the rebels who took Channel 4.

The people's uprising engulfs the helicopters which had just defected, above and upper right. The objects of awe and curiosity: Sikorsky helicopters which are swift, agile, ferociously armed high-tech gunships. Guarding one of them are soldiers who flash the Laban sign, middle right. Clearly visible is the muzzled 57 mm rocket which could have reduced the rebel headquarters to rubble. Rebel soldiers tie a streamer saying "Defection Center" to the Crame grandstand, lower right. Monday was a day of major defections. Aside from the gunships, the defections included the 3rd Marine Brigade Commander Rodolfo Biazon who came from Davao City with 600 of his men and staff officers as well as the crowd disturbance control

unit of the Marines who were ordered to assault Crame at dawn that day. By Monday afternoon, General Ramos claimed that over 50 per cent of the armed forces had shifted to the rebels' side. It was a giant leap from the three batallions—one in Crame, two in Aguinaldo—with which the rebellion started on Saturday.

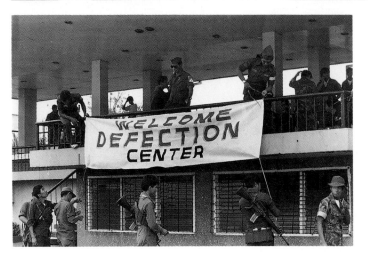

Minister Enrile and General Ramos share the good news about the helicopter defection with the people massed on the street outside Crame, above and far left. They brought with them a statue of Our Lady and the Philippine flag. Later, in the same place, opposition leader Butz Aquino gives a pep talk to the crowd, left.

Early Monday morning, rumor swept the street barricades that Mr. Marcos had left the country. People erupt in joy, above; with one hand, General Ramos waves the Philippine flag in jubilation, right. The rumor was false.

x

222

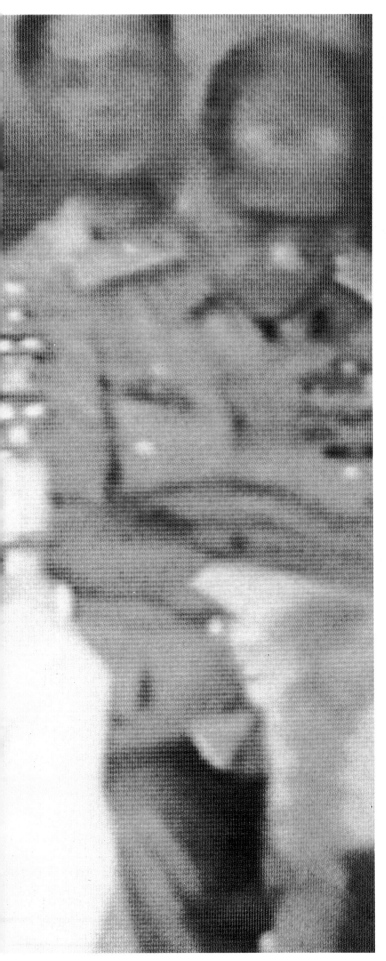

Unedited Video Tape

24 February 1986, before noon: Mr. Marcos appears live on government television to say that he was in control. His entire family, including his grandchildren, were shown to dispel the rumor that they had left the country. The telecast was shown over US television which ran the confirming indication that it was an unedited video tape. In Metro Manila, however, this live telecast was cut short when the rebel forces took the government Channel 4 exactly when Mr. Marcos was on the air.

Rebel troops surround Channel 4, the government station, above, shortly before they took it over. Artists and performers stage a show outside the station to celebrate, right.

24 February 1986, 1 p.m.: This is the historic first telecast of the liberated Channel 4, which had hitherto been devoted to Marcos propaganda, above. Declaring it a free and open station for the people, the first telecasters were: Colonel Mariano Santiago who led the rebel forces which captured the station; Orly Punzalan, the station manager of Radio Veritas; Maan Hontiveros, host of a television talk show; and Father Efren Dato, an anchorman of Radio Veritas.

Monday, the day of many victories, ended still at the barricades where people settle down for the night, right and opposite page. With the full moon lighting the sky, a priest celebrates the Mass—in thanksgiving for the day's victories, in prayer for yet more, above.

25 FEBRUARY 1986

Voices

AMADO L. LACUESTA, JR., screenwriter
Tuesday Morning:

It still feels unreal to watch Channel 4.

Seeing Noel Trinidad and Subas Herrero, I remember how, at dinner Friday night, Noel had been firmly convinced that before Cory could sit, violence was inevitable. Subas and I had argued the opposite, basing our conviction only on faith. We had broken up at nearly 2:00 a.m. of Saturday, unable to convince Noel, little knowing that before the day was over, our convictions would be put on the line.

It is past mid-morning when the videotape of Cory's inauguration is finally shown. It is a heartwarming scene, especially when newly promoted General Ramos salutes Cory, who does not expect it and returns the salute sheepishly, evoking good-natured laughter all around. Still, it is almost anticlimactic in the wake of all the events that have preceded it and made it possible.

Before noon, Channel 9 is showing another farce. Another set of Three Stooges is setting the stage for Marcos' inauguration. One of them is the retired general from last night. Another is a regular TV newscaster with a long, sour face who obviously wishes he were somewhere else and keeps flicking cigarette ash on the floor. They all look like wet chickens.

The retired general painstakingly explains the wonders of Marcos' mandate, gushing over how understanding Marcos has been in not ordering the arrest of those who violate his curfew. You see, General Moe explains patronizingly to his fellow Stooges, many people may not have adjusted their schedules yet to the curfew hours. As an example, he cites those businessmen delivering goods to the markets before 6:00 a.m. By now, the farce is no longer funny.

When Channel 9 finally starts transmitting Marcos' "inauguration," I still cannot decide whether Marcos and his family and loyalists are insane or just extremely brazen.

The ceremony starts with an invocation. When the screen suddenly goes haywire, signalling the untimely end of the transmission, I am relieved. It is only much later that I learn the reason for it.

SISTER SHEILA LUCEY

Along EDSA: yellow, Cory Aquino's campaign color, also associated with the hope surrounding Ninoy's return, was everywhere. Venders were selling yellow ribbons, yellow t-shirts, yellow fans and umbrellas, yellow pennants, yellow everything.

Because this is the Philippines, the people's faith was as eloquent as the yellow emblems. Outside the gates of the camp and at other strategic points, altars had been set up. The Rosary was recited at these centers at different times, usually by a small group of people who came to pray. When the people faced the tanks early on Monday morning and again on Tuesday, they had a statue of Our Lady with them and they were praying the Rosary. Devotion to Our Lady is a deep and constant feature of Philippine spirituality. The people knew their Mother would save them. They merely kept reminding her.

EDITH A. BATALLA, teacher

At about 3:00 a.m. Tuesday, I was awakened by gunfire coming from the vicinity of Malacañang. (We live near the area.) I couldn't go back to sleep, because all the while I was practicing how to play dead.

I was determined to go back to the barricades as soon as it was light although I expected killing. "I'll bury myself under dead bodies," I thought, "so I have to learn how to control my breathing to avoid detection."

It was thrilling to realize that I was capable of some rebellious action against the dictator, that I was no longer a sitting duck. On February 13 at the *Batasang Pambansa* when I was feeling desperate about the situation, I showed my nails to some friends. "They're not even long enough," I said. "How can I use them to help topple the Marcos dictatorship?"

CESAR B. UMALI, Jr.

By 3:00 a.m., we were so sleepy we decided to go home. By this time, I "guesstimated" that there were about 500,000 people around the two camps. "Nothing will happen tonight," I said. On the way home, we saw that the corner of Santolan and Ortigas was already barricaded by some 300 civilians. I was glad that there were other barricades at a distance from the camps.

Reaching home a few minutes later, I was alarmed to hear that a long convoy of the elite First Ranger Division of the Marcos army was headed towards Guadalupe Bridge toward the two camps. It turned out, however, that they were going to surrender, not to attack. The most amusing observation about the whole siege is that all those ordered to attack Camps Crame and Aguinaldo defected to the side of the rebels just before they reached their target. They did not fire their guns at the mass of unarmed civilians. To me, this inability to shoot civilians was the single most crucial enigma during those days, resulting from just the right blend of faith and patriotism.

NINO NUÑEZ

A slight drizzle at 5:30 a.m. woke up the thousands of vigilantes lying on makeshift cardboard and newspaper mats along Mother Ignacia Street and Bohol Avenue. It was a sight: a tire was still burning on the street littered with papers and dirty plastic cups, two Manila Transit buses with flat tires blockading the area from Quezon Boulevard, and two fallen acacia trees blocking it from EDSA.

While the youngsters hustled to get their coffee and bread in plastic bags from the soldiers at the TV station gate or from the sisters of St. Joseph's College inside a Fiera marked "Food Van", young scavengers hurriedly picked up their instant loot of cardboard and papers.

Three soldiers in fatigues came out of the gates to talk with the people milling around. "Where are you from?" asked one soldier. "How long have you been here?" asked another. "Thank you," the third soldier told another group inside a jeep nearby.

At the end of the avenue, two buses were filling up. "It's a long way to Batangas," the conductor told some girls running after his bus. "We should try to get there before lunchtime." In the middle of the street, two jeepneys marked "Fish Dealer" were parked with some sleeping passengers inside, all of them women, except for the drivers.

As the line for steaming coffee in yellow cups became longer, a dozen Metro Aides arrived and started sweeping the streets. More soldiers came out to mix with the young crowd. Two men from the neighborhood came with bolos to cut away the acacia trunks blockading the road. Five morning joggers in shorts who chanced to run by stopped and helped them carry the logs to the roadside.

The buses left. The jeepney with a Quiapo-Cubao signboard was filling up. A group of some twenty residents from Apalit, Pampanga, decided it was time to go.

Art Director-Scriptwriter Ruben Arthur Nicdao and Production Designer Danny Evangelista with an image of Our Lady of Fatima passed by with their God's Brigade from Laperal Apartment on Recto. Some 20 college boys carried the standards of saints on white silk. "We started at Ortigas last Saturday night, then at Camp Crame last Sunday. Tonight we keep vigil here. I have lost my voice leading the Rosary," said Danny.

The sun was rising when I decided to go. The

soldiers at the gate were still giving out plastic bags of food and some medicine. The sisters from St. Joseph's College were still giving away sandwiches and coffee from their parked Food Van. "Don't be shy," a nun told the crowd. "All the food is from our donors." She told me they had yellow t-shirts for the soldiers too, also from their donors.

CONCEPCION Q. SONON

February 25, 7:00 a.m., Scout Borromeo Street, a street at the back of Channel 4.

When we arrived, we heard several shots, and we all scampered to take cover. Onlookers told us that four persons had been shot by the snipers perched at the tower of the Channel 9 transmitter. The snipers wore white bands on their forearms. These reports did not scare us. We believe in people power and we were ready to face any consequence.

We then spotted a van with the image of the Blessed Virgin on top. We decided to use this as a shield as we proceeded to the Channel 9 transmitter. We believed that the snipers would not shoot because they still feared God. Everybody on that street was reluctant. But we led the group and everybody followed.

We inched our way toward the transmitter. Bullets rained as the snipers continually shot at us. Luckily no one was hurt. Though it would usually take less than five minutes to cover the distance from Channel 4 to the Channel 9 transmitter, it took us almost 30 minutes.

BRAHIM KADATUAN, logistics foreman

I cannot forget how tense the situation was. It was tense because you didn't know if the soldiers were going to shoot or not. We didn't know which side the soldiers would take.

RUDY LAO, unemployed

I went to the area near the Channel 9 transmitter just for curiosity and some excitement. But when a 6 x 6 truck full of soldiers arrived with two jeep escorts, the people ran away shouting: "These are Marcos loyalists!" But the soldiers gave the *Laban* sign.

The people went back, but I saw that the soldiers were wearing the white armband of Marcos loyalists. Someone pointed this out and the people ran away again.

Then someone from the crowd yelled: "Don't be afraid. I will lead you. Let us use people power." The people came back and joined him. I joined too even if earlier I did not really care about what was happening.

Boy at play: the day the armored car came

EDITH A. BATALLA

The possibility of death was very real to me, having heard all that gunfire, so when my brother and his wife, a cousin, and I were ready to go I said aloud: "Let's cross ourselves first." To myself very quietly, I said: "We might not see each other again." It took us some time to muster enough courage to go out because the radio announced that there were tanks in Quezon Boulevard where we were going to pass on our way to Channel 9 where, I heard over the radio, civilian reinforcement was needed.

I had difficulty spotting the Marcos loyalist said to be perched halfway up the tower of Channel 9. By about 11:00 a.m. when it was getting hot — I could imagine how searing it would be up there — I finally saw the man. He ran back and forth, maybe frantically looking for a good aim or just getting crazed with fear.

Then rat-tat-tat! The shots sent people ducking (but me jumping up, I guess my reflexes were different) but not leaving their places. A radio announcer covering the event said of the recalcitrant civilians who didn't heed the warnings of danger: "Maybe they want to see how a bullet pierces the human body."

DIONISIA NORA, wife and mother

At about noontime, shooting began again at Channel 9. I quickly dropped to the ground. When I looked around, I couldn't see my son. I was trembling. We looked for him and I thought: "Where is he, my God?" I was feeling very cold. As we walked, I saw the tanks. On top of one of them was my son. "Get down!" I said to him. "That's a tank, it might fire at you." He said: "I'm looking for its opening, Mother. How can it drive without any person?" He was really naughty.

OMPOY PASTRANA, DYFM-Iloilo reporter, assigned to Manila

It was like witnessing a war movie. When the attacking reformists started their siege of the defenders atop the transmitter, we were carried by the people who backed out and fled at the first burst of automatic gunfire. We were carried by the human wave as far as 200 meters from where we were before and when I looked around, my friend Greg was nowhere.

FREDDIE AGUILAR, singer

Someone woke me up to say that he had heard over the radio that June Keithley wanted me to go to Channel 4 which was seized by reformists the day before. There were snipers at the Channel 9 tower, which was near Channel 4. There was shooting there. I was about to go when my mother confronted me: "Why do you want to go where there is shooting?"

"Mother, that is where I'm needed," I answered.

So I went to Channel 4 and they put me on the air for about three hours. I even spoke to Marcos on the air. I was the only one who did that. I said: "Ex-President Marcos, please tell your people not to launch an attack, because you will be hurting your countrymen."

While the Channel 9 tower was under siege, we were asking for blood donations for the wounded. Then we heard that pro-Marcos men were barricading the road from Bulacan and were forcing people to go to Malacañang instead of Crame to attend his oathtaking. I felt that nothing was happening at Channel 4; it was all talk. So I went out. The people in front of Channel 4 saw me. They stopped me and applauded, some shouting: "Freddie! Freddie!" They asked me where I was going. I said I was going back to Crame.

RAFAEL G. ONGPIN, student

Negotiations between Cory's camp and the military revolutionaries had been going on since early evening of the 24th. The reformist generals were professionally appalled at Cory's announcement that she intended to hold the ceremony at 8:00 a.m. at Club Filipino, a heretofore unruffled suburban country club just a kilometer away from enemy lines.

"It's within mortar range, and we can't seal it off. It's almost totally indefensible — a tactical nightmare," said reformist generals Paiso and Gutierrez, in charge of security arrangements. "From a security standpoint, we'd be far better off if we held it on the Crame parade ground. We could fly her there in an unmarked civilian chopper."

"We could discuss this all night," said a sleepy and haggard Peping Cojuangco, Cory's brother and secretary general of her party. "But you must realize that in the end, it's all up to her. Nothing we can say or do will divert her from what she decides."

"First of all, we must remember what Crame means to me, and to the people," Cory began to explain. The sun had barely risen, but she was as fresh as a daisy, in contrast to the drawn and drowsy faces of her advisers and the generals around the dining table of her modest Times Street residence. "Camp Crame was the first place where Ninoy, where every political detainee was brought during the martial law years. Filipinos once lived in dread of being taken there. Today, it may be a place of heroism, but unfortunately, a lot of tortures, executions, and summary detentions took place there in the past. The second thing is, I have already told the people that I will be at Club Filipino, and I fully intend to keep my promise. I chose it because it is a neutral and public place. And I absolutely refuse to take a helicopter."

She would not, indeed, be moved. The generals and advisers left to make whatever security arrangements they could. Cory chatted amiably with Father Joaquin Bernas, S.J., president of the Ateneo de Manila University, Father Jose Blanco, another Jesuit, and Jaime Ongpin, my father, who took me along with him to Cory's house that morning. All three belong to her inner circle of advisers.

Her daughters wandered about the house, getting their dresses pressed for the ceremony. Eldon Cruz, her son-in-law, answered the constantly ringing phones.

Suddenly, there was a loud slamming of machine gun fire, very close by. It was answered by the popping rattle of M-16 rifles. Everyone in the parlor ducked into an adjoining stone corridor as Noynoy, Cory's son, dashed out of the house with his Colt .45 automatic, a flak jacket thrown over his pajamas.

Shortly afterwards, he returned, and announced that a firefight had started at the Channel 9 television station a little over a block away. The reformist forces were attempting to capture it. He indicated the tall antenna tower, clearly visible through the huge picture window. There was a sniper perched on one of the beams. He was perilously close — surely within rifle range. He was looking the other way.

Cory told her children to pack and calmly announced to her disbelieving advisers that she was going to take a shower and get dressed. Glum and nervous, they paced the narrow stone corridor, starting at the occasional bursts of fire. They sounded very close — too close. Father Blanco prayed the Rosary, the beads shifting deliberately in his pale fingers. Father Bernas, while outwardly calm, seemed as if he was trying studiously not to tremble. Jaime Ongpin, nervously adjusting his glasses, answered a steady stream of telephone calls.

Finally, Cory emerged, and the party climbed into cars to meet the rest of the opposition, and continue to the proclamation. To the terror of the rest of the motorcade, Cory's Chevrolet Suburban cruised through the crowd-littered streets at Sunday promenade speed, pausing respectfully at every red light despite the scarcity of other traffic. Fortunately, no one recognized her through the heavily tinted, bulletproof windows.

By this time, the heat out on the naked asphalt around Club Filipino was blistering. But the crowd stood in closed ranks, sweating and murmuring quietly. She was over an hour late so far, yet no one complained. Some toyed with their idle video cameras or bought cool juice for their kids from wandering venders.

Occasionally a ripple of applause broke out as an oppositionist Member of Parliament, justice, ex-senator, or congressman was recognized wading through the crowd into the clubhouse.

Outside the Sampaguita Room, where the inauguration was to be held, Cory supporters looked longingly over the balcony behind them, at the sparkling, inviting swimming pool. In a field visible some blocks away, a squad of snarling helicopter gunships touched down after their 45-second flight, and General Ramos and Minister Enrile alighted amid the swirling, flapping grass, surrounded by their ferociously armed guards. They strolled to the crowd, who engulfed them in a wave of delighted, appreciative cheering as they made their way to the clubhouse. The crowd called out their nicknames, as if they were rock stars: "Eddie! Eddie!" (Ramos); "Johnny! Johnny!" (Ponce Enrile).

Some time after they disappeared into the clubhouse, a distant, rhythmic roar was heard slowly approaching. The crowd knew what it was instantly, and they took up the chant: "Co-ry! Co-ry! Co-ry!" Her Chevy could now be seen in the distance, as if borne on a sea of people with their arms upraised, toiling slowly onward, a swarm of dark and shiny Mercedes seething in its wake. The roar was deafening by the time the van and its entourage reached the driveway. In addition, a knot of foreigners had brought an air horn, whose blasts competed with the psychotic wail of an air raid siren some other enthusiast had dug out of his closet.

The crowd suddenly quieted as Neptali Gonzales, Mandaluyong MP and staunch opposition warrior, began the ceremony in his low, musical voice. The makeshift PA system was hardly audible and most of the crowd huddled around their AM radios, which in these last few days had become the most indispensable survival equipment for every *barricadista*. Gonzales read name after name of signatories to the proclamation, halting often for applause, variously joyful or respectful. Long after he finished the first page, he was still being given pieces of paper, many of them Club Filipino cocktail napkins, passed hand to hand from as far as outside the clubhouse; they bore the names of more and more signatories, active and retired justices, mayors, governors, labor leaders, military officers, diplomats, senators and congressmen from the old legislature, and assemblymen from the new.

Justice Claudio Teehankee, the most respected and courageous member of the otherwise Marcos-dominated Supreme Court, had been chosen to swear in the new President and Vice President.

Not one person in the huge crowd spoke, starting from the pause as Justice Teehankee stepped up to the rostrum, and as he read the words of the oath with quiet but forceful and solemn dignity, Cory answered in a similar tone. As Justice Teehankee uttered the final words of the oath, a tremendous cheer broke loose from every throat. Flags waved, hats and bandannas were thrown into the air. Outside, there was dancing in the street.

Eventually, the crowd quieted down enough to sing the Lord's Prayer in Pilipino and then *Bayan Ko* (My Homeland), the melancholy, yet defiant early-twentieth-century protest song that in this decade had become the "second national anthem" of the Philippines. Tears were in many eyes.

Above, the protecting gunships howled in lazy sweeps around the china-blue sky. Elsewhere in the city, Mr. Marcos was having an altogether different kind of inauguration.

CORAZON C. AQUINO, President of the Philippines
(Inaugural Address, 24 February 1986)

My brothers and sisters, I am grateful for the authority you have given me today. And I promise to offer all that I can do to serve you.

It is fitting and proper that, as the rights and liberties of our people were taken away at midnight twenty years ago, the people should firmly recover those lost rights and liberties in the full light of day.

Ninoy believed that only the united strength of a people would suffice to overturn a tyranny so evil and so well organized. It took the brutal murder of Ninoy to bring about the unity, the strength, and the phenomenon of People Power. That power, or *Lakas ng Bayan*, has shattered the dictatorship, protected the honorable military who have chosen freedom, and today has established a government dedicated to the protection and meaningful fulfillment of the people's rights and liberties.

We became exiled in our land — we, Filipinos, who are at home only in freedom — when Marcos destroyed the Republic fourteen years ago. Through courage and unity, through the power of the people, we are home again.

And now, I would like to appeal to everybody to work for national reconciliation, which is what Ninoy came back home for. I would like to repeat that I am very magnanimous in victory. So I call on all those countrymen of ours who are not yet with us to join us at the earliest possible time so that together we can rebuild our beautiful country.

As I always did during the campaign, I would like to end with an appeal for you to continue praying. Let us pray for God's help especially during these days.

Barbed wire souvenir: never again

AURORA A. AQUINO, mother of Benigno Aquino (Ninoy)

When Ninoy was young, he saw a picture of President Roxas being sworn in. On the President's right was his wife and on his left was his mother, Mrs. Picazo. "Why is she Mrs. Picazo and not Mrs. Roxas?" asked Ninoy. "Because Mrs. Picazo was formerly Mrs. Roxas; when her husband died, she married again." "Well, Mama," he said, "I will aim for Malacañang on one condition. I must have a Mrs. Aquino on my right, and a Mrs. Aquino on my left. Is it a deal?" "It's a deal," I said.

Aim for Malacañang! He was only joking. When I was holding the Bible during Cory's inauguration, I felt that Ninoy was between Cory and me. After the oath taking, I asked: "Cory, did you feel the presence of the invisible President?" Cory laughed: "Yes, I felt the presence of the invisible President. I felt that he was around."

Aim for Malacañang! And he did not make it. Ninoy never thought I would be the one holding the Bible, that his wife would be the one sworn in, and he would be in the middle, invisible.

MAX SOLIVEN, newspaper columnist

The euphoria inside and outside the Sampaguita Hall of Club Filipino yesterday worried me. There were tears and jubilation. The people who elected Cory Aquino President of the Republic and Doy Laurel Vice President deserve their hour of triumph, no one can deny. They fought long and hard and sacrificed much for this moment. But we must not forget that there are still many battles ahead. The people must not proudly sing *Bayan Ko* (My Homeland), and then go home. They must be back at the barricades, not relaxing their vigilance. For it is darkest just before the dawn.

The presence of Defense Minister Juan Ponce Enrile and Lieutenant General Fidel Ramos at the head table at Cory's inauguration attests to the fact that this nation is still on a war footing.

RAY DANTE L. SOÑOSO

At about 11:30 in the morning, my friend and I went to Malacañang to attend the inauguration of Marcos. We easily got in because we were wearing KBL shirts. Many people were at the palace grounds. People were waving flags and shouting: "*Marcos pa rin!*" (Marcos Still!). I also shouted with the crowd because I was loyal to

Marcos. Anyway, I witnessed Marcos' last speech and his duet with Meldy. My friend, who is a dedicated loyalist and admires Marcos very much, began to cry as the couple sang "*Dahil sa Iyo*" (Because of You). Some of the loyalists beside me were also deeply touched.

At about 2:45 p.m. we volunteered to be defenders of Malacañang against possible attacks by Enrile and Ramos supporters. We were given ID's which read "I hereby pledge that I am a Marcos Loyalist." We were promised by a woman coordinator that we would be given .38 guns plus instructions later in the night. I got scared and persuaded my friends to back out. We left the palace at about 6:00 p.m. with packed food that was given to us — it was exclusively for volunteers.

DELFIN QUIAMBAO, utility man

I remember when Marcos called the loyalists and said he was going to give them jobs. Marcos was also going to give 100 pesos to those who would come to Malacañang. I just went there to eat. While he was saying it was good of us to come, someone announced that the food was already there. The 500 people who were there ran to where the food was and nobody was left to listen to Marcos.

LILIA CAPRESO, wife and mother

It was nearly one o'clock in the afternoon when we entered the Malacañang compound on Tuesday. I was terrified, because tanks were facing us and there were many soldiers.

I told my son, Zaldy, to be courageous. We were already there, I said, and we wanted to earn the hundred pesos we were promised if we attended the inauguration of Marcos. We needed the money to buy rice.

Zaldy told me he wanted to go home. He was afraid. I told him just to be alert. I told him that if there was some shooting, we should drop to the ground, face down.

I saw Marcos. He was so thin. They all looked sad.

AMADO L. LACUESTA, JR.
Tuesday Afternoon:

The radio reports that the situation at Mendiola is getting dangerous. A large crowd has gathered at the barbed-wire barricades and is reportedly getting restless and starting to taunt Marcos' troops. I am concerned that before the day is over, the revolution will no longer be bloodless. Only succeeding reports that priests and nuns and the leaders of certain cause-oriented groups are attempting to calm the people ease my worry. But I am still convinced that the worst is over, especially with Enrile and Ramos alternately reporting continuing defections of Armed Forces units all over the country.

JOSE MULACRUZ, supervisor

When we were fighting the Marcos loyalists near Mendiola, some priests formed a barricade between us. They shouted for us not to fight anymore. Suddenly, a rock was thrown from the loyalist side. It hit one of the priests. The priests still kept on shouting for us not to throw rocks. But I said: "Father, it is hard for us to stop throwing rocks when your face is bleeding."

COLONEL GREGORIO CAGURANGAN,
Philippine Army

On Tuesday afternoon, I got in touch with Colonel Vic Batac, one of the brains behind the Reform Movement, to find out the developments in the revolution. He told me: "This won't take too long. The end of the revolution is near. Marcos is already negotiating for a safe-conduct pass." So as early as that afternoon, we knew that Marcos would be leaving.

JAMES B. REUTER, S.J.

On Tuesday afternoon I was in the War Room of Johnny Ponce Enrile and Fidel Ramos, in Camp Crame. By this time they had 87 per cent of the Armed Forces of the Philippines on their side. About fourteen generals and colonels were standing around Enrile as he put on his bullet-proof vest and buckled on his pistol. Enrile did not plan to make a speech. He was just talking to the men as he finished dressing. He said: "I just spoke to the President." Cory had already been inaugurated, so I thought he was talking about her. But he was not. To Enrile, "the President" meant Marcos. He said: "He is willing to negotiate for a graceful exit. I promised that we would not harm him, or his family. He asked: 'What about Ver?' I said that I would have to discuss this with the men."

He had finished dressing and was now standing still. Suddenly it was a real message. He said: "Gentlemen, we can no longer offer allegiance to our old commander-in-chief. If you watched the inauguration this morning, you saw that the people really want Cory. Our allegiance is to the people. And the people are represented by Cory."

Everyone was standing stock still. There was a hushed silence. It was like a funeral. "The King is dead. Long live the King!"

Then Enrile said: "This morning, on my way to the inauguration, I heard the people shouting: 'We love our soldiers!' I never heard that before in my life. In all my years with the military, I never heard that—people shouting: 'We love our soldiers!' We have to be worthy of that. Our allegiance is to the people."

Beside me was Flotz Aquino, who is a general. Flotz turned to me, and his eyes were wet. As we started out of the room, he said: "It gets you, right here!" And with his closed fist, he struck his chest, just over the heart.

FR. ARNOLD BOEHME, O.C.D.

On Tuesday, the 25th, I heard the urgent call on Channel 4 for priests and seminarians to go to Mendiola Bridge. The people who went there were those who had suffered under Marcos. They were angry and wanted to storm Malacañang Palace. Priests in cassocks were needed to be with the people and try to avoid bloodshed. I did not have to think twice. We gathered over 30 priests and seminarians — from our own Carmelites and some seminarians from Saint Andrew's.

For the first time in my 18 years in the Philippines, I found myself in the front line of a demonstration. After a few minutes my fear was gone; there was only love for the people and concern for their well-being. As I stood between the people and the Marines, I felt that I was one with all of them in their aspirations for a new just society. When I looked around I noticed that the only foreign priests I could see were the three Carmelites — Father Herman Esselman, Father Alan Rieger, and me. I felt proud and greatly honored to be one with my Filipino brothers. Before long a foreign correspondent approached me and asked how long I intended to stay at Mendiola Bridge. Without hesitation I answered: "All night, if necessary."

I soon found myself part of the negotiating panel between the clergy and the military. When we saw the helicopters leave Malacañang, we joined the people who were shouting for joy, with the hope and a prayer that Marcos was aboard. Within a few minutes it was confirmed that he had indeed left. But there were still many Marines between the Palace and ourselves. They had switched allegiance to General Ramos and Minister Enrile, but they did not know how or where to surrender. They were now concerned for their own safety. We negotiated with Father Bernardo Perez, O.S.B., who allowed the Marines inside San Beda College.

Shortly after this, the people heard over the radio that Marcos had left. With that news a huge mass of humanity ran towards Malacañang shouting: "Marcos is gone! We are free! Malacañang is ours!" I just stepped aside, knowing that our work was done. We had answered the call for help. We put our lives on the line. The Philippines was free at last. I went back to the Carmelite Monastery full of peace and joy. I was praising God.

The human barricade: numbers count

VICENTE T. PATERNO, former Minister of Industry

Sometime in 1974, I was in the study room of President Marcos to brief him about developments in small- and medium-scale industries. He had just finished playing golf and was in a reflective mood. He told me that he was worried about the possibility of a revolution in a country in Southeast Asia. He said: "I hope the man who is in charge of that country realizes that there are only two causes of a revolution — the first is corruption and the second is injustice."

AMADO L. LACUESTA, JR.
Tuesday Evening:

Throughout the day, Enrile kept calling for more people to reinforce those already at EDSA.

After dinner, we prepare to go back. This time, we take along our second son, Kite. We bring the same provisions, but we load them in a yellow Land Rover pick-up instead. The canvas-roofed pick-up bed promises to be more comfortable than a car-seat.

We make an appointment to meet Lolly's sisters at the corner of White Plains Road and EDSA.

We park about a block away from EDSA, intending to walk the rest of the way. Even at first glance, there are obviously more people tonight than Sunday afternoon. But we are unprepared for the sight that finally greets us.

There must be millions on EDSA tonight. People everywhere as far as the eye can see from north to south, and still more people arriving without pause. Banners and placards proudly proclaim the origins of some of these pilgrims: San Pedro, Laguna; Mindoro; Masbate; Tarlac; Bulacan; Pampanga; Bicol; etc.

There cannot be more people here than there were at the Luneta just over a week ago. But somehow, this is different. The millions at the Luneta were there mainly to look, to listen, to hope. Here, tonight, as for the past three days and nights, these millions have come also to fight, after a fashion.

Watching them, listening to them, feeling them, I suddenly realize that these millions have already transcended Cory, Enrile-Ramos, and Marcos. Cory, Enrile-Ramos, and Marcos have, in fact, become incidental to the situation.

These people are here to assert themselves, to declare their freedom, to reclaim their dignity after a generation of silence, of fear, of self-deprecation. And even though this pure moment, this pure feeling, cannot last, I have seen it and felt it. If only for this, I feel my whole life has been worth it.

We try to walk toward Crame, wanting Kite to experience something of this incredible phenomenon.

The going is extremely difficult. Not only are millions already here but most of them are moving around singly, in pairs, in families, in hordes. And everywhere, everyone is singing, cheering, talking, laughing, teasing, congratulating, bragging, smiling. It is almost as if all of these acts had been suppressed for a generation and then let loose suddenly and completely tonight in a carnival of euphoria.

Still some distance away from the main gate of Crame, we give up. It hardly seems possible to penetrate such a dense, shifting mass of humanity without losing a shirt or an arm in the process. Again and again, the word "incredible" comes to mind.

During the next two hours, confining ourselves to the vicinity of the White Plains Road-EDSA corner, we run into a Filipino Jesuit friend and then a neighbor and his grown-up children. We note two or three long, serpentine lines of people queuing for three meals and realize that what we have heard about seemingly inexhaustible supplies of food during this revolution is entirely true.

At sometime past 10:00 p.m., we give up on Lolly's sisters.

Then, as we work our way back to the pick-up, we begin to hear that Marcos and company have finally, really, fled Malacañang. We hear it from radios, of which there must be at least one per square meter of EDSA. We hear it from people although everyone seems to be very skeptical now after yesterday's letdown. Pockets of confident cheering here and there. But I am not really that anxious. If I am anxious at all, it is only that Marcos' resignation or flight, even though it is a foregone conclusion, may be delayed a day or so more than necessary. Please, God, I pray, let him leave now, let him be gone already.

Soon, it is confirmed that Marcos has indeed finally fled. At Mendiola, the impatient crowds are marching into Malacañang already. It is all over. We have won. We are free.

Strangely, although I do feel victorious and happy, the feeling is subdued.

Perhaps, it is because the victory had, in fact, already been won yesterday and Marcos' ignominious flight is the foregone conclusion.

Perhaps, it is because, having already achieved its purpose, this incredibly beautiful revolution must now wind down, and tomorrow must be just an ordinary day again.

Perhaps, it is because of a sense of loss, or more aptly, a fear that, having already tasted blood, in a manner of speaking, we may be more easily led to take this path again in the future, for less noble ends and with less pleasant outcomes.

In any case, it is certain that EDSA will erupt in celebration tonight. But Lolly, Sarge, Kite, and I pile into the Rover and head home. As on Christmas, New Year, and other such days of joy and triumph, we will celebrate at home as a family. I have been saving a bottle of champagne just for this day and occasion.

Perhaps, tonight, we will open it. After all, we have won.

MAR UN OCAMPO III

On Tuesday night at about 8:00 in the evening, a young couple approached our camp on EDSA. The woman was very pregnant and the man looked like a very poor laborer. They came carrying a few carton boxes. They told us they were from Tarlac and then shyly they said: "We can not afford to give you anything. But last night we saw you sleeping on the cement pavement — please accept this, this is all we can afford to give." They gave us their carton boxes.

We did not even get the chance to use the boxes to sit or sleep on. In less than an hour, the revolution was over. But we decided to bring the boxes home to remind us of that poor young couple who shared what they had.

SISTER SARAH MANAPOL, volunteer VHF radio operator

Shortly before 9:00 p.m., the lights went off. We checked and learned that the whole street was dark but that the rest of Manila had electricity.

Our contact at the US embassy called and said, "Okay, Sister, I better tell you." I asked: "What is it?" He replied: "Didn't you say it was your birthday?"

This must be a code, I thought. I said to him: "Well, not really. Not yet, I think." I think he understood that I understood.

"Well, it is the dawn of your birthday," he said.

"Are you sure?" I asked.

"Don't jump the gun," he answered. I promised I wouldn't and asked him what his message was.

239

"Okay, Sister, it is your birthday. And you have a birthday gift, compliments of the United States of America," he said.

"Honestly? Is he really leaving?" I cried.

"Sister, you promised not to jump the gun," he said firmly. "Now put down that phone. I have other calls to make."

So I put down the phone and I was jumping in the dark. I told the people who were with me: "It's our birthday. That was the embassy. They said: 'Our birthday is coming nearer and nearer.' "

The lights went on, and the radio and the television went on, and we heard the news that the helicopters had just taken off to take Marcos and his family to Clark Field.

DYFM Station, Bombo Radio (Iloilo)

At about 9:20 p.m., there was an unconfirmed report from a source near Malacañang that a helicopter had taken off from there. Since it was unconfirmed, Varon announced: "Marcos might have left Malacañang already." Arcones followed by relating a series of reports he had received earlier that pointed to the preparations for the Marcos departure.

At past 9:30 p.m., the phone rang. It was Jenil Demorito confirming the report that Marcos had indeed fled Malacañang. At that moment, revelry broke loose inside the DYFM station. Everyone was dancing and shouting. Later on, we learned that the same thing happened in all the other Bombo stations and in the streets. People everywhere danced in mad revelry.

LYCA B. BROWN, DZRB volunteer

By Tuesday evening Marcos had left the country. We received a tip from a caller who identified himself as a "hostage" in Malacañang. He claimed he was released five minutes after four helicopters left the palace grounds. I called "Falcon" at MIA, who confirmed three sightings on his radar: one over Malabon and two over the US Embassy heading toward Clark Field. I rushed to June Keithley, who called General Ramos' office. The party at the other end finally admitted: "It's over."

JAIME CARDINAL SIN, Archbishop of Manila

I was not able to sleep for three days and three nights, monitoring the events, calling the American Embassy, calling the White House. The White House wanted me to go to Malaca-

ñang to negotiate. I said that was impossible. The American Embassy also told me: "Get out now, because there is an order to kill you." I was on the hit list. The American Embassy asked me: "Would you like to come to our embassy?" I saw no need to go to the American Embassy.

When Marcos left, I was very sad. So we all went to the chapel. And I called the nuns again. "The victory is won. Pray for Marcos." I was sad for him.

It was good that we declared Marian Year in 1985 because that prepared our people: in conversion, in trying to be more spiritual, in trying to conscienticize them. Our preparation was great. The Marian Year was a kind of penance, an offering, and a reparation. Since the Lord was appeased by the penance and the sacrifices of the people, the scourge was taken out. It is very clear that when the people start asking pardon, the Lord will never refuse.

CECILIA MUÑOZ PALMA

On Tuesday evening, I was with Cory in the home of her sister, Josephine Reyes. There Cory received the phone call from US Ambassador Bosworth, telling her that Marcos was ready to leave but was asking to stay for at least two days in Paoay, his home in the North.

Cory's initial reaction was: "Poor man, let us give him two days." But we did not agree with that idea. We thought that given the chance, Marcos may regroup his forces or extend his stay indefinitely.

Cory then called Ambassador Bosworth to say that she could not grant the request. Marcos should just leave the country.

When Ambassador Bosworth called her back, it was to say that Marcos had left. Cool as always, Cory turned to us after she put the phone down. She said simply: "Marcos has left." She said it as if it was the most ordinary thing. We all shouted jubilantly. Cory did not.

DANILO BELO, student

My mother and I were in Kelly's Cafe in Clark Air Base when we heard that Marcos had left Malacañang. I was awakened by the sound of helicopters. I was scared. I grabbed a pair of binoculars and peeped through it. I was surprised to see ex-President Marcos and the ex-First Lady come out of a helicopter.

CARLOS CARBONELL, student

Over the radio at about 10:00 p.m., I heard that Marcos had left Malacañang. I was then on Mendiola Street with the *Alyansang Makabayan* (Nationalist Alliance) League of Filipino Students. At that moment, I really felt down to my bones that I am a Filipino. It was hair-raising. Church bells rang. There was dancing in the streets. Some people were cheering: "Cory! Cory!"

I saw people enter the administration building of Malacañang; maybe the people thought that it was Malacañang itself. They tried to bring out appliances and office equipment, but they were intercepted. Instead, they ate the food they found. "This is ours," they said. "This is our money. We worked for this, therefore we should get it."

SAMUEL DUGUILES, student

It was about eight in the evening, and we could not enter Malacañang, because about five hundred Marcos loyalists were blocking the gates. We asked them to surrender, but they shouted: "President Marcos will never abandon us!" It was a pitched battle, with the two groups throwing stones at each other. We had to bring ten of our injured companions to ambulances. At about ten in the evening, after we heard that Marcos had left Malacañang, the loyalists still held on. It was then that a group of Cory supporters attacked. The loyalists were dispersed. Some were beaten up while some clambered over the fence into the Malacañang Palace grounds. We beat up one of the loyalists whom we had seen throwing stones. One of the foreign journalists intervened. I felt a pang of guilt and so I helped him ward off the many attackers. He was badly hurt and was taken to the hospital. I was angry with him and all the other loyalists, but I just could not leave him to the mob. He would have been killed.

Young revolutionist: she too was there

EDITH A. BATALLA

The real fun was in Malacañang at about 11:30 p.m. after Marcos fled. There was so much rushing and jostling at the Mendiola entrance that we decided to take the dimly-lit San Rafael Street with a handful of other people. When we got near V. Mapa High School, we heard shots. We stopped. When the shooting ceased, we walked on. We heard shots again. The urgent firing that followed sent us running in all directions and I thought it was the end of me. When we passed by the barricades, a companion tried to stop to get a piece of barbed wire, but I shouted: "Keep running! They'll blast us off!" We slowed down only when we got back to Legarda Street.

At about 1:00 a.m., we finally got to Malacañang via Mendiola, but we weren't able to enter the gate. Neither were we able to get a piece of the barbed-wire barricade. My brother found a souvenir which he said he would preserve for posterity: a worn-out combat boot.

RICHARD WILHELM B. RAGODON, antique restorer

Frenzy preceded the onslaught to Malacañang. The people became unruly. They started pushing towards the gate, some started climbing the gate and the fence. People started shouting "No pushing!" and "Open the gate!" When the gate opened, all hell broke loose.

During the melee, many were bruised and stepped on. My slippers were stepped on and destroyed instantly. I proceeded barefoot to the Malacañang grounds.

Most of the people went directly to the palace doors, which were locked when we arrived. After a while, they were opened. Like flash floods, people rushed in. This time, the shouts were "Don't break anything, Cory will use them," and "That is ours."

All the doors inside the first floor were locked. Most of us went directly to the small garden facing the Pasig River. I heard people saying: "It's lovely here." "It's so big!" Some people, in their eagerness to go inside the different quarters, tried to climb up the balcony. The windows had iron grilles, while the doors near the balcony were also locked. They were only able to peep in.

In the palace garden, fronting the river, people collected whatever articles they could salvage from the burning piles of paper and documents. Others ate the dinner packs that were left within the grounds. The packs consisted of rice, chicken stew, stringbeans with squash tidbits, and a piece of cake.

I went to the radio and study rooms on the second floor. The sophisticated radio transmitters were still functioning. The loaded M-16 Armalites that were left behind were still in place, ready to be used. I was taken aback by the grandeur of the President's study room. For a while, I was stunned and confused. I did not know where to go or what to look at first. Everything inside was clean and in order. The wooden floors and old walls were shining magnificently. Books were neatly arranged, preserved, and enclosed in glass. The room had expensive decorations, furniture, and paintings. Everything seemed to be preserved in time for a person of the future to discover. In this fleeting moment, right in the abode of the former President, I never imagined that I would be able to enter the sanctuary which had been heavily guarded for twenty years.

NELSON TRINIDAD, geologist

I finally became part of history when I joined the first group that entered the palace. In the rush I lost my shoes. So I wandered around the palace grounds on my bare feet. I can honestly say: "I have set foot on Malacañang."

TONY GO

I was among the first to enter the Palace on the night of February 25. We hooted down men who in their unbridled excitement were scaling the buildings, smashing windows, looting. This was the big letdown for me. These people who might have had the notion that they were merely exacting just vengeance were in reality inflicting graver wounds upon themselves, not realizing that they were invariably contributing to the further desecration of a heritage already in tatters. We shouted ourselves hoarse when that great hanging flag began to be torn. We formed human barricades to prevent further entries.

Joy must present itself occasionally as a tremor, but freedom is, as always, as everywhere it must be, an earthquake. The very earth shook from the dancing, the vent of so many happy feet. We were engulfed with wonder, with fear, with exultation.

But in the midst of what was New Year's Eve in February, Malacañang seemed to be the repository of all that is sad in this world. The deserted hallways leading into empty rooms echoed the wail of victims of the former occupants' unending lust for power. On an opulent divan sat the ghost of a people betrayed;

upon its cold floors were prostrate the discarded dreams of a race broken. The Pasig seemed to me that night, even with the moon reflected on its surface, a flood of sorrows. How ironic that a fully-lit tree, once an instrument of wanton merriment, could only look infinitely desolate.

I saw people touch the ground on which the Palace stood. One pocketed a pebble, many uprooted plants for transplanting in their own backyards, thinking perhaps that history might indeed be tangible. I so loved to touch the buildings themselves, as if to touch were already to possess, and to know. Two massive frogs in the still lit pool elicited much laughter: not a fish swam in this almost magical water. I wondered about the garbage piled by the riverbank, half-expecting that it would not smell. Coming into the Palace grounds was like stepping on totally alien terrain. I shuddered at finding the mystery as tenuous, as vulnerable as Malacañang was that night. It was a most painful experience.

RENATO CHAVEZ, mason

I think I was one of the few who first entered Malacañang. There was no one in the building but the lights were on. I was afraid. I went from room to room. It was very beautiful, especially the chandeliers. I saw the chair used by Marcos when he had conferences. It had his seal as president of the Philippines. I sat on the chair and felt really happy.

I saw a pin cushion and I wanted to take it, but someone said to me: "Don't get it. Cory might be able to use it."

I was able to enter the library. I saw grapes, fresh grapes, on a dish. I ate them all.

One woman kept saying to us: "Please don't touch anything."

I entered Marcos' room. It was beautiful. I saw a new black suit and I wanted to take it but didn't. Instead I took a *barong tagalog* shirt. There were many of these shirts but I took only one, because I was carrying only a clutch bag. Some people were taking guns and typewriters and putting them inside sacks.

FREDDIE AGUILAR

On Tuesday night, I had a show in Hobbit House. Along the way, I heard people cheering and saying that Marcos had fled. I did not want to believe it and said that I would have to go and see it for myself.

At Hobbit House, I sang a few songs. Then I told the audience: "Come with me to Malacañang. I heard that Marcos has left." The tourists cheered and some of them came along with me to Malacañang. Traffic was very bad. We had to walk from Mendiola Street.

In Malacañang, there was pandemonium. An old man came up and said to me: "Freddie, they are looting the place. Maybe they will listen to you. Ask them to stop."

I borrowed a megaphone from a reformist soldier. I asked the people not to destroy Malacañang, to think of our new President, to realize that we do not want her to enter a dilapidated Malacañang. Some people answered back and assured me that they would watch Malacañang for Cory.

I decided to go to Channel 4 to tell them what was going on in Malacañang. I was put off when some people in the channel told me not to say anything about the looting. I said that if they do not want me to tell the truth, I would simply leave. When I finally got in front of the cameras, I told the truth: I asked the people in Malacañang to please stop looting the place.

Outside Channel 4, there was some confusion. Since Marcos had left, the people at the barricades wanted to go home. But Jim Paredes thought that they should stay. I went up to the makeshift stage and pleaded with the crowd to stay: "Let's not leave yet. The Marcos loyalist troops have not surrendered. They might still attack Channel 4." I sang to them for more than an hour. When I made as if to leave, the people asked me to stay and so I did. I sat with them on the road through the night on Tuesday.

JOSE MARIA SISON, political ex-detainee

I think the left had a major participation in this EDSA happening. BAYAN and other organizations were part of the hard core, the cause-oriented organizations from left to right were at EDSA. Of course, the majority of the people at EDSA responded to the call of Cardinal Sin and the leaders of the cause-oriented organizations. But there had to be a hard core who would stay all throughout. During the three-day happening, the spontaneous masses came and went but the hard core was there.

In the operation to seize Channel 4, I think BAYAN had a major part. They cooperated with Colonel Santiago in the operation.

And the flight of Marcos was hastened by the constant pressure of BAYAN at Mendiola and at the foot of Nagtahan Bridge.

Street shrine: reminders to pray

JUNE KEITHLEY, radio announcer

It was very dramatic shortly after midnight at Channel 4. Father Efren prayed, Bong cried, and I cried. I said: "I am going out to dance."

As I was going out, I got a call on the hot line. It was Crame. They said: "June, please go back, there are some elements in Malacañang who are trying to turn the tide. Don't mention who they are. Try to get the people away from Malacañang if you can, because they're going to do it now." They were leftists who tried to create some havoc and the soldiers couldn't shoot because there were too many people.

Throughout that day, we had people calling with messages like: "We have taken Caloocan." We were not aware then that they were leftist signals, although we already knew that there were some plans afoot. But I did not think that they would do it that night.

The people were celebrating and jubilant. These leftists were riding on this. I was angry, so angry. How dare they rob us now, when our freedom is at hand? How dare they put their personal interest above the interest of this country and its people? I was furious. That was why I looked so red and serious on camera.

The General said: "June, we leave it up to you. This is what is happening." I said: "Okay. I'll just announce that there are people in Malacañang taking advantage of the situation."

CORAZON C. AQUINO

At last, we are home. Let us remember the day, February 25, 1986; the time, nine in the evening; the occasion, the coming of freedom.

Freedom from twenty years of dictatorship, twenty years of oppression, hardship, repression, injustice, corruption, greed, waste and near-despair—ended. Ended by a revolution of peace, prayers, Rosaries, radios, and above all, raw human courage.

It is true: the Filipino is brave, the Filipino is honorable, the Filipino is great.

I have never felt prouder to be a Filipino. I am sure I share this feeling with millions of Filipinos. I am told that in other cities, when they learn that you are a Filipino, they shake your hand and praise the nobility of your race. In the streets of New York, I am told that Filipinos are being stopped and congratulated for moral courage as a people. The Filipino stands proud before the whole world.

I can't help but remember Ninoy. I cannot resist comparing his death to Good Friday and our liberation to Easter Sunday. I am sure that Ninoy is smiling at us now from the life after, for truly we have proved him correct: the Filipino is worth dying for.

In the dark days before liberation, I said that I believe God is on our side and that we have nothing to fear. I truly believe that He is not only on our side, He actively intervened and fought by our side. How else can we explain many of the events in the days that just passed?

I pray that He will continue to be by our side in the difficult yet challenging days to come. I am confident that He will not fail us: our cause is just. God is beside us. We can face the coming trials.

CONSTANTINO TRILLANA, hotel employee
(From a letter dated March 7, 1986, Washington)

The day after Marcos fled, my officemates greeted me with placards: "Happy Filipino new year!" "Long live Cory!" "People power!" There was a yellow ribbon tied around my word processor monitor.

One of my bosses began to shred some yellow paper for confetti. I had to stop him because I knew I was going to clean up after him. Three of my best buddies treated me to lunch and during our toast to Cory, we were overheard by the huge restaurant crowd who spontaneously joined. That was so euphoric!

Later, the president of our outfit passed by my desk. He stopped to say that I could take the afternoon off so I could join the Filipinos milling in front of our building on Massachusetts Avenue on their way to the Philippine Embassy. I went home instead and made flan — good for 30 people. I brought the flan (which was very yellow) to the office next morning. They all asked for the recipe and I said that they had to ask Cory.

VER AUDIENCAL, employee,
Jeddah, Saudi Arabia
(From a letter dated March 3, 1986)

Our radios here were all tuned in to BBC and VOA for fresh reports from Manila. The tension here was high when both sides seemed geared for a bloodbath. We have a lot of sympathizers here: the Saudis, the Syrians, the Jordanians, the Egyptians, the Sudanese, the Palestinians. They are all pro-Aquino. They listened to the Arabic broadcasts which they translated for us. They all know the *Laban* sign and if I meet anyone of them in the office, they flash the L sign and say "Aquino." They also know the meaning for us of the color yellow.

When Marcos left, they did not stop until I treated them to Pepsi and sandwiches. I spent a few hundred bucks for that celebration.

These non-Filipino supporters of Aquino in our offices have high praise for the courage and unity of our people and for people power. They cannot imagine how the Filipinos united and responded to just a single call from Radio Veritas. They said that if what Filipino did could be done by other people, there could be peace.

SYLVIA L. MAYUGA, writer

The world has heard by now of what took place in the Philippines from February 22 to 25—the rebellion of Enrile, Ramos, and the reformists, that radiant explosion of people power encouraged by Cardinal Sin and bishops of the Catholic Church, the Rosaries and flowers that confronted tanks, the defection of the 15th Wing of the Philippine Air Force, the takeover of the government Channel 9 that interrupted Marcos in mid-sentence during his fake inaugural, the fiesta all over Camps Crame and Aguinaldo and the TV station with civilians defending the military, and soldiers and civilians side by side for the first time since the nightmare of Marcos began.

Through four days that elongated the seconds, minutes, and hours, Juan Ponce Enrile made public the frustration of martial law gone sour, making an "act of contrition" for having been one of its chief architects, and told the world of the electoral cheating he had been privy to in his own bailiwick. "My heart is clean," he said. "I am ready to die. I know in my heart that Mrs. Aquino has won."

General Fidel Ramos, for his part, made a vow: that the long dark years when the Armed Forces of the Philippines lent themselves as a black magician's wand to the wishes of one man's heart would never happen again. "We are the New Armed Forces of the People, the New Armed Forces of the People," he said over and over again, triumphantly, like a child, over the radio and the liberated TV stations as defections to the reformist camp grew and grew… and tears fell in the Ministry of National Defense and its commands, down the cheeks of Ramos, Enrile, the soldiers, and all over the thirsty land.

She, the Virgin, graced the corridors of power again. Through all the televised briefings with which Ramos and Enrile guided the four-day "revolution" to its peaceful conclusion, Our Lady of Fatima, Enrile's private icon, stood circumspectly over a bowl of yellow chrysanthemums on the center table of the war room for all the world to see—and history to remember.

PHILIPPINE DAILY INQUIRER, Manila
(An editorial dated February 27, 1986)

Every Filipino in the world today stands a little taller and a little prouder.

No longer the butt of jokes and the object of pity or derision, Filipinos can take their place in the council of nations because they are one of the few races who have done the impossible.

They have deposed a dictator without the help of anyone but themselves, and they have unshackled their country from a decade of bondage with minimal bloodshed.

When Filipinos first voted out Marcos and their will was frustrated, it seemed as if the depths of degradation as a people had been plumbed. Years of being the world's prostitutes, coolie labor, international criminals, apathetic subjects of a repressive ruler had made the Filipino a laughingstock in the international community.

But redemption was forthcoming.

When the revolution now popularly called People Power began, it was triggered by two Filipinos—Juan Ponce Enrile and Fidel Ramos. But neither of them would have survived if the people had not put themselves between the attackers and the leaders of the revolt.

People all over the world then saw the unbelievable.

Filipinos charging at giant tanks with Volkswagens. Nuns and priests meeting armored cars with Rosaries and prayers. Little children giving grim soldiers flowers and urging them not to fight for Marcos. People linking arms and blocking tanks, daring them to crush their fellow Filipinos, which they did not.

It was a lesson in passive resistance that will be the model for all oppressed people of the world, and it was uniquely Filipino.

And in the end, when the dictator had been deposed, his followers were treated with compassion rather than anger, with charity rather than vindictiveness, and national reconciliation at last became possible.

Filipinos have regained not only their liberty but their pride, not only freedom but dignity, not only honor but the respect of other men.

FR. FRANCISCO J. ARANETA

We are dazed, and we ask: "What happened?" What made three million men, women, and youngsters from all walks of life converge at EDSA, completely unarmed, except for religious statues and rosaries? And what gave them the generosity and the valor to turn themselves into human barricades?

What was the power at work by which hardened soldiers trained to kill could not bring themselves to hurt unarmed civilians?

For years to come, historians, psychologists, sociologists, and political scientists will be studying the 77-hour revolt. They will write a whole library of articles and books dissecting the whole thing, learnedly analyzing what happened and what made it happen.

If we sit quietly and pray over the matter a little bit, we will know in the depths of our heart what happened and what made it happen.

What happened was conversion. What has been happening in our midst these past few years has been a gradual but nationwide change of heart.

We had many people who prayed, but who thought that to stand up for one's political rights was beneath the dignity of a Christian. Now they came to realize that the love of neighbor called for defending his rights.

We had many activists, ready to march up and down our streets, ready to risk their lives if need be to bring down an oppressor. Many of these had thought that to pray was pointless. Somehow they learned that prayer was the source of strength, courage, dedication.

Our rich people looked down on our poor as a lazy, dishonest, ill-smelling breed. Our poor people looked on the rich as an arrogant lot. More and more over the years, they have learned to look on each other as brothers and sisters in Christ.

What brought about these changes?

God's gift of His own love. What we learned in our catechism to call "grace."

And so it was that on a three-kilometer stretch of cemented road, between two army camps, a new people was born, a people of God, whom the world calls Filipinos.

Nun at barricade: mine eyes have seen

TERESITA ESTRADA MERCADO, wife and mother

For me in Malaybalay, Bukidnon, Tuesday began shortly before dawn. Our parish had organized a penitential procession as our way of helping the revolution in Manila. The invitation went out even to the barrios. That morning on my way to church, I saw the barrio people coming in from several directions; they formed mini-processions and held candles to light their way into town.

We went all around Malaybalay on foot early that morning. We said three parts of the Rosary and attended the first Mass. Many people attended the dawn Rosary and the Mass; it was made clear to us that praying was our vital participation in what was going on in Manila.

In the evening, we planned a noise barrage in response to Cory Aquino's call during her post-election rally in Luneta. She said she would talk over the radio at 8:00 p.m. on Tuesday and that after her talk, we should have a noise barrage. Because there was no notice to the contrary, the Malaybalay supporters of Cory decided to go ahead. We got into our cars, honked the horns, and banged tin cans, while driving all over the town. We cheered: "Cory! Cory!"

We made the noise barrage for over an hour. At some point, we saw many people going out of their houses and cheering and dancing. We thought they were supporting us. All the more, we made noise.

It was close to 10 o'clock when we broke up. When we got home, we were told that Marcos had left Malacañang. The people we had seen cheering and dancing were celebrating his departure; many of them thought we were making noise to celebrate it.

MSGR. NICO BAUTISTA

On Sunday, March 2, in my parish in Magallanes, I talked about "People Power Is Prayer Power." I said that prayer touches the hearts of people. As an illustration, I spoke about the pilot who was instructed to strafe Crame but had a change of heart and defected to the rebels instead.

After my homily, four men followed me to the rectory. The first man introduced himself: "Father, you talked about the pilot who defected. I am that pilot. I am Colonel Antonio Sotelo. My family and I come to Magallanes every Sunday."

I asked him if it would be all right if I introduced him to the congregation. He agreed.

After the Mass, I went up again to the rostrum and told the people that the pilot who defected was with us. There was a long ovation for Colonel Sotelo, who said, among other things: "Father Nico's homilies reinforced my decision to defect."

A revolution is not a single act which erupts at a particular point. It is a series of many independent acts converging at a single definite point.

CRISTINE LAZARO PALMER

My pastor said it was not just people power that caused the miracle—a first ever for any nation in the world. It was "praying people power," as evidenced by the different creeds, denominations, and nationalities who manned the barricades.

What a privilege it was for expatriates to have been in the Philippines and to have witnessed this! For Filipinos: what pride to be able to hold our heads up again before the world and show what unity and prayer can do against insurmountable odds!

KAA BYINGTON, writer

Though I was here only during the last three weeks of the revolution—from Election Day on—I somehow managed to see most of its great events: people guarding ballot boxes, demonstrations, the Radio Veritas newsroom, Cory's incredible meeting at the Luneta, Javier's funeral at the Ateneo, the siege of Camp Crame, the battle for Channel 4. I saw the jets and helicopters screaming overhead and the people power reaction, heard the gunfire, even twice ran into Marcos loyalist troops. I did not see a tank, thank God. I stayed up two nights running, glued to Radio Veritas, with the crazy idea that somehow just listening would keep the tank columns or the helicopters away. I knew I could never have the courage to lie down in front of a tank, so I sat up in front of a radio.

FRANCISCO RODRIGO (SOC)

People power in Pilipino is *lakas ng bayan*. LABAN, the name by which we call our umbrella opposition group, stands for *Lakas ng Bayan*, People Power.

I can still remember when we were thinking of a name for the opposition. I said that the acronym must be LABAN, which means fight. Everyone agreed.

I suggested that we use the name: *Lapian ng Bayan*, People's Party. Neptali Gonzales objected: "I am a member of the Liberal Party. *Lapian* means party. I cannot be a member of two parties. But I can belong to an umbrella organization." Juan David raised the same objection. *Lapian* was out.

Neptali came one day with Ninoy's suggestion: NO—for *Nagkakaisang Oposisyon* (United Opposition). He said that we would be saying NO to corruption, to tyranny, to repression, etc. But Charito Planas thought that it was too negative.

We were back to LABAN and the problem with the word *Lapian*. We had to think of another Pilipino word that begins with *la*. Then Alfonso Policarpio, Ninoy's associate, suggested: *Lakas*, power. I thought it was excellent. The name was unanimously approved for our umbrella opposition group: LABAN, *Lakas ng Bayan*, or people power.

FREDDIE AGUILAR

I recorded the song *Bayan Ko* (My Homeland) in 1979—seven years before the revolution. I felt that foreign culture was beginning to swamp local pop music. I thought that maybe a patriotic song would jolt back those who were starting to forget who we really are. *Bayan Ko* was the best I could think of, because it has been my favorite since I was a child. I think it is truly beautiful.

When I was singing that song, without accompaniment, beside the coffin of Ninoy Aquino, I broke out in goose pimples. I was thinking: "I am full of conceit. All I do is talk. This man gave his life." From then on, I became part of the protest scene—all the way until the revolution, still singing *Bayan Ko*.

WILFREDO ARCE, Ph.D., sociologist
(From a letter dated March 26, 1986)

I have thought on and off about our brief conversation the other day and I decided that I should write you this note.

You recalled then that in an earlier conversation I had said something to the effect that "revolution is not a picnic," the implication being that it must necessarily be violent. But, you asked, how come the recent "revolution" was relatively peaceful? In my response, I made these points, in order: the revolution had already been won even before the 77 hours at Crame and Aguinaldo and "revolution" is a term that has different meanings to different people.

As you can see, regardless of the validity of those points, I did not answer your question directly. Part of my problem is that I have always thought of "revolution" in the way sociologists and anthropologists generally view it: an abrupt, radical, and irreversible transformation of a social system. Thus, if this term was used in our earlier conversation that you referred to, my mind would have automatically conjured up pictures of changes far greater than the February happenings have accomplished so far. Such changes usually require a great deal of human sacrifice as witness, e.g., the widespread and inhuman exploitation of labor that accompanied the industrial revolution in Great Britain, and the systematic extermination of the kulaks during the Bolshevik revolution in Russia. In this sense, revolution is indeed not a picnic, to use a hackneyed phrase.

But at the risk of sounding like an intellectual turncoat, let me refer to the everyday (dictionary) definition of revolution as a forcible change, especially in a government. If one follows this definition, the February happenings could properly be called a revolution. They did force out a despot and installed a new head of state committed to leading a democratic government. Why did the change take place peacefully? One could always come up with a laundry list of factors, especially from hindsight. Let me focus on the gut feeling that a friend and I have had about what one may call the Filipino national character.

Some years ago, I had a job in Singapore but decided against renewing my contract on its expiration and to return to Manila instead. Dr. Eduardo (Ned) Roberto of the Asian Institute of Management was visiting at the time and, in a conversation, I mentioned my decision to him.

"But why go back at this time? Marcos' rule will have to end sooner or later and some believe the end can only come with large-scale violence," Ned remarked in a manner that indicated he was asking questions to which he already had answers.

"If by violence they mean widespread and prolonged street fighting, I just find it difficult to see that happening," I replied.

"So do I," said Ned quickly. "Not the Iran or Beirut type of fighting anyway. There may be some shooting for, at most, three days. Then somebody will say: 'That's enough. Let's all go home.' And that would be a consensus."

Ned put his thoughts and mine on the subject (change from Marcos' rule to somebody else's; no mention of "revolution") so well that I have had occasion to repeat his words to a few friends after that and before the 77 hours of February. However, the precise manner in which the people brought about the change was certainly something difficult to foresee. Like everybody else, I could only admire the way it was done and rejoice in it.

TONY GO, writer

In the four days of the revolution, I came to know of pagans having all of a sudden encountered God on some lonely street corner, and of broken families coming together. Before the revolution, barbed-wire symbolized slavery and oppression. On the night of February 25, I went down to the muck below Mendiola Bridge to retrieve a length of this same material for safekeeping, recognizing it now to be a manifestation of freedom taken.

Inside Malacañang: jubilation

I am proud that in crucial moments at the two camps, at Channel 4, and at Malacañang, I was there. Our separate little acts of heroism contributed to a great whole—even if each time we went out for the nightwatch we were secretly in our hearts bidding the kids a final, sad goodbye.

And that is why, nowadays, I perceive the flowers in my garden as having become more intensely white, or as having a more pervasive scent. They also proffer memories of a little people's collective heroism and how feathers, gathered together, finally sank a boat.

POY PANTALEON, wife and mother

It was the Battle of Lepanto and La Naval all over again, where Our Lady was at the helm, the tireless frontliner of an army whose weapons were rosaries, holy medals, scapulars, and prayer cards.

Borrowing Mary's childlike faith and tender compassion, the "revolutionaries" placed their trust on soldiers who could not find it in their hearts to fight against weapons of faith.

It was a revolution that seemed more like a barrio fiesta—a people honoring its saint with Masses and song: colorful and prayerful scenes full of comings and goings of friends and strangers who easily became smiling acquaintances because of a common cause. And there was plenty of food. Cardinal Sin called it a laughing revolution. People didn't seem to be going to battle—they were going on a pilgrimage. Faith in Our Lady was so thick, so deep, that you saw her image in processions along the barricades of EDSA in the late, late hours of the nightwatch. People not only prayed the Rosary incessantly; they wore rosaries around their necks or held tightly to the beads as if they were holding the hands of Our Lady herself. Mary's image was everywhere: atop a bantam car surrounded by candles; at the ramparts of Crame and Aguinaldo, on banners held aloft in the heat of day and in the cold night, on holy medals pressed to the heart, on hearts and minds lifted on trusting conversation with her. One's heart leapt with emotion at the sight of all these.

The Filipinos' victory was a Marian victory. During those three shining days of courage, Our Lady was a Filipino. You just knew it. Your heart told you. You couldn't explain it. It did not have to be explained. The Filipino was never more Christian than when he won fighting his most precious battle—the battle for freedom, democracy, and peace.

Let no one write the history of this brave, noble revolution and forget that God was with his Filipino children and Mary led the battle. Our Lady begged and pleaded for us. And God pulled the stops and the flood of graces was like a tidal wave sweeping us to victory, overwhelming and leaving us breathless and speechless at the suddenness and the magnitude of it all.

GEORGE WINTERNITZ, insurance manager

People talk of the "carnival revolution" when they remember the lighter moments of the four-day confrontation with the Marcos government: the Ati-atihan dances, the impromptu talent shows and performances outside Crame, the popcorn and dumpling venders, the traffic at the barricades. All these disappeared instantly when the danger was signalled with the cry: "Tanks! Tanks! The tanks are coming! Hurry up, line up, the tanks are coming!" But Our Lady was constant. She was with us again during the moments of triumph as we celebrated.

It was touching to see the people come together to offer thanks. How they flocked to the Masses and offerings of thanksgiving following the victory over the dictator. Churches were filled for the thanksgiving Masses. Luneta overflowed with people at the thanksgiving Mass on the Sunday following the victory, the crowd exceeding that of the pre-revolution rallies. In the parable of the ten lepers, nine forgot to thank our Lord for having healed them. The Filipinos remembered.

As we look back, we think about how silly the talk was about whether the Americans helped us or not. How empty! It was Our lady who helped and she showed it by being everywhere. Before, during, and after this big event in Philippine history. After all, she is the patroness of the Philippines.

LULU HIDALGO

Everybody is talking of people's power, but it was really God's power that we saw. God was the real hero.

JAIME CARDINAL SIN

We celebrate the victory of our people—a victory won with only the weapons of faith, a victory for brotherhood and peace won by hands and arms not bent by the weight of guns but by hands and arms opened out to the brother in love and peace.

MARGARITA COJUANGCO (TINGTING), opposition leader

It is not yet time to celebrate. There is yet so much to do. It is time for a lot of hard work.

God made us win but it is for a purpose that we still have to accomplish.

MAXIMO V. SOLIVEN

The truth is that the Communists and their front organizations were caught flat-footed by the People Power Revolution, the barricades, the turnabout by the military led by Defense Minister Juan Ponce Enrile and the Chief of Staff, General Fidel V. Ramos. What must be most galling to the NPA is that the once-hated military, cannily christened by Ramos the "People's Armed Forces," managed to gain instant popularity.

The Communists wanted to boycott the February snap elections. Their newspaper, *Liberation,* had been for it. But Cory Aquino and Salvador "Doy" Laurel had rallied the nation to battle—and won in the struggle for the ballot box (although the COMELEC and the *Batasan* had frustrated this victory). The Communists were left stranded, high and dry. They had called it all wrong.

But they had "Plan B" up their sleeves. In the weeks before the elections, they had infiltrated hundreds of cadres (fully armed) into Metro Manila and such major cities as Cebu. These cadres had been instructed to lie low and be ready to take advantage of any violent demonstrations that might arise in the wake of anger and disillusionment following the inevitable fraud at the polls.

Alas, for the Reds, this opportunity did not arise. They were again caught flat-footed by the forthright pastoral letter of the Bishops (who seized the initiative away from them) and taken by surprise by the sudden events of the revolution of February 22 to 25. Before they could act, the confrontation at the barricades was over. Those people-power battalions sent to stop tanks and Marines by Jaime Cardinal Sin even stole the word *people* away from them.

Of course, in the waning hours of the barricades, the Communists managed to give eager-beaver foreign correspondents and television crews a few bold interviews—but their hoped-for offensive had been stymied, and liberation from Marcos won without their leadership or, worse, without their help.

President Aquino had leaned over backward to fulfill her campaign promise of releasing all political prisoners—including the Communist leadership—and now they cannot even attack her for not having kept faith with her word. They are in sad disarray.

But their wisdom is as old as the devil's. Now they are patiently waiting for the Great Cory Crusade to falter, and human nature—with its propensity for Original Sin—to take the sheen off the reform government of Aquino and Laurel.

Don't expect the NPAs to come in from the cold. If at first you don't succeed, according to the Red bible, dig in and obfuscate. Tomorrow you may get a second chance.

CORAZON C. AQUINO

I am determined to make a success of this government. I am not doing it for Cory Aquino but for the people who are hoping and praying. I am doing it for democracy. If I fail, it might be said that democracy itself does not have a chance to survive here. It is determination, more than anything else—and I keep telling people: "You have to help me." They do help and, for some of them, it is a big sacrifice.

CECILIA MUÑOZ PALMA

During those four days in February, we demonstrated through military power, people power, and prayer power. Prayer power first, then people power, then military power third. As Cory had said in a statement, she had done everything humanly possible for her candidacy in presenting to the people the need for a change. She said God had to intervene. I was touched by that statement of hers. So I said: "God, You'd better intervene."

When Marcos was proclaimed by the *Batasan*, where was God? Why did He not intervene? But in a few days, He did. The assassination of Evelio Javier, the breakaway of Enrile and Ramos—God was working on them. That was how I felt. The military, Enrile and Ramos—as I envisioned it—could not have succeeded if people did not come to their assistance. They could easily have been captured, arrested, or could have fallen into the hands of Ver and his group.

VIC SISON

What happened in Camp Aguinaldo and Camp Crame was a miracle. One of the things that made this miracle happen, I believe, was the death of Evelio Javier. He practically offered himself up to make this victory a reality. He died at the right moment and at the right time to fire up the people. I would dare say that many of the people who went to EDSA were inspired to offer their own lives by the memory of Evelio. That was the meaning of Evelio's death. Ninoy Aquino's death was an impetus to the protest movement, but Evelio's death was the more immediate goad. His martyrdom was right there in our midst, and when we were mourning, we were saying to ourselves: dare I do anything like that for my country? Cynics may disagree. I believe Evelio's death was a source of inspiration to many people—and that inspiration was carried through into a miracle.

Moreover, I felt that the demonstration of strength, solidarity, and absolute courage in EDSA was an extension of the secret ballot for Cory Aquino into a *viva voce* vote. If Marcos, other Filipinos, and the world did not believe that Cory had her victory won, it was proved by the raising of the hands on EDSA.

I had the privilege of seeing this phenomenon grow from practically nothing, even from outright fear, when we were gathering a million signatures for Cory's candidacy. People were timid then; they had to make some comment or excuse when they signed. I remember that we gathered a whole lot of signatures at the cemeteries during All Souls' Day. We had to be where the people were in order to get their signatures. Less than three months later, those signatures became alive on EDSA.

ALBERT G. GRUPE

My entire family was at EDSA together with millions of people who went wild with joy as the radio announcers confirmed the departure of Marcos. Suddenly the unseen Power who had led the people to victory gave us the impulse to organize instant parades on the initiative of the people who had come from the provinces to support the exhausted Manila barricade brigades. There were spontaneous prayer meetings right there on the highway, amid fireworks, dancing, and bonfires. I cannot remember ever feeling so happy in all my life. A Jesuit priest, Father Tanseco, summed it up for me during his spontaneous prayer: "Thank you, Lord, for allowing us to witness a real miracle during our lifetime."

C.A. GAMBOL

I saw, heard, and overheard many vignettes during the revolution. I saw an old woman hugging a dumbfounded Marcos loyalist soldier who had defected. She was saying: "I love you, I love you." The poor man did not know how to react. I saw a young man caressing a helicopter and saying: "So this is what a Sikorsky is like." Another young man was jubilantly holding up his right hand: "I'll never wash this hand. It pushed back a tank."

I saw a crowd getting unruly on EDSA. The people were pushing and shoving. My sister, a nun, stood up from where we were seated along EDSA and went near them. The people just automatically lined up when they saw her. She didn't need to say a word.

I saw seminarians forming a ring to enclose soldier-defectors going into Crame. The seminarians looked like young boys; my sister called them God's brigade.

Right at the middle of EDSA, while taking chances that they would be safe from tanks and artillery fire, some young people were taking chances at cards. They were playing Crazy Eight and *Cara y Cruz*.

An old woman said she walked all the way from Cubao. She was carrying a gallon of water, which she offered to the nuns: "This may be of some help."

I saw a large, potbellied man with an entourage of servants, all carrying food—not for himself but as his contribution to the food brigade. A huge delegation from Lipa City came with a band which played cheerful music on EDSA. A delegation of fishermen brought their fishing torches.

I saw faith that was alive. Where in the world will you find a people whose faith is so strong that they believe holding up a statue of the Blessed Virgin before tanks would stop them? Where will you find battle-tested soldiers who stop their tanks when faced with people at prayer? I saw a living faith when I heard my friend shout at the top of her voice as tanks revved up: "Let's pray out loud so that the soldiers will hear!" And at the top of their voices, the people around her cried: "Glory be to the Father and to the Son and to the Holy Spirit"—three times, out loud like a cheer. The tanks turned away.

I saw and heard a Swiss journalist remark: "Is this a revolution?" He watched unbelieving as people chanted and chatted, prayed and sang, ate and listened to the radio—in between facing tanks and tear gas. My husband replied to the puzzled Swiss observer: "We Filipinos like to do things differently."

And, yes, I saw the new look that girls were proudly sporting after three days at EDSA. It is called the "Crame Tan."

FR. VIC HELLY, S.J.

It was a revolution begun and won by the people of God. The Church was the people of God liberating themselves. The means the people of God chose as the means to effect their liberation were chosen precisely because they gave expression to the Gospel values: respect and love for the human person, respect for human life. They chose a nonviolent resistance that harmed no one and drew all together.

Young men and gestures of hope

253

SR. TERESA OF JESUS AND MARY, Carmelite nun

The odyssey of our liberation was a pure gift of God to us. We lived our Carmelite calling—to keep faith and prayer alive in this world—at its purest. We never forgot even for an instant that we were doing battle. We daily called God in prayer to assist us all: those outside and we inside. Our solitude was not strained nor disciplined; rather, it was a fierce and ardent attachment only to God's will. Our silence was not just obedience to our Rule; rather, it was a sweet, gentle, and full response to God's words: "Be still and know that I am God." Our fasting was not only more rigorous but was directed to inner fasting. Our penance was not more material and exterior; rather, it was a brave, generous, constantly renewed oblation—a plea to absorb into our poverty the doubts, the weaknesses, the deceit, the rapacity, the cruelty, the wickedness, the wanton betrayals—all in the spirit of Jesus taking on Himself our sins.

Perhaps for the first time in Carmel in the Philippines, Radio Veritas regularly sequenced our adoration, Rosaries, and personal meditations. All calls for help we addressed to Our Lord in the Blessed Sacrament: "Give them the courage and generosity, Lord. Send them there, but protect them!"

We were everywhere in spirit. We were there, responding to all calls for urgent help; there where fear and danger were greatest—EDSA, Bohol Avenue, Fort Bonifacio, Nagtahan, even Malacañang. We were there, everywhere with our Army: led by Our Lady, St. Michael, the Holy Innocents, all the angels and saints, all the souls in purgatory, and Blessed Lorenzo Ruiz commissioned from on high. Our faith knew no bounds; our hopes soared the more deeply immersed we were in prayer. And the usual recessional of our daily Mass was *Bayan Ko* (Our Homeland).

The papers kept us updated and we thrilled to witness God's empowerment in the hearts and minds of the EDSA multitude that had gathered to form a human cross—four streets intersecting each other. This is the Mystical Body on the Cross: it was happening all over again (and not just to one person in the depths of her interiority) but to millions truly become one person in Christ on the cross.

Deeply grateful, awed beyond thought, groggy from lack of sleep, we were at our posts of prayer, overwhelmed at the mystery of God's ways: We saw somehow that the good God wanted us to have Mary's Holy Saturday grace. For just as in Jesus' time, between Good Friday and Easter Sunday, when the world was plunged in darkness and despair, in the whole wide universe, there was one little candle burning fiercely, steadily, and seen through all creation. It was Mary's unwavering faith in her Son's resurrection.

She was our model in a very special way. We were asked to be Mary on our country's Holy Saturday. From February 22 to 25—especially on all of Monday and Tuesday—we had nothing, absolutely nothing to go by, except for that dazzlingly white point of perfect peace in our inmost souls. In our heart of hearts, we knew there would be no bloodshed, the Marcoses would go, Cory would really be President, and the whole gaping, watching world of nations would say of God and our country: "Truly, God has wrought marvels in that little country! What a people! What faith! What a lesson for the whole world!" And the glory is God's.

MARIA PILAR MISA, immigrant, Melbourne, Australia
(From a letter written March 18, 1986)

Mabuhay ang Pilipinas! (Long live the Philippines!) I did expect some amount of heroism from you, but I certainly did not, still cannot, see you lying on that hard EDSA floor. But I am proud of you, all of you. The image of John Cabato standing with a bayonet aimed at his belly and later sitting on that throne at Maharlika Hall was just too much. Jimmy Hofileña was right: Filipinos are stupid, stupid enough to face tanks. That's why not one foreign political observer predicted the situation correctly. Am I glad we are all so stupid! Was Rizal right? Are Filipinos inherently lazy, too lazy for a civil war? Now I can laugh, and so can you all.

Having had to watch it all on TV this far away was sheer torture. I was imagining all sorts of things: you guys manning the barricades, being dispersed, fearing for your lives. How I wish I could hug you right now!

KAA BYINGTON

I had long before realized that the only reason Marcos got away with martial law was that he first cut off the media—television, radio, newspapers—and then controlled them. There is a reason why the First Amendment to the

American Constitution guarantees free speech. Two hundred years ago my ancestors, the colonial Americans, had been subject to a sick tyrant, too. In the two years that I lived under martial law, I developed an insatiable hunger for truth, for a free press. All the old saws that I learned mindlessly in school suddenly became real to me. Every day, for four years of college, I had walked under the words carved in stone above the door of the university library: "The truth shall make you free." It took Ferdinand Marcos to make me understand those words.

I left the Philippines, reluctantly, in 1974. Back in America I indulged in an orgy of newspaper and magazine reading, getting illicit thrills out of it—I couldn't get over the idea that I could be arrested for possessing a newspaper or magazine critical of Marcos until one memorable day a couple of years later at a cocktail party, of all things. It was held on a ferryboat on San Francisco Bay, and was to "honor the local diplomatic corps." One of the honored guests was the Philippine consul general. I was standing in a group next to him, and he was holding forth on "smiling martial law." I listened for a few minutes, sipping my champagne and eating my caviar, and then all of a sudden it dawned on me that I could say anything I wanted to. So I did. I looked at him and said, loudly: "Bullshit." I, too, expatiated on martial law. Everyone was appalled, of course, and I was lectured on manners by my friends. But nobody in America will ever understand how that liberated me.

I didn't have a lot of contacts with Filipinos in the States—after all, all of my friends were *in* the Philippines. I knew from them, not the press, what was going on. About 1980, I started seriously thinking of writing for a living. The one thing I wanted most to write about was the Philippines, but I knew that I might get my friends in serious trouble there if I did. I had noticed, for instance, that every time an article critical of Marcos came out in a newspaper or magazine (and there was no other kind), there was an immediate indignant reply from somebody, usually a consulate somewhere. They didn't miss a thing. Even radio talk shows—you never heard a Filipino accent on a talk show, unless the subject was Marcos, and then a paean of praise came in. But I was still operating under the "bullshit" theory—I had the freedom guaranteed under the US Constitution. But I was wrong, as it turned out.

A prominent American journalist heard through the grapevine that I had a bunch of letters I had written from Manila during my years there. He asked if he could see them, for a book he was doing on the Philippines. However, he told me, to my astonishment, I had to be very circumspect about delivering these letters to him or being associated with him in any way, because the FBI was tapping his telephone, and he was under surveillance. He and his co-author, who lived in New York, were both getting death threats as well. I was flabbergasted. It seemed that in 1981, one of the first acts of the Reagan Administration had been a promise from Alexander Haig, the new Secretary of State, to Marcos that the full force of the US law-enforcement agencies would be brought to bear on anti-Marcos "terrorists" in the United States. I was aware from the local papers that one man, Steve Psinakis, was being investigated, but I also naively thought that the American justice system would work, and he would be cleared by a grand jury. The prominent journalist, however, told me that the FBI had picked on him because he had interviewed Psinakis and other anti-Marcos Filipinos—they now assumed that *he* was a terrorist. In other words, my own government was an agent of Marcos. Now I had to be afraid of Marcos from ten thousand miles away.

And I was. But I did a stupid thing—figuring, I guess that I would never win, I entered an essay contest in a national magazine, on the First Amendment, using martial law in the Philippines as my example. Among other things, interestingly enough, I said that I knew two people (names on request) who saw Ponce Enrile shoot up his own car in Wack Wack Village the night before martial law was declared. (I had been fascinated now that Enrile mentions that as one of his great *mea culpas*.) The essay won the contest, was printed, and then reprinted by *Newsweek* in a special packet on press freedom to be used in high schools.

Shortly after that (and certainly after my daughter applied for a student visa for the Philippines), my telephone started acting up. But I was too busy with personal matters to think much about it. A year later, I learned (from the telephone company) that it was tapped. I assume it is not anymore, and I also have to assume that it was Marcos' people doing it. The only recompense for it all is that they must have had to listen to hours and hours of teenage conversations about rock concerts—it would have been one of the least productive phone taps in history.

I think now that was the reason I came to Manila. Partly, of course, it was to be where the action was, to see what I sensed would be history. Another part was to be with my friends. But more of it was purely personal—I wanted to vote against Marcos, too. Or more than that, I saw the remarkable Cory Aquino as Joan of Arc—as truth and honesty and light. Someone to stand up and be counted.

Before I arrived, I knew vaguely that I had seen more of Cory Aquino on American television than Filipinos had, but I had not been really aware of the meaning of that. I had to be forcibly reminded. To see Cory Aquino, I had to go to where she was. Even to hear Cory Aquino, I had to go with tens of thousands, sometimes millions of people, and walk a long, hot way. She was never on television, and on only one radio station. I watched every minute of the one TV show that the opposition was allowed on—and even that wasn't really opposition—the infamous Ronnie Nathanielsz/Rita Gaddi-Baltazar "Let's-Get-NAMFREL" panel discussion. It was nauseating, a parody of "equal time" and "fairness," and it was, I suddenly realized, on "my" old station—the former ABS-CBN, whose previous owners were living in San Francisco and being hounded by the FBI.

And I noticed the irony of the fact that Americans must have seen the two million at the Luneta on 16 February (because there was a satellite transmitter there), but all Filipinos could see was Marcos telling foreign correspondents that the crowd was the "usual Sunday" crowd of 100,000. Even more did I resent the fact that we had to hear, via a phone call from Singapore, that General Ramos and Minister Enrile had "rebelled." It had been announced by BBC three hours before anyone here heard about it. Even Radio Veritas could only replay it on tape here. Then, Channel 4 showed another lurid comedy: Marcos and his assassination plot—hours of it. The following morning people were rejoicing, dancing, whooping, and yelling, thinking that Marcos had fled the country. Channel 4 was dead—nothing but static. Then I happened to glance over and see it was broadcasting the face of General Ver. My heart dropped right through the floor in stunned silence.

The next day, there was the crackle of gunshots, jets overhead, and our only source of information, actually June Keithley, was transmitting from some secret place in "Ver territory," unprotected. Channel 4 suddenly went off the air—what did that mean? Would the face of Ver appear again? As the world now knows, it did not. Instead we heard the words, "This is Channel 4, serving the people again." One wise friend, Tony Mercado, said it perfectly: "That's all we needed, just one television station."

Pouring from that TV tower which had overshadowed my life first in Manila, and then from afar in San Francisco, came at last, the truth. And it made me free. I was not afraid any more. Ninoy was right: "Courage *is* contagious."

Now that I am back in San Francisco, eating porridge and *camote* tops to make up for the cost of that airline ticket which took me to Manila, my head is till spinning from the sheer velocity of all the events I witnessed. People here keep asking me: "Is it true? Did we really see that on TV? Did the Filipinos really pull off a miracle?" I tell them: Yes, it's true, I saw it with my own eyes, and it was a miracle. They really did overturn a tyrant and his armies, using only faith and prayer and love. For me, I tell them, the experience of the Philippine revolution was like lifting a corner of the universe to see the way God works.

My friends ask me: "And what did you do?" I say: Well, I did what everyone else did. I prayed a lot, and I wept a lot, and I was scared sometimes, and jumping with joy at others, but when I think back on it, I think that what I did most was laugh. "Laugh?", they say incredulously. "Are you crazy?" I answer: "A little, I suppose, but so is everybody else in that country. That's why I like it so much."

Yes, indeed, it *was* a lovely revolution. It changed the Philippines, and it made the whole world a better place. And it changed me, too. When I hear someone in the Reagan Administration saying "the United States' brilliantly planned and conceived policies caused the overthrow of Marcos" or when Ronald Reagan tells me that sending $100 million in arms to the Somozista Contra goons in Nicaragua is the moral equivalent of People Power in the Philippines, I no longer scream and throw bricks at my television set. I just laugh and turn it off.

To me, the lesson of the Philippine revolution is that one should never doubt that Good will overcome Evil, that Truth will overcome the Lie.

Someday my own country may truly stand for what the Philippines now represents: justice, decency, courage, democracy, freedom, truth. Not now, not yet, but I have hope that it will. The Philippines showed the way. Meanwhile, laughter helps.

RICHARD WILHELM B. RAGODON

I entered the dark dining hall of Malacañang. There was a piano. A guy went directly to it and started playing "*Ang Bayan Ko*" (My Homeland). Another person pointed his flashlight directly on the keys of the piano. Others gathered around and sang the song loudly and proudly. Everybody was happy. Some even cried while singing.

ALICIA YAEL HONASAN, sister of reformist leader Colonel Gregorio Honasan
(From her diary)

They won. They really, really won!

We just got back from an incognito tour of the surroundings. In our nightgowns, we rode around the area of Channel 4 and Quezon Boulevard, with Loloy and a carful of security guards tailing us. We just had to see the people for ourselves.

If I could have given the Filipino people a collective hug, I would have jumped off the Hiace and grabbed every yellow-ribboned being in sight. Without them, who knows what would have happened? No killing, no blood, no nothing. The guys from the Ministry of Defense didn't get to fire a shot and Marcos was gone. It's so unbelievable, it's awesome.

I was thinking in terms of compromises. Greg and the guys would get killed, but Marcos would leave. Or Greg would be okay, but Marcos wouldn't let him be. But no. No compromise, no hitch. We got Greg and the country back at the same time, and it was unbelievable.

Tita Lyd's neighbors took out some New Year leftovers and lit firecrackers all over the place.

God, you are something else. You knew all along, didn't you?

It feels so good to be here, now, even if I missed the rally of all rallies.

It feels so good to be Filipino, right here and now.

VICENTE T. PATERNO

I think that we were all surprised that there was very little violence. I think that this was because, to a large extent, it was a religious revolution. It reminded me really of the Crusades. People were willing to die but not to kill. And I thought that even if some soldiers were willing to shoot the people, they were not willing to shoot the crucifixes. Many of them come from the provinces where they were raised to fear God. They could never shoot at people who were praying. They could have shot people who were throwing stones, as they did during the rallies. But this was the first time that they were confronted with prayers. They did not know how to react. I think this was crucial to the whole nonviolence stance.

The people were there to defend the camp. They were not aggressors. We cannot pray and be violent at the same time. The religious character of the revolution made the revolution very unique. If you took away the religious flavor of the revolution, you would have removed the essence of it.

The red flags which had characterized the period between August 31, 1983 and the BAYAN Congress in 1985 were not there in Crame. Their boycott of the elections alienated them from the people. They tried to make a show but they were not really there. They were actually in Malacañang. While the stance on EDSA, Channel 4, and Veritas was defensive, in Malacañang it was offensive and aggressive. And that is characteristic of BAYAN and the National Democratic Front. I cannot imagine BAYAN in a religious revolution. It is antithetical.

ERNESTO B. FRANCISCO, JR.

Earlier, I talked to the barricaders. I told them that the reports we were getting did not mean that our job was through. Our task was to man the barricade and we were to stay till all was clear. They all agreed.

At four o'clock in the morning, our barricade seemed to be the only one left in the Crame-Aguinaldo area. There was an attempt to break it up when somebody stormed in to agitate that we join the celebration in Malacañang. We just stared him down.

Many vehicles tried to pass through our barricade. To give even a little way to them would subject the group to a shower of dust. On the first attempt, I submitted the issue to the group. The denial was unanimous. It was our first taste of the new democracy at work!

Before the sun was up, all indications were that this time it truly was all over. We decided to break up camp. There were congratulatory handshakes everywhere. We cleaned up the whole place.

Before finally leaving, we formed a small circle and prayed.

25 February 1986, late morning: Passersby cower as reformists and Marcos loyalists shoot it out for the control of the Channel 9 transmitter, above. At this time, Channel 9 was the only channel carrying Mr. Marcos' live telecasts. The Marcos loyalists arrive and surround the transmitter, right. Three of them climbed the transmitter tower to gain a vantage point but were gunned down from a reformist helicopter. His shroud flapping in the wind, one of the Marcos troops is lowered from the transmitter girders, opposite page. The gunbattle took place in a quiet residential area of Quezon City, far from the human barricades around Camp Crame.

A priest negotiates with Marcos loyalists in one of several AIFVs halted on Roces Avenue in Quezon City on its way to the battle for the TV stations, above. Out on the street, while battling for a TV station, a reformist and a Marcos loyalist embrace, right. They were classmates in the Philippine Military Academy. Looking on is Col. Mariano Santiago, who led the successful reformist take-over of Channel 4. As Marcos loyalists pull out from Channel 9, a nun shields them from the crowd, opposite page.

Marcos loyalist troops pull out from Channel 9 amid cheers from the crowd, above and opposite page. Earlier, a girl and her brother persuade some of these Marcos loyalists to join the people's side, left. In this manner, soldier by soldier, little by little, Mr. Marcos' military support dwindled.

With umbrellas and rosary beads, citizens kneel on the street in front of a column of tanks approaching the Circle in Quezon City, above. Most of the people in this area were defending their turf, a neighborhood which includes the residence of Cory Aquino, just behind the large building in the background. In the same place, two men hold their hands up in supplication as Marcos loyalists avoid looking at them, opposite page. The priest had been facing them alone, until another man joined him.

After praying on his knees in the middle of the street, this man takes up rosary beads and umbrella to confront the Marcos soldiers with guns cocked in their military vehicles in the Circle neighborhood, above. Emboldened and with one of them carrying a statue of the Blessed Virgin Mary, the people surround an armored personnel carrier, right. One of the soldiers on board holds out an appeasing hand. Patience, persuasion and prayers succeed: the military vehicles pull out of the Circle neighborhood, overleaf.

Guido Santos blows out nine candles on his birthday cake, left. Busy at the barricades on EDSA, his parents decided to hold Guido's party right there. "You'll have the biggest birthday party ever in the whole world," his father, Dr. Vivencio Santos, told Guido that morning, February 25. Guido shares his birthday fare with people at the barricades in front of Camp Crame, above and right. When his party was over, Guido joined his parents at the barricades.

With hands raised in the L sign for "Laban" (Fight), the guests in the presidential inauguration sing "Bayan Ko", led by President Corazon C. Aquino (right), Vice President Salvador H. Laurel (middle) and General Fidel V. Ramos (left). The sad but defiant 19th century protest song came to be the opposition anthem during the Marcos regime and often evoked tears, particularly during this hardwon Aquino-Laurel inaugural.

25 February 1986, late morning, Club Filipino in Greenhills, Metro Manila: As the seventh president of the Philippines, Corazon C. Aquino takes her oath of office on a Bible held by Doña Aurora Aquino, the mother of her slain husband. Her voice quiet and firm, President Aquino's oath was followed over the radio by millions of Filipinos. As she said "So help me God" to seal her oath, a tremendous cheer broke loose in the jampacked hall, outside on the street and all the way down to the barricaded EDSA nearby. People waved flags, threw hats into the air, drank toasts and danced at the barricades and at home in support of the Aquino presidency delivered to her by people power.

Meanwhile, in Malacañang, the official residence of the President, another crowd gathers for the Marcos inauguration despite the fact that his election was under strong public protest, above. The people were given special passes, free lunch and the opportunity to roam around the decorated Malacañang front garden, right. In the periphery, tanks and armored personnel carriers, like this one, guard Malacañang, left.

Paper flags drown the crowd at the Marcos inauguration in Malacañang, left. Besides the flags, the inaugural guests got t-shirts, hats and pins like those worn by the woman, above. Volunteers were also asked to help protect Mr. Marcos. Some did; they got identification badges which read: "I hereby pledge that I am a Marcos loyalist".

From the balcony of Malacañang, Mr. Marcos addresses the crowd at his inaugural, left. His entire family was with him but not Arturo Tolentino, his running mate, who did not take the oath of office as Vice President. Even before the people's uprising, not a single diplomatic mission accepted the invitation to attend this Marcos inaugural. As Mr. Marcos leaves the balcony, Imelda Marcos lingers in farewell, above. As it turned out, this was the last public appearance of Mr. Marcos for whom departure arrangements were already being made by the US embassy.

At the barbed wire barricades placed across all approaches to Malacañang, the crowds are restive as they pluck out the wires one by one, upper left, or run off with the barriers, lower left. Some individuals, however, simply and quietly stand at the barricades with their prayers, opposite page.

In Camp Crame, General Ramos monitors information about the pending departure of Mr. Marcos, above; then he confers with the commanders of the police and the constabulary about peace and order measures for Malacañang when it is vacated, upper right. Said Ramos with regret: "Mr.

Marcos is no longer the same President we used to know, to whom we pledged our loyalty and dedicated our services. He is no longer the able and capable commander-in-chief on whom we used to count. He had already put his personal interest above the interest of the people."

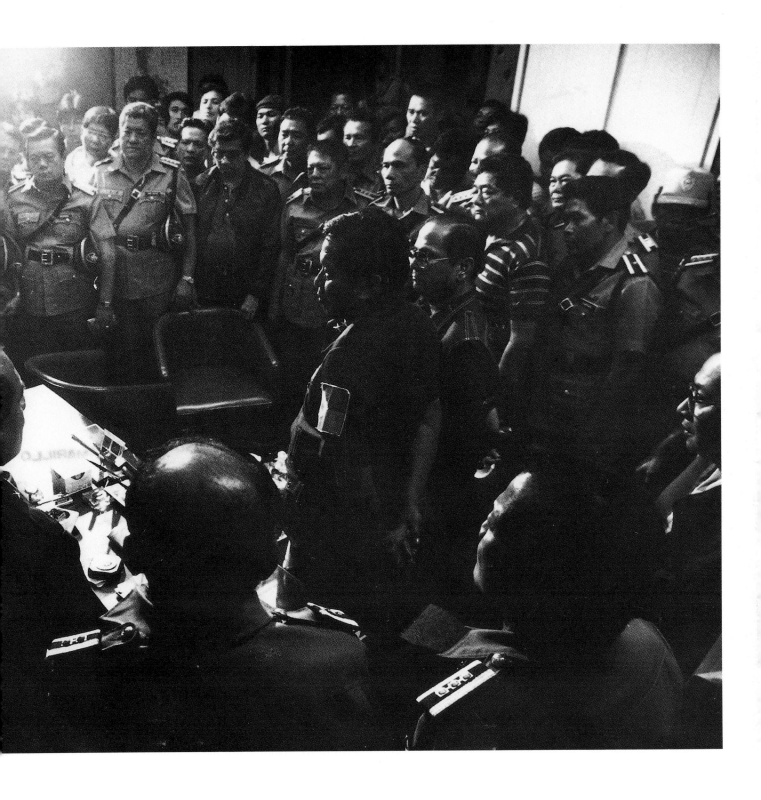

25 February 1986, evening: People surge into Malacañang within the hour after it was confirmed that Mr. Marcos and his family had left, above. Since 1972, when Mr. Marcos imposed martial law, only the officially invited people were allowed to enter Malacañang. In fact, traffic was closed for several blocks around Malacañang itself. On Tuesday night, all barri-

cades were lifted. The jubilation is clear in this housewife's smile as she cradles the gun of a reformist soldier, sent earlier by General Ramos to secure the premises, right. A statue of Our Lady presides on a stage in the Malacañang garden, overleaf. The statue was installed upon an instant shrine by devotees who carried it in procession into Malacañang.

Curious, unbelieving people move freely into the public and private rooms of Malacañang and scan, unchecked, the papers and books on Mr. Marcos' desk, above. They also saw the remnants of a barely eaten dinner and the bedroom of Mrs. Marcos, far right, upper and middle photographs. Outside, one of ten tanks which had

earlier guarded Mr. Marcos and his family, stands abandoned and festooned with the white cloth of surrender, lower right. The following day, newspapers carried front page news of Mr. Marcos' departure. A farmer in Agoo, La Union province, reads about it as he stands in front of the Marcos monument, overleaf.

Boys ring the bell of the San Pedro cathedral in Davao City the night Mr. Marcos left Manila, above. The celebrations continued the next day in many cities and towns: in Baguio, there was a parade on the main street, left; in Davao City, too, opposite page, upper left; and in Iloilo, there was dancing on the streets, opposite page, lower left.

28 February 1986, morning: Thousands hear a Thanksgiving Mass at the main setting of the four-day people's uprising on EDSA itself, left. Where before, there was a thicket of placards with various messages, there was only one message that morning: gratitude to the leaders of the uprising and to God's providence. A flagbearer raises the Philippine emblem high above the heads of people celebrating the victory on EDSA, above.

In prayer at the Thanksgiving Mass, Minister Enrile and General Ramos join a chain of linked hands, above. Singing "Bayan Ko", the theme song of the opposition, the people raise their hands as customary but this time not in protest but in victory, right.

The thanksgiving celebration on EDSA also served to introduce new heroes such as the members of the Reformist Movement who, by necessity, kept a low profile. Mostly graduates of the Philippine Military Academy, the reformist leaders formed the core support of Minister Enrile and General Ramos when they broke away from the Marcos government. Atop an armored personnel carrier, they savor victory, right. Nuns—the unexpected heroes of the people's uprising, whose prayerful resistance earned for them labels such as "the unarmed forces" and "anti-tank weapons"—meet their military counterparts, above.

2 March 1986, Rizal Park, Manila: In the same place where two times before in political rallies, Cory Aquino had gathered crowds estimated at above two million each time, they gather again—in greater number—to share the victory, right. They are of all ages but of the same celebrating mood, above and left. Amid thunderous cheers, President Corazon Aquino addresses her people, overleaf.

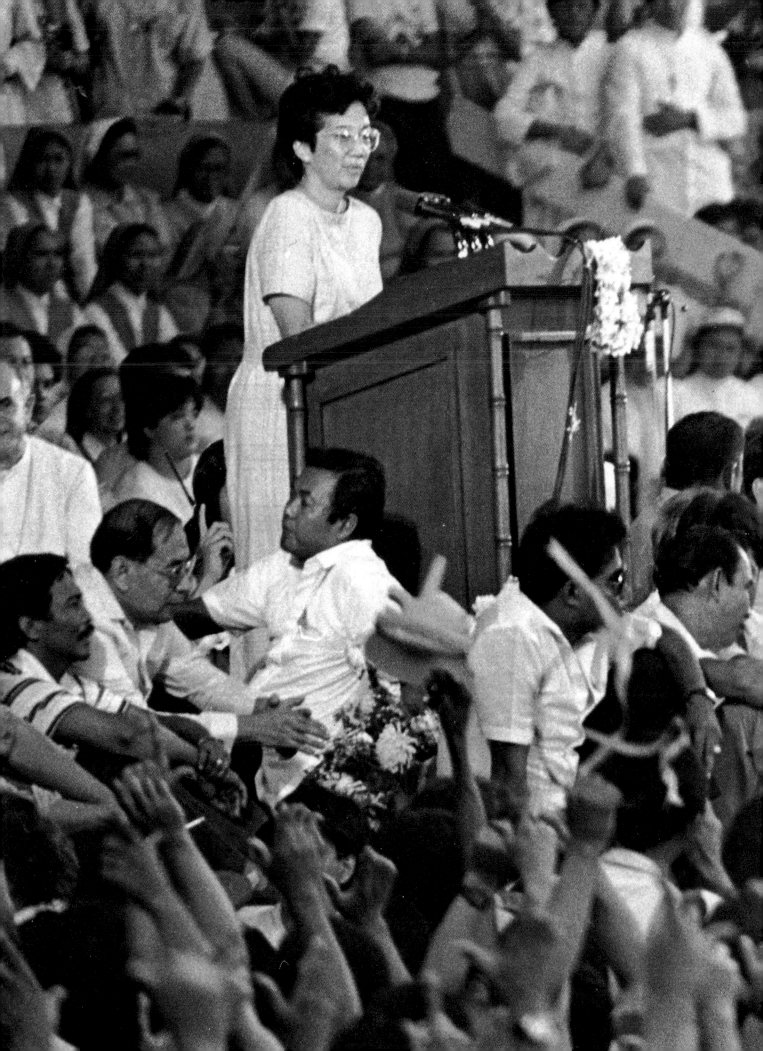

Epilogue: The Wisdom of Nonviolence

Withstanding injustice and violence from physical harassment with small weapons or with tanks and assault troops or with goons—this is people power. The will not to give in to the injustice or the violence, the determination to pay the price even to death—this is people power.

The action in small numbers and in big numbers from 30 computer tabulators to 30,000 NAMFREL volunteers to 3,000,000 defending Camp Aguinaldo, Camp Crame, Radio Veritas, and MBS Channel 4—this is people power.

Going to the polls and voting according to their conscience for Cory in spite of the harassment and intimidations or the effort to guard the ballots and the tally sheets, being hurt and perhaps killed in the process—this is people power. And doing this in the millions through an electoral process—this is people power.

Gathering in the millions to assert victory in spite of the cheating and in the face of a *Batasan* proclamation that Mr. Marcos won and to do this with an air of festiveness—this is Filipino people power.

The effort of NAMFREL volunteers and watchers to ensure honesty and the sanctity of the ballot, to do this in the face of threats and knowing the history of killings in the elections of 1984—this is people power.

Why or how could Filipinos do this? Is there a way of explaining this? Is there anyone among 54 million Filipinos who had an inkling this would come about? Winning our freedom, forcing Mr. Marcos into exile, and doing all this in the most nonviolent way in all world history?

We would like to attempt an answer.

Our answer will run along lines of faith and sequencing of events, and the ordinary human factor of the patience of the Filipino. We will dwell on each of these points. But we will also show how the elements mesh and reinforce each other.

We would like to start with some external event which all of us know as a data of experience—the death, the martyrdom of Ninoy Aquino. People began to move as one and in numbers when literally millions—in all hours of the day and night, in rain and sun—filed past the bier of Ninoy to do him honor. Yes, they came to honor Ninoy. But they also came to register their silent and quiet protest against such a public act of murder.

By their coming to see Ninoy, people were saying No to Marcos. In the first and biggest show of people power, they took part in the long funeral march. They lined the streets. All told, there were two million of them. This people power was initiated and triggered by the death of Ninoy.

Never had people moved with a cause in such huge numbers as they did for Ninoy's funeral. It went for a whole day. It went in sunshine and in rain, in thunder and in lightning. It wound up by candlelight in the night in Manila Memorial Park.

Following this was the formation of cause-oriented groups, marches, demonstrations, and rallies. The seed that had fallen to the ground and died bore a hundredfold of critically conscious, unafraid, liberated Filipinos. For the most part, they desired to be nonviolent, but did not always succeed. During these rallies, people were being prepared and trained to withstand police and military harassments. And this came in handy in facing the tanks, Marine assault troops, and Scout Rangers.

There were those gatherings—on August 21 and September 21, 1984, of mixed groups of red and yellow, then the November 27 birthday of Ninoy in 1984, only yellow showing up; the split demonstration and rally of August 21, 1985; next the million signatures which persuaded Cory Aquino to lend her person to lead in a presidential election; then the revelation in the final campaign rally of a crowd in the millions led by a charismatic and well-loved leader in the person of Cory. People knew—they felt in their bones—that they had numbers, they had power. Add to that the thousands that gathered in other big cities. People were so sure Cory was going to win. Only massive cheating could prevent her from becoming President of the Philippines.

When the massive cheating came to light, the people, reinforced by the Statement of the Bishops, for a second time gathered in the millions to tell themselves, the whole nation, and the world that Cory, their candidate, was President. They were going to stand by this truth. They went home with a program of activities to show they were not submitting to Mr. Marcos' spurious show of authority.

That was people power. With all these sequence of events, of exercises and flexing of muscles, a feeling of power, unity, and capability was being forged. People were saying that by Easter, at the longest within three months, Mr. Marcos would be unseated.

But the sequencing of events brought in one factor that no scenario ever provided for—Mr. Enrile's and General Ramos' defection from Mr. Marcos. They had inside information that the President had an arrest order for Mr. Enrile. They conferred and decided to dig in. They also asked the people—people power—to come and protect them.

There is great humility in that. There is also great wisdom. When an army asks to be protected by its people, that is a humbling posture. When an army decides to go on people's power and nonviolence, that is wisdom. And these have been proved.

This sequence of events tells us that people power did not come about in a day, not even in months. It took a good two years and a half since the martyrdom of Ninoy.

But nobody was programming these two years and a half. No one had set a time table. Who then was orchestrating all these events and activities? For us Christians and for others who believe in a Supreme Being, we can assign this orchestration to God. This does not detract from the human element and factors that contributed to people power and its astounding result. We can say for example that God was working through and in Mr. Marcos' decision to have snap presidential elections before 1987 when it is stipulated. Whatever the intentions and motives of Mr. Marcos, we had the snap elections and every event connected with it brought us to where we are now. If there had been no snap elections, we would still be waiting for 1987.

In the same vein, whatever the causes and emergency situations that Mr. Enrile and General Ramos saw in their predicament, they decided to cut their allegiance to Mr. Marcos and forged that people power-military combine. I think we can all agree that, if the two did not decide and act the way they did, we could still be boycotting San Miguel Beer, Rustan's, and getting several banks to have a run in protest against Marcos. And who knows how long that would have taken? God acts through human purposes and human decisions. Without violating our freedoms, he can set a series of events to erupt or come about.

God wants this proclaimed to the world: Nonviolence can work. It does work.

But a deeper interpretation needs to be given about the role of faith in this people power that we acted out and experienced with such amazing and unexpected results.

From the Bible, particularly that of Exodus, we know that divine revelation—God's communication of his saving acts—comes through events. Externally these events are part of ordinary political, social, and ideological affairs and struggles. But those who have faith can see beyond political movements the pattern of God's designs and purposes. A Christian has been defined as one who knows. Knows what? That God has empowered him or the community to carry out and continue the saving designs of God. Where or how does one read in the events of February 22-25 the saving acts of God?

We will cite one or two examples and those of us who took part and went through the experience can unravel how God was carrying out the salvation that has resulted in our political liberation. No matter what dispositions of fear and uncertainty or sheer adventurism or calculated risk or deep commitment we carried within us, we went to man the barricades in Crame, Aguinaldo, Channel 4, Radio Veritas.

We knew in our hearts that the defection of Minister Enrile and General Ramos was the beginning of disintegration in the camp of Mr. Marcos. Since they needed to be protected, even defended, we went to shield them with our corporate bodies, presence, and number. We must not miss at this point that the willingness to pay the price—the possibility of death—all of a sudden possessed us.

This quality of commitment, as we explained earlier was little by little firmed up in us through many rallies and challenges and experiences within the last snap elections. This commitment is a grace of God, a gift of God, the spirit of Jesus sharing his own commitment to the cross with us.

The other grace of God is simply this: facing the tanks and armored personnel carriers and the combat-ready soldiers with our bodies, our prayer, our Filipino piety with images of Mary and the crucifix. Our faith has made us this kind of people, both us who were resisting as well as the soldiers who were ordered to attack. We have not interviewed any of the soldiers or tank personnel, but we venture to suggest that when the soldiers saw praying unafraid people, cheerful, offering flowers and cigarettes, willing to come under the tank treads, these effectively tied their hands and changed their will not to carry out their mission of destruction.

They might as well not have had guns,

because they had no will to squeeze the triggers. They might as well have had no tanks and armored cars, because their human concern for the lives of thousands was a stronger brake that kept their armored vehicles at a standstill. They had only one gear available: reverse gear. That is what they used.

God who is the author of life, who is more interior to us than we are to ourselves, was powerfully at work within us and was powerfully at work with the soldiers. What we say of the soldier, we can say the same of Colonel Antonio Sotelo. "I followed my conscience," he said. He led 16 combat pilots to land in Crame to join the rebels instead of attacking the stronghold. Acting according to conscience, whether in diverting one's attack helicopter to friendly allies or writing down Cory in the ballot in the face of threats and money, this is God's grace working deeply within the believers' hearts.

Many have called the concatenation of events a miracle. And it is. The miracle is the mystery of God's grace powerfully working in the hearts of each one of us. The miracle is God bringing about events both big and small, which no one of us thought about, much less planned.

Cory has been performing as an inspired woman-leader. Another quiet gentle woman, loved by Filipinos, was instrumental in the miracle or victory through nonviolence. She is Mary, our mother. Her instrument was the Rosary, the unrelenting Hail Marys that filled the atmosphere; the mantle of her protection was her many images and statues—one of them was prominently displayed on General Ramos' table.

She took care and made sure that we, her devoted children, who had already suffered for so many years, would be completely delivered from bloodshed. God was actively present during those February days. So was Mary.

People power then is people with God, people with Mary, people with Cory, people with the military.

People power is grounded and based on God's saving activity within us as a people. In the dictum of Augustine: God created us without us, but God will not save us without us. Our political liberation has been our work and struggle and sacrifice—but equally and internally it has been the work of God.

Because we interpret the events in the light of faith and acknowledge God's saving activity in all that has happened, we must ask what God wants to communicate to us by his saving activity and presence. What does God wish us to proclaim to the world through our nonviolent revolution? Simply this: the political problems of people can be solved without recourse to arms or violence.

The world's problems are best solved if we respect the humanity, the dignity of every human person concerned. The desire to be violent or to use violence can be tamed and diminished, if we show love, care, joy to those who are unjust and wish to be violent. Violence addresses the aggressor. Nonviolence searches out and addresses the humanity in the enemy or oppressor. When that common humanity is touched, then the other is helped to recognize the human person within and ceases to be inhuman, unjust, and violent.

One does not have to be a Christian to reach out to the humanity in the other. Christian or not, believer or unbeliever, every single human being has been created as an image of God. To recognize that image and to respect it in an absolute way is to live the Gospel radically and in the nonviolent way.

Our darkest hour could not take away our humor. Our tensest moments could not cancel out our joy. Our patience, our resilience, our humor paid out. Sweeping away Marcos and his government, installing Cory and initiating a new revolutionary government—it was a bloodless revolution.

Unless we take these qualities of ours as a people, we will not understand Filipino people power. This patience, this resilience, this humor and joy will be—along with the grace of God—our most valuable assets as we move to reconstruct and build our nation from the ruins.

The eyes of the world are upon us. Let us share with all peoples these great things that the Lord has done to us. Let us show that we can gain liberation in a nonviolent way. Let us show that we can construct a world without guns and without arms.

The world is best reconstructed by valuing people and human lives, by reaching out in joy and dialogue. That is Filipino people power. This will be our contribution to human progress and peace. By this, we proclaim to the world that God, in whom we believe, has a hand and will continue to have a hand in our history as a people.

JOSE BLANCO, S.J.
Secretary-General, Aksyon Para sa Kapayapaan at Katarungan (Action for Peace and Justice)

Appendix

HISTORICAL NOTES

THE PEOPLE'S REVOLUTION
(February 22 to 25, 1986)

February 22, Saturday At 6:45 p.m., Defense Minister Juan Ponce Enrile and Vice Chief of Staff Fidel Ramos announce at a news conference their withdrawal of support for Ferdinand Marcos. Enrile charges Marcos with committing massive fraud in the snap elections—an offense, he says, that has forfeited the mandate of the people. Enrile and Ramos declare that the rightful President of the Republic is Corazon Aquino. Ramos calls on the Armed Forces to join the rebellion against the government. With 200 supporters, Enrile and Ramos barricade themselves in the Ministry of National Defense at Camp Aguinaldo to await an attack.

The news conference is broadcast nationwide over Radio Veritas at 9:00 p.m. An hour later, Marcos calls his own news conference to report an aborted coup by Enrile and Ramos. He urges them to "stop this stupidity."

In a message aired over Radio Veritas, Jaime Cardinal Sin, Archbishop of Manila, calls on all peace-loving Filipinos to bring food to the soldiers at Camps Aguinaldo and Crame, pray, and keep vigil. "They are our friends," he says. The call is heeded. Assembling at the camps, people form almost at once a human barricade, hoping to block an attack. Even soldiers loyal to Marcos will not shoot defenseless Filipinos—or so they hope. For once, the civilians are out to protect the military.

For that night at least, they are safe. Enrile and General Fabian Ver, Armed Forces Chief of Staff, have agreed that neither side will make a move until morning. Military officers begin to defect to Enrile and Ramos, but they are still too few.

Presidential candidate Corazon Aquino, caught by surprise by the rebellion while leading rallies in the South, hears reports that there will be an attempt on her life. Her supporters hide her in a convent.

February 23, Sunday Morning: At dawn, armed men destroy Radio Veritas transmitter, cutting off the people in the provinces from events in the capital. The station switches to its standby transmitter, which is limited in range and can only broadcast for a few more hours.

People continue to come to the camps. Barricades are set up. Food comes in abundance. Priests say Sunday Mass for the people.

Afternoon: At a news conference, Marcos claims that he has control of the situation. Enrile and Ramos demand that he step down to make way for Corazon Aquino.

At 3:00 p.m., a large Marine force led by tanks and armored personnel carriers heads for the camps. They are stopped a mile from their target by tens of thousands of people forming a human barricade. The Marine commander, Brigadier General Artemio Tadiar, threatens to shoot if the blockade is not lifted. The people do not budge. They pray the Rosary, offer the soldiers cigarettes, and ask them to join the rebellion. The Marines start the tanks' engines and edge them forward. Still the people will not move. The Marines withdraw without firing a shot.

Evening: Radio Veritas signs off as its standby transmitter fails.

February 24, Monday Morning: At half-past midnight, the search for another radio station pays off. Civilians commandeer DZRJ and begin broadcasting reports of government troop movements and other vital information to the people in the barricades. DZRJ is now DZRB, Radio Bandido. Mindful of what happened to Radio Veritas, the announcer June Keithley keeps the station's location secret. Bandido's broadcasts help the people get into position and keep morale at the barricades high.

At dawn, 3,000 Marines attack and capture the Logistics Command on the east side of Camp Aguinaldo. The people at the barricades are teargassed and dispersed.

The 15th Air Force Strike Wing takes to the air with orders to attack the camps. The seven helicopter gunships, under Colonel Antonio Sotelo, have enough firepower to destroy the camps. But the pilots cannot bring themselves to do it. They land and defect to the rebel forces.

At this time, Keithley receives reports that Marcos has fled the country and that he has been seen in Guam. She broadcasts the report. The people at the camps break into celebration. There is cheering, weeping, dancing in the streets. Hundreds of thousands come to the main gate of Camp Crame and hear Enrile and Ramos declare themselves members of the "New Armed Forces of the People."

At 9:00 a.m., however, Marcos appears on television, on government-owned Channel 4. He declares he will never leave. General Ver appears on screen and asks permission to finish off the rebel forces but is restrained by Marcos. Then Channel 4 goes off the air.

Reformist soldiers under Colonel Mariano Santiago have taken over the station. The channel that used to broadcast government propaganda is now the People's Television.

Afternoon: Rebel helicopter gunships attack Villamor Air Base and destroy enemy helicopters on the ground. A helicopter fires a rocket at Malacañang, causing minor damage. Defectors have begun to come in droves. By now the rebellion that began with a couple of hundred men has the allegiance of the majority of the 200,000-member Armed Forces.

Marcos imposes a dusk-to-dawn curfew; it is ignored.

He announces that he will not resign, determined to go on with his inauguration the next morning. Corazon Aquino announces that she will set up a provisional government by morning.

February 25, Tuesday Corazon Aquino takes her oath of office at Club Filipino before Supreme Court Senior Justice Claudio Teehankee. An hour later, Marcos holds his own inauguration at Malacañang. Channels 2, 9, and 13 cover the ceremony. They are cut off suddenly.

Reformist troops have taken the transmitter tower of the three channels. Without television, Marcos finally loses control.

He calls Enrile to offer him power in a provisional government; Enrile turns him down. Marcos calls Senator Paul Laxalt to ask for advice. He is told: "Mr. President, I think you should cut, and cut cleanly."

Marcos makes a final call to Enrile asking for safe conduct for his family. The Marcoses then pack hurriedly. At 9:00 p.m., four American helicopters fly the Marcos party from Malacañang to Clark Air Base. The next day, they stop over at Guam, then fly to Hawaii.

FILIPINOS FOR FREEDOM:
AGAINST ALL ODDS

Filipinos have been fighting for freedom for the past 400 years. Chronicled below are some of their most heroic moments.

1521 The Battle of Mactan. Ferdinand Magellan tries to claim the Philippines for Spain. The chieftain of Mactan Island, Lapu-Lapu, defies Magellan's demand for tribute. Magellan invades Mactan, confident of victory against an enemy armed only with clubs, spears, and arrows. He is hacked to death, and his fleet suffers heavy losses. The Spaniards are barely able to make it back home.

1565-1898 Muslim Resistance Against The Spaniards.
The Muslims of Maguindanao and Sulu put up the fiercest rebellion against the Spaniards. After Miguel López de Legazpi establishes a foothold in the Philippines, expedition after expedition is sent to pacify the Muslim South. But the Muslims will not be defeated. Sultan Kudarat of Cotabato leads the rebellion with such audacity and vigor that he is even able to take the offensive. Even the Spanish strongholds in Zamboanga and in the Visayan islands are not safe from him. Kudarat's heirs carry on after his death. The Muslims are never conquered.

BATTLE ZONE METRO MANILA

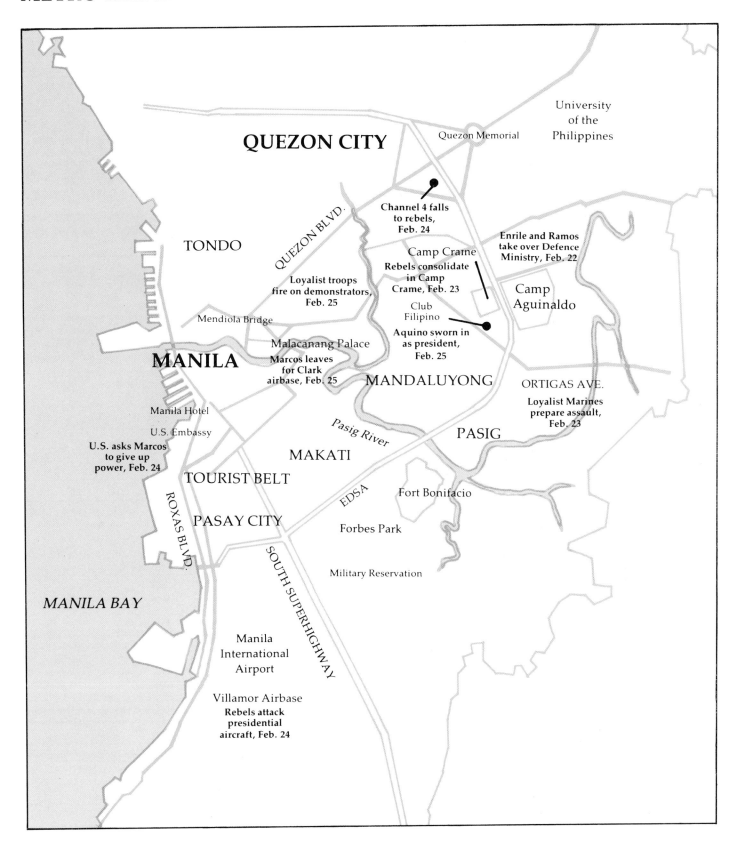

QUEZON CITY

University of the Philippines

Quezon Memorial

Channel 4 falls to rebels, Feb. 24

TONDO

QUEZON BLVD.

Camp Crame

Enrile and Ramos take over Defence Ministry, Feb. 22

Loyalist troops fire on demonstrators, Feb. 25

Rebels consolidate in Camp Crame, Feb. 23

Camp Aguinaldo

Mendiola Bridge

Club Filipino

Aquino sworn in as president, Feb. 25

Malacanang Palace

MANILA

Marcos leaves for Clark airbase, Feb. 25

MANDALUYONG

ORTIGAS AVE.

Loyalist Marines prepare assault, Feb. 23

Manila Hotel

U.S. Embassy

Pasig River

PASIG

U.S. asks Marcos to give up power, Feb. 24

MAKATI

TOURIST BELT

EDSA

Fort Bonifacio

ROXAS BLVD.

PASAY CITY

Forbes Park

Military Reservation

MANILA BAY

SOUTH SUPERHIGHWAY

Manila International Airport

Villamor Airbase

Rebels attack presidential aircraft, Feb. 24

1744-1829 The Longest Revolt. Francisco Dagohoy leads 3,000 men in revolt on Bohol Island after a Spanish priest refuses to grant his brother a Catholic burial. Dagohoy's stronghold in the Bohol mountains remains impregnable for many years, during which his men have virtual control of the island. After 85 years, the Dagohoy revolt, now numbering 20,000 men, is finally suppressed by an overwhelming force of Spanish and native troops.

1762-63 The Silang Revolt. The British attack and capture Manila. Taking advantage of the situation, Diego Silang leads an uprising in Ilocos province, north of Manila. His forces score many victories. He tries to strike an alliance with the British, but is assassinated by the Spanish. His wife, Gabriela, takes command of his forces. In a few months, she too is captured and hanged.

1840-41 The Tayabas Rebellion. Apolinario de la Cruz, a devout Catholic, seeks entry into the Franciscan Order but is turned down because he is a native. He organizes his own religious sect, the Cofradía de San José, and attracts adherents in Tayabas, Laguna, and Batangas. He becomes known as Hermano Pule, or Brother Pule.
The Spaniards grow suspicious of his sect and mount a campaign against him. The rebellion ends when Pule is captured and executed. A few faithful followers return to the mountains of Tayabas, where they continue to practice their own religion.

1872 The Cavite Mutiny. The privileges exempting workers in the arsenal and barracks of Fort San Felipe in Cavite province from forced labor and paying tribute are withdrawn. The workers mutiny but are quickly crushed.
The Cavite Mutiny is in itself a minor incident. But it assumes national significance when a number of prominent liberals, including the Filipino clergy, are rounded up on the charge that they had conspired in the revolt. Three Filipino priests—José Burgos, Mariano Gómez, and Jacinto Zamora—are found guilty and garroted. Their deaths spark the nationalist movement that will eventually result in the Revolution of 1896.

1892-98 The Katipunan Revolt. A secret society, the *Kataastaasan Kagalang-galangang Katipunan ng mga Anak ng Bayan* (Supreme and Most Honorable Association of the Sons of the Motherland), begins organizing a rebel army. It is discovered in 1896, and is forced to take to the hills.
In the famous "Cry of Balintawak", the *Katipuneros* tear their *cedulas* (receipts for tributes) in a symbolic gesture of defiance against Spanish sovereignty.
In the early skirmishes in Rizal province, the force led by Andres Bonifacio, the *Katipunan's* founder, suffers heavy losses. In the nearby province of Cavite, however, the *Katipuneros* under Emilio Aguinaldo win battle after battle. Cavite becomes the rebel stronghold and Aguinaldo takes over the rebel forces. Factional strife, however, divides the rebels and allows the Spaniards to regain lost ground. By 1897, Aguinaldo's weakened forces are forced to agree to a truce. Aguinaldo then goes into exile in Hong Kong.

1899 The Filipino-American War. War breaks out when an American sentry shoots a Filipino soldier at the San Juan Bridge.
It rages for three years, the Filipinos eventually having to resort to guerrilla tactics. In March of 1901, Aguinaldo is captured in Palanan, Isabela. The Americans declare the war officially over. Pockets of resistance remain, but the guerrillas are considered by the Americans to be no better than ordinary bandits and thieves.

1902-06 The Sakay Revolt. General Macario Sakay continues the war against the American forces after the majority of Filipino generals surrender. He gathers the remnants of the army in mountain strongholds. He draws up a constitution, sets up a provisional government, and conducts successful guerrilla operations. After four years, Sakay is finally captured. The Americans declare him guilty of banditry and execute him. Sakay protests to the very end that he is not a bandit but a patriot fighting for his country's independence.

1935 The Sakdal Uprising. Shortly after the inauguration of the Philippine Commonwealth, a group of nationalist peasants from the provinces of Laguna, Rizal, Bulacan, and Cavite take up arms against the government, which they consider anti-nationalist. These rebels are members of the mass-based Sakdal Movement, organized by Benigno Ramos. The uprising, not sanctioned by Ramos, is quelled within a day by the Philippine Constabulary. Ramos, however, is in Japan at the time and so eludes arrest.

1942 The Battle of Bataan and Corregidor. The Filipino and American forces make their last stand against the Japanese in the Bataan Peninsula and the island fortress of Corregidor, which guards the entrance to Manila Bay. With American troops and supplies committed to the war in Europe, no help is forthcoming. Their effort is valiant, but lack of supplies, the spread of malaria, and Japanese firepower prove to be too much. On April 9, 1942, the defenders of Bataan surrender. They begin the infamous "Death March" to the Japanese prison camp in Capas, Tarlac. The Battle of Corregidor ends a month later.
Though it ends in defeat, the effort of the defenders of Bataan and Corregidor is not in vain. It buys time for the Americans to regroup. In 1944, they retake the islands.

FERDINAND EDRALIN MARCOS
(1917-   )

The man who would be President: his was a story of success. It was a long, arduous climb to the highest office in the land. He worked hard to achieve it. It was not an easy road—there were frustrations, obstacles, and public scandals along the way. But he made it. Despite seemingly irreversible defeats, he fulfilled what he promised his mother: "For every tear you shed now, there will be victory."

September 11, 1917 Born in Sarrat, Ilocos Norte, the eldest son of Mariano Marcos and Josefa Edralin, both teachers.

1923-29 Studies in several elementary schools as his parents' assignments change constantly: Sarrat Central School, Shamrock Elementary School, Laoag; and Ermita Elementary School.

1929-33 Enters the University of the Philippines High School.

1933-36 Enrolls in a Liberal Arts course, University of the Philippines. Commissioned as third lieutenant (apprentice officer) in the Philippine Constabulary Reserve after having been a battalion commander, with the rank of cadet major, and team captain of the university rifle and pistol team.

1935 Assemblyman Julio Nalundasan, newly declared winner from Ilocos Norte and political rival of ex-Representative Mariano Marcos, is shot dead while brushing his teeth in front of his dining-room window. Suspicion falls on the Marcoses.

1936-39 Enters the University of the Philippines College of Law. Joins the Upsilon Sigma Phi Fraternity, which specializes in political heckling of Manuel Quezon's Commonwealth government. Excels in academics and oratory, and joins the debating team.

1938 Arrested on a charge of conspiracy in the murder of Julio Nalundasan.

April 1939 Receives his Bachelor of Laws, *cum laude;* would have been class valedictorian and *magna cum laude* if imprisonment had not prevented him from attending several weeks of class. Reviews for the bar examination in prison.

August 1939 Posts bail in order to take bar exam.

September 1939 Stands trial in Laoag Provincial Court of First Instance along with his father and two uncles.

November 1939 Emerges bar topnotcher. Summoned by university dean on suspicion of cheating in the bar exam, withstands the interrogation, and justifies his high scores.

Within the year, Judge Roman Cruz of the Laoag Provincial Court finds Marcos guilty of murder and sentences him to imprisonment.

October 1940 Appeals his own case and defends himself before the Supreme Court. The Supreme Court, under Chief Justice Jose P. Laurel, having found the prosecution's case and testimonies contradictory, grants Marcos an acquittal. (He has not even begun his practice of law but has already won his own case before the highest court of the land.)

1941-42 Sees action in Bataan.

1943-45 Joins guerrilla units in Luzon.

1946 Returns to Manila to resume law practice.

1947 President Manuel Roxas invites him to be a member of the Philippine Veterans' Commission.

1948 Gives up planned studies at Harvard to serve as technical assistant to President Roxas.
Campaigns for a seat in Congress with the promise: "Elect me a Congressman now, and I pledge you an Ilocano President in twenty years."

1949 At 32, elected congressman of Ilocos Norte, under the Liberal Party. Becomes the youngest member of the House of Representatives.

1953 Re-elected congressman of Ilocos Norte as a Liberal despite the *Nacionalista* sweep under Ramon Magsaysay.

May 1, 1954 Marries Imelda Romualdez, a 23-year-old beauty from Tacloban, Leyte, after an 11-day courtship and a civil wedding. Principal sponsor is President Ramon Magsaysay and the reception is at the Malacañang Palace grounds. The Marcos children: Maria Imelda (Imee), born in 1955; Ferdinand, Jr. (Bongbong), in 1958; and Irene in 1960.

1957 Re-elected congressman for the second time, the only one in the district to be given three terms in the legislature. Serves as minority floor leader and acting temporary president of the Liberal Party.

1959 Runs for the Senate and tops the election, besting 22 other candidates. Is the first minority party candidate to top the senatorial elections. Becomes minority floor leader of the Senate.

1961 Gives way to Diosdado Macapagal as Liberal Party presidential candidate on the agreement that Macapagal will support his candidacy in 1965. Serves as Macapagal's campaign manager and is elected Liberal Party president.

1963 Elected Senate President, replacing 80-year-old *Nacionalista* Party president Eulogio Rodriguez.

April 1964 Sworn in as a *Nacionalista* by Jose B. Laurel, Jr., after incumbent President Macapagal refuses to honor their agreement and decides to run for re-election.

November 1964 With Imelda's help in her first active political role as campaign manager, wins the *Nacionalista* Party presidential nomination, besting other NP stalwarts.

1965 Involved in one of the most vicious and expensive presidential campaigns in Philippine electoral history up to that time. Harnesses Imelda's capacity to campaign extensively with her coterie of Blue Ladies. Both candidates spend nearly 32 million pesos for the campaign; at one point, even Imelda's betrothal and wedding rings have to be pawned.

November 1965 Elected sixth President of the Republic, defeating Macapagal by 670,000 votes.

January 1966 In his State-of-the-Nation address, vows to be a "leader of the people." Reiterates his inaugural vow "to make this nation great again."

1969 Re-elected President for another four-year term, defeating Sergio Osmeña, Jr. This is the first Presidential re-election in Philippine history.

1972 Declares martial law and suspends the 1935 Constitution, which would have denied him a third term.

1973 Promulgates a new Constitution. Written under his influence, the document entitles him to stay in office. Through a manipulated referendum, he is "mandated" to continue as President until the end of martial law.

1981 Lifts martial law and allows holding of presidential elections. Re-elected President for a six-year term.

1985 Calls for snap presidential elections a year ahead of schedule, hoping to renew his mandate for another six-year term.

1986 Proclaimed winner of the snap presidential elections by his controlled National Assembly despite the discrepancy in the poll count and the opposition of assemblymen in the minority party. Deposed by a people's revolt, initiated by a defection of a segment of the military; but not after he has himself inaugurated in a private ceremony in Malacañang Palace as the re-elected President. Flees the country into exile.

THE MARCOS REGIME: MAJOR EVENTS

Ferdinand Edralin Marcos came to power in 1965 and remained President for the next twenty years. By using the martial-law provision of the 1935 Constitution, he was able to impose authoritarian rule and prolong his tenure. Popular protest against his regime came to a boil in 1972 but was driven underground or stifled during the rest of the decade. Marcos consolidated his regime into one of the most powerful and entrenched political dynasties in modern history.

1965 Ferdinand Marcos, running against re-electionist Diosdado Macapagal, wins the Presidency.

1966 U.S. President Lyndon B. Johnson, seeking support for American involvement in South Vietnam, calls a summit meeting in Manila among his allies in Asia and the Pacific. The Marcos government responds by sending an engineering battalion to Vietnam despite popular clamor for non-involvement.

1968 Jose Maria Sison, founder of *Kabataang Makabayan* (KM) [Nationalist Youth], a militant student group, organizes the Communist Party of the Philippines. The CPP takes over the struggle from the old *Partido Komunista ng Pilipinas* (PKP) [Communist Party of the Philippines], whose leaders were mostly in prison.

1969 The CPP forms an alliance with the remnants of the old *Hukbong Mapagpalaya ng Bayan* (HMB) [National Liberation Army], the military arm of PKP, under Bernabe Buscayno, alias "Kumander Dante." It is renamed the New People's Army (NPA).

January 1970 A series of rallies is launched by radical and moderate student groups protesting the inclusion of politicians in the forthcoming Constitutional Convention and the constitutional provision being considered which would allow the incumbent President to run for a third term. Violence erupts when riot police are unleashed on the students. The first Battle of Mendiola is fought when students overrun military lines and ram a commandeered firetruck against the gates of Malacañang. The bloody episode begins a wave of protest known as the "First-Quarter Storm."

February 1971 Students barricade the University of the Philippines campus and establish the "Diliman Commune."

June 1971 The Constitutional Convention convenes to replace the 1935 Constitution written during the American colonial period.

311

August 1971 Two hand grenades are thrown at the stage of a Liberal Party rally at Plaza Miranda. Several LP stalwarts are injured, among them Jovito Salonga and Gerardo Roxas.
President Marcos suspends the privilege of the writ of habeas corpus.

November 1971 The Liberal Party wins the majority of the Senate seats. Only two of Marcos' party candidates are elected.

January 1972 Constitutional Convention delegate Eduardo Quintero of Leyte exposes Marcos' bribery attempt. He alleges that Marcos has been giving the other convention delegates bribe money to make them vote against the Rama resolution which would bar him from running for a third term and his relatives from seeking the Presidency.

July 1972 Government authorities seize a shipment of contraband firearms found abroad a Philippine merchant ship, M.V. *Caragatan,* docked in Palanan, Isabela. It is meant, allegedly, for the NPA.

September 1972 Bombings rock Metro Manila. Targets are department stores and government buildings.
Senator Benigno Aquino denounces before Congress "Oplan Sagittarius," a plan to place certain areas of the country under martial law.

September 22, 1972 The car of Defense Secretary Juan Ponce Enrile is "ambushed." No one is killed.

September 23, 1972 President Marcos declares martial law. Scores of opposition leaders and media personalities are detained, among them Senators Benigno Aquino and Jose Diokno. Congress is closed and the Constitution suspended.

January 1973 The final draft of the 1973 Constitution, approved by the Convention in the absence of opposition delegates, is ratified not through a plebiscite but by a dubious *viva voce* vote of so-called citizens' assemblies.

March 1973 The Supreme Court rules that since no legal obstacle exists, the 1973 Constitution is in force.

July 27, 1973 President Marcos holds a referendum to find out if the people want him to continue serving beyond his term so he can finish the reforms he began under martial law. According to official figures, 96.7 per cent of the 18 million voters vote "Yes."

September 21, 1974 Anniversary of the declaration of martial law. Marcos issues Presidential Decree 557 creating the *barangay* as the smallest unit of government. This, according to the decree, would enable citizens to take part in the shaping of government policies. September 21 henceforth becomes *Barangay* Day.

February 27, 1975 Marcos holds another referendum in which two questions are asked. One: do the people approve the manner by which Marcos issues decrees and proclamations with the force of law? Two: do they want him to continue exercising such powers? Out of 22 million voters, 88.69 per cent answer "Yes" to question number one; 87.51 per cent say "Yes" to question number two. Calling of an interim Legislative Assembly as provided for in the new Constitution is delayed as a result of this.
The First Lady, Imelda Marcos, becomes Governor of Metro Manila by virtue of a "popular draft."

October 16, 1976 Another referendum is held asking the people whether or not they approve of amendments to the new Constitution that 1) allow for the creation of a *Batasang Pambansa* (National Assembly) in lieu of the Interim Assembly; 2) allow Marcos to exercise his power until martial law is lifted; 3) give Marcos emergency legislative powers (Amendment 6) when the *Batasan* is not in session or when he deems it necessary; 4) give him immunity from suits even after his term. The results are in Marcos' favor.

1977 Jose Ma. Sison, CPP head, is captured. Bernabe Buscayno

and Lieutenant Victor Corpus, a Philippine Military Academy instructor who defected to the NPA, have been arrested a year earlier.

April 7, 1978 Elections for representatives to the Interim *Batasang Pambansa* were held. The Liberal Party boycotts the elections. The *Kilusang Bagong Lipunan* (New Society Movement), an umbrella organization of politicians supporting Marcos' "New Society" ideology, wins 187 seats to the opposition's 13. In Metro Manila, the KBL, headed by Imelda Marcos, wins all 21 seats, trouncing the *Lakas ng Bayan* (LABAN) [People's Power (FIGHT)] headed by Benigno Aquino, who ran from his jail cell. LABAN organizes a march to protest the conduct of the elections. Its leaders—Lorenzo Tañada, Francisco "Soc" Rodrigo, Aquilino Pimentel, and Teofisto Guingona—are detained.

June 12, 1978 The Interim *Batasang Pambansa* (IBP) is convened.
The Ministry of Human Settlements is created with Imelda Marcos as Minister.

January 1980 Elections for governors and mayors are held, the first since martial law was declared. The Liberal Party and LABAN boycott. The KBL wins 69 of 73 gubernatorial positions and 1,450 of 1,560 mayoral positions.

January 1981 Marcos lifts martial law. But he retains extralegal powers, such as the Presidential Commitment Order (PCO) that allows him to order the detention of a person suspected of subversion or rebellion.

June 16, 1981 The first presidential elections since the declaration of martial law are held. The opposition parties call for non-participation. Marcos wins overwhelmingly over Alejo Santos, a former Defense Secretary, and Bartolome Cabangbang, leader of the Statehood USA movement. Marcos wins 88 per cent of the votes and is proclaimed President for a six-year term. Finance Minister Cesar Virata becomes Prime Minister. General Fabian Ver, head of the National Intelligence and Security Agency and the Presidential Security Command, replaces General Romeo Espino as Chief of Staff of the Armed Forces.

August 21, 1983 Benigno Aquino is assassinated at the Manila International Airport. His alleged assassin, Rolando Galman, is killed by Aquino's military escorts. Mass demonstrations follow. Opposition newspapers blossom. For the first time people openly protest.

September 21, 1983 As the government celebrates *Barangay* Day/National Thanksgiving Day to commemorate the declaration of martial law, thousands of Ninoy supporters hold a "National Day of Sorrow" and call for unity in the ranks to topple the Marcos regime.

May 14, 1984 Elections for the *Batasang Pambansa* are held. The United Nationalist Democratic Organization (UNIDO) and the Pilipino Democratic Party-*Lakas ng Bayan* (PDP-LABAN) coalition decide to take part. Cory Aquino, Ninoy's widow, throws her support behind the opposition candidates. They surprise Marcos by winning 56 seats out of the 183 amid familiar allegations of fraud.

October 24, 1984 The Agrava Board, tasked with investigating the Aquino assassination, concludes that there was a military conspiracy behind the killing and implicates AFP Chief of Staff Fabian Ver.

February 22, 1985 General Ver, 24 soldiers, and one civilian stand trial before the *Sandigan-bayan* (court for government employees accused of crimes) for the Aquino murder. Ver takes a leave of absence as Armed Forces Chief of Staff.

August 1985 Opposition MPs file a motion for impeachment against Marcos in the *Batasan,* citing culpable violation of the Constitution and "hidden wealth." The majority party squelches the motion.

November 3, 1985 Marcos suddenly announces the holding of snap presidential elections after alleged prodding from Washington.

December 2, 1985 General Ver and all his co-accused are acquitted by the *Sandigan-bayan*. Marcos reinstates him as Chief of Staff amid widespread protest.

December 3, 1985 Corazon Aquino declares her candidacy for President. Salvador Laurel, who earlier has wanted to run for the same position, agrees to be her running mate.

December 5, 1985 Opposition standard bearers are proclaimed and Cory Aquino and party take to the hustings.

February 7, 1986 A heavy voter turnout and the juggling of the voters' list create confusion during the presidential elections, resulting in the disenfranchisement of three million voters. Incidents of fraud, vote-buying, intimidation, and violence are reported. Election returns are tampered with. The Commission on Elections (COMELEC) tally board shows Marcos leading while the National Citizens' Movement for Free Elections (NAMFREL) consistently shows Cory Aquino ahead by a comfortable margin.

February 9, 1986 Thirty computer workers at the COMELEC tabulation center walk out, protesting the tampering of election results.

February 11, 1986 Oppositionist ex-Governor Evelio Javier of Antique province is murdered in front of the provincial capitol where canvassing is being held. Primary suspects are the bodyguards of the local KBL leader.

February 13, 1986 The Catholic Bishops' Conference issues a statement condemning the elections as fraudulent.

February 15, 1986 The *Batasang Pambansa* proclaims Marcos the winner as opposition assemblymen walk out.

February 16, 1986 Corazon Aquino leads the *Tagumpay ng Bayan* (People's Victory Rally) at the Luneta, where she launches a nationwide campaign for civil disobedience to force Marcos to step down.

February 19, 1986 The U.S. Senate passes a resolution condemning the Philippine election as fraudulent, while a House subcommittee votes to cut military aid to the Philippines as long as Marcos is in power.

February 22, 1986 Defense Minister Juan Ponce Enrile and General Fidel Ramos announce their withdrawal of support for President Marcos and call for his resignation. With about 300 soldiers, they barricade the Ministry of Defense in Camp Aguinaldo and the Philippine Constabulary-Integrated National Police (PC-INP) Headquarters in Camp Crame. Cardinal Sin makes an appeal over Radio Veritas for people to bring food and lend moral support. The overwhelming response results in the four-day people power revolt that topples the Marcos dictatorship.

February 25, 1986 Corazon Aquino takes her oath of office as the seventh President of the Republic. In the evening, Marcos, realizing the futility of his stand, flees Malacañang with his family and supporters.

BENIGNO SERVILLANO AQUINO, JR.
(1932-1983)

A young man in a hurry, he was always a step ahead of his generation, venturing into worlds open only to his elders. But he was always outstanding, despite his youth.

He was being groomed to be the next President of the Republic after the incumbent President Marcos' term expired in 1973. Instead, he became Marcos' number one political prisoner.

Ninoy—as he was fondly called—deserves that phrase: "The good die young." For many who witnessed the brutal manner in which he was killed in 1983, Ninoy's legacy will live on.

November 27, 1932 Born in Concepcion, Tarlac, the second child of Benigno Aquino, Sr., and Aurora Aquino.

1935-41 Begins elementary education at St. Joseph's College and eventually finishes at the Ateneo de Manila in Intramuros.

1945-48 Finishes high school at San Beda College.

1948-49 Enrolls at the Ateneo de Manila for a Liberal Arts course. Works as a copy boy for the *Manila Times* under Joaquin (Chino) Roces. Eventually becomes a regular reporter.

1950 As a 17-year-old, covers the Korean War as foreign correspondent of the *Manila Times*. Becomes the "baby" of the press corps. Awarded the Philippine Legion of Honor, Officer Degree, by President Elpidio Quirino for his meritorious service to the country in covering the Philippine Expeditionary Force to Korea.

1951-53 Becomes foreign correspondent of the *Manila Times* for Southeast Asia; named foreign editor until 1955. Enrolls at the University of the Philippines, College of Law.

May 1954 Negotiates the surrender of Huk leader, Luis Taruc, for which he is awarded the Philippine Legion of Honor, Commander Degree, for exemplary meritorious service to the Filipino people by President Ramon Magsaysay. Serves as special assistant to the President.

October 11, 1954 Marries Corazon Cojuangco, also of Tarlac, at the Our Lady of Sorrows Parish Church, Pasay. President Magsaysay serves as principal sponsor. Does not finish his fourth year of law at U.P. Never took the bar.

1955 At 22, elected the youngest mayor of his hometown, Concepcion, Tarlac. His opponents protest that he has not yet fulfilled the age requirement, which is 23 years old.

1956 Serves as press officer, Philippine-American military bases agreement negotiations.

1957 Becomes special assistant to President Carlos Garcia after Magsaysay's death. The Supreme Court unseats him as mayor of Concepcion, upholding the decision of the Court of First Instance in Tarlac that his election was "unlawful and illegal," as he is still 19 days short of the required age.

1958 Becomes administrator of Hacienda Luisita and Tarlac Development Corporation.

1959 At 26, elected youngest Vice Governor of Tarlac province.

1960 Voted one of the Ten Outstanding Young Men of the Philippines (TOYM) in the field of public service.

1961 At 28, appointed provincial governor of Tarlac.

1963 At 30, elected provincial governor of Tarlac, winning in all 17 towns and posting the highest majority ever garnered by a gubernatorial candidate in the province.

1964 Becomes special counsel to President Diosdado Macapagal, whom he accompanies on state visits to Cambodia and Indonesia.

1966 Becomes project director of the Tarlac Project Spread, a joint undertaking of the National Economic Council and the United States Agency for International Development (AID), designed to increase rural income.

1967 At 34, elected youngest senator, the lone opposition Liberal Party candidate to survive the election sweep by Marcos' Nacionalista Party. Again, his opponents protest that he is underaged, since he is a few days short of 35 upon his election. This time, the protest is not upheld. Elected secretary-general of the Liberal Party.

1968-71 Does unrelenting and incisive fiscalization work in the Philippine Senate.

1971 The Liberal Party wins six of the eight senatorial seats, bolstering Ninoy's hopes of being the Liberal Party presidential contender. Becomes the arch-critic and nemesis of President Marcos, who continually accuses him of Huk-coddling and fraternizing with the Communists.

September 1972 Denounces and exposes President Marcos' "Oplan Sagittarius"—a plan to declare martial law in Metro Manila and surrounding areas.

September 22, 1972 Arrested and detained hours before President Marcos makes the declaration of martial law public. Would become the longest held prisoner among Marcos' political opponents and critics.

April 1975 Trial of Ninoy before a military commission begins. Refuses to take part in what he believes are sham proceedings. Stages a 40-day hunger strike to protest the military order forcing him to attend the military court sessions.

November 1977 Found guilty of subversion, illegal possession of firearms, and murder, and sentenced to die by firing squad—by a decision of the military tribunal.

April 1978 Heads the *Lakas ng Bayan* (LABAN) [People's Power (FIGHT)] ticket which challenges the ruling party for seats in the Interim National Assembly. Campaigns from his prison cell and is allowed a brief television appearance.
The night before Election Day, April 6, citizens of Manila hold a "noise barrage" as a show of support for his candidacy and to make Ninoy "hear" that they are behind him.
Eventually loses to Imelda Marcos, head of the *Kilusang Bagong Lipunan* (KBL) [New Society Movement], which sweeps the 21 seats for Manila.

December 1979 Granted a three-week furlough to be with his family for his 25th wedding anniversary, the first time he is ever released from detention.

May 1980 Allowed by President Marcos to go the United States for heart surgery.

1980-83 Becomes research fellow and lecturer at Harvard University and also a research fellow at the Massachusetts Institute of Technology, 1982-83.

August 21, 1983 Shot at the Manila International Airport upon descending from a China Airlines plane.

August 31, 1983 Buried at the Manila Memorial Park after an 11-hour funeral march from Sto. Domingo Church through 30 kilometers of Manila's streets. Nearly two million people participate in or line the route of the cortege, making it one of the most memorable in Philippine history.

MENDIOLA: CATALOGUE
OF PROTESTS
(1970-1986)

Mendiola Street is one of three approaches to Malacañang Palace, official residence of the Philippine President. The street is about a kilometer long starting from the bridge intersecting Legarda up to J.P. Laurel Sr. (formerly Aviles), which leads to Gate 4 of the Palace.

On both sides of Mendiola are some of the older and more established schools in the Philippines—San Beda College, Centro Escolar University, and the College of the Holy Spirit.

Before the seventies, Mendiola was a special meeting place, a typical promenade where families gathered while old folk went to the San Miguel Pro Cathedral, farther to the right, to pray.

At the turn of the seventies, however, Mendiola became a veritable battleground. As protest marchers and activist groups were frustrated by government troops from ventilating their grievances in public areas like Plaza Miranda, they started going direct to Malacañang through Mendiola. Because President Marcos did not want such mass actions to embarrass his Administration, he ordered all approaches to the Palace closed. Gradually, he isolated the people from Malacañang. Mendiola became a fearsome place.

Chronicled below are six of the more famous encounters over Mendiola Bridge, the mute witness to over a decade of protest.

January 30, 1970 The First-Quarter Storm. After being turned back by Constabulary soldiers and riot policemen in the grounds of Congress four days before, militant students, farmers, and workers picket Malacañang Palace to demand that President Marcos assure the people of a nonpartisan Constitutional Convention and that he should not run for a third term. The President meets with student representatives inside the Palace, but makes no comment. The students linger outside, along Mendiola.
By evening, as the lights outside the Palace are suddenly turned off, the situation goes out of control. Military troopers, in riot gear, attack the students, who in turn respond with stones, molotov bombs, and a commandeered firetruck which they ram into Gate 4 of Malacañang. The law-enforcement agents are able to disperse the crowd, but only after scores of students have been injured and arrested. This encounter is later dubbed "The Battle of Mendiola."

August 31, 1983 Ninoy's Funeral. Thirteen years later, August 31, 1983, Mendiola once again is the scene of protest. It is the funeral of Ninoy Aquino, killed by an assassin's bullet at the airport ten days earlier. Throngs of supporters line the streets. Thousands are in the 11-hour-long funeral march.
By late afternoon, a splinter group of students holds a demonstration at the University Belt area close to Mendiola Bridge. It begins as a peaceful demonstration, but by evening, as students face riot policemen and the latter fire water cannons into the crowd, it turns into a free-for-all. One person is killed.

September 21, 1983 National Day of Sorrow. As the government commemorates the declaration of martial law and *Barangay* Day, opposition leaders and supporters, headed by Ninoy's widow, Cory, stage a rally at Liwasang Bonifacio, mourning the death of Ninoy a month before and the death of democracy in the land. As the rally ends, a breakaway crowd of 15,000 mass in front of Mendiola Bridge and face a solid phalanx of Marines, riot police, and firemen ready to hose the crowd.
There is a standoff as the demonstrators jeer and stone the police, who are standing their ground. Suddenly, explosion rocks the government lines, killing two firemen. The Marines charge and sniper fire is aimed at the students and protesters. A riot ensues as the demonstrators regroup and try to charge the Palace. At the battle's end, 11 people are dead, and hundreds are wounded on both sides.

July 13, 1984 Peaceful Rally on One-Half of the Bridge.
On this day, 20,000 people, students, urban poor, professionals, nuns, and workers march to Mendiola, headed by Butz Aquino, Ex-Senator Ambrosio Padilla, and Ex-Con-Con delegate Teofisto Guingona. They have a permit from Mayor Ramon Bagatsing to hold a rally at the intersection of Legarda and Recto, but are not allowed to cross the bridge.
The rally's leader negotiates with the head of the riot troops to be allowed to occupy at least half of the bridge. Surprisingly, the police accede. The demonstrators occupy half of the bridge, to a point about 25 feet from the foot of the bridge.
Shortly before dark, the ranks march forward, until they are eyeball to eyeball with the first line of riot police, only to turn back peacefully. Having conquered half of the bridge, they make a vow to be back, to conquer the rest of it.

September 21-22, 1984 Anniversary of Martial Law: National Day of Sorrow. Once again, the opposition commemorates the declaration of martial law by declaring a National Day of Sorrow and Protest. After listening to opposition leaders speak at Liwasang Bonifacio, the rallyists make their way to

Mendiola Bridge. The area is now barricaded with barbed-wire fences. They can no longer occupy any part of the bridge. But the demonstrators, numbering more than several thousands, decide to stay put.

Then begins a 15-hour vigil. As the crowd slowly thins to about 3,000, both sides manage to maintain peace. The demonstrators stay overnight and camp at the area around Malacañang. At around 6:30 a.m., while they pray the Rosary, they are ordered to disperse by the authorities. The rallyists refuse and plead for more time.

The police, losing their patience, fire tear-gas cannisters and aim water cannons at the rallyists, among them the priests who said Mass and some nuns. Troopers then attack the remaining protesters with truncheons. The demonstrators are forced to disperse. Six are arrested, 18 are injured, and about a hundred are unaccounted for.

February 25, 1986 The Fall of Malacañang.

Militant citizens gather around Malacañang Palace, which is heavily fortified with armed guards, sandbags, machineguns, and even tanks. Barbed-wire fences have been around the streets to the Palace since before the elections. The crowds slowly snip pieces of barbed wire for souvenirs.

The crowd has been dispersed with water cannons the day before. But now they are back. So are some Marcos loyalists who attended the President's inauguration earlier, and are now staging their own version of people power. At around 9:30 p.m., the news finally breaks out: the First Family has fled the Palace.

The crowd surges. The more violent ones attack the loyalists who have stayed behind. The rest climb over the fence, storm the Palace, and ransack the rooms. In anger and jubilation, they vandalize portraits of the First Family and loot whatever valuables have been left behind.

MALACAÑANG PALACE

Malacañang Palace, on the north bank of the Pasig River, has stood as a symbol of power for three centuries. It was originally a villa in an exclusive part of Manila. Malacañang became the summer residence of the Spanish governor general in the nineteenth century and then the official governor general's residence after the governor's palace in Intramuros was destroyed by an earthquake. When the Americans took over Manila at the turn of the century, Malacañang became the residence of the American civil governors. The Palace was turned over to the Philippine Commonwealth in 1935. It has since been the official residence of Philippine Presidents.

All told, 14 Spanish governor generals, 13 American civil governors and 9 Philippine Presidents have stayed in the Palace. Some of them have made their mark on its architectural structure by adding azoteas (porches), annexes, buildings, and galleries.

Controversy surrounds the origin of the name Malacañang. Some say the name comes from may lakan diyan, meaning "there are nobles there," or from ma-lakan-iyan, meaning "place of the chief." Others say the name derives from mala cana, or "bad cane," since bamboo groves that used to abound in the district were believed to have been inhabited by evil spirits.

Between 1972 and February 1986, Malacañang stood for the autocracy of Ferdinand E. Marcos, who occupied the Palace for 20 years, from his first term in 1965.

1802 Colonel Jose Miguel Formento of the Spanish Army buys the original villa from the Spaniard Don Luis Rocha, for 1,000 Mexican pesos.

1825 The government buys the estate from Colonel Formento, using funds raised from the Chinese head tax.

1847 A royal decree designates the estate as the summer residence of the Spanish Governor General.

1863 After an earthquake destroys the Intramuros Palace, Governor General Rafael de Zulueta takes up permanent residence in the summer house.

1869-1898 More than P300,000 is spent on numerous repairs and extensions. The summer residence of the Governor General becomes a sprawling government complex.

1902 William Howard Taft becomes the first American civil governor to occupy Malacañang. The Palace undergoes radical changes.

1921 General Leonard Wood becomes Civil Governor. The Executive Building is built on the left side of the Palace. This building, which in the Marcos regime housed the Presidential Library and the Office of Media Affairs, is ransacked and looted during the 1986 revolution.

1935 Manuel Luis Quezon becomes the first President of the Philippine Commonwealth and the first Filipino occupant of Malacañang. During his term, the property across the Pasig is developed and becomes part of the Palace complex.

1953 Ramon Magsaysay, the third President of the Philippine Republic, opens the Palace to the people for the first time.

1965 Ferdinand E. Marcos becomes President. His wife, Imelda, begins the first of several renovations.

1970 Militant students ram a commandeered firetruck through a Palace gate. Molotov cocktails and pillboxes are lobbed into the grounds. The Palace grounds are closed to the people.

1977 A full structural renovation of the Palace is ordered by Imelda Marcos. The changes are so thorough that former occupants do not recognise it.

1983-85 Malacañang is completely isolated from the people. The barbed wire across Mendiola Bridge becomes a symbol of oppression and the isolation of the Marcoses from reality. The bridge is a kilometer away from the Palace gates. Crossing it becomes a symbolic victory for the people.

1986 At 9:05 in the evening of February 25, Ferdinand Marcos and party leave besieged Malacañang aboard four helicopters. Minutes later, the people, massed at the gates, clamber up and storm the Palace, which for almost a decade was off limits to them.

THE PHILIPPINE PRESIDENCY

The 1935 Constitution of the Republic of the Philippines provided for the election of a President as Chief Executive and a Vice President for a term of four years and, at most, one re-election.

Traditionally, elections were held toward the end of a year (usually, November). The newly elected President assumes office in the first month of the first year of his four-year term.

This setup prevailed from 1946 to 1972, when the constitutional process was disrupted by the declaration of martial law. In 1973, a new Constitution came into effect which significantly altered the powers and conditions for election of the President.

April 1946 First postwar presidential elections are held. The once-dominant Nacionalista Party of the prewar period is split into factions. Manuel Roxas, who formed the Liberal Party, and challenged the incumbent President, Sergio Osmeña, Sr. (who took over the office when Commonwealth President Manuel Quezon died in exile in August, 1944), emerges the victor.

July 1946 The Philippine Republic is inaugurated after nearly 48 years of American colonial rule. Manuel Roxas, first President of the postwar Republic, and Vice President Elpidio Quirino face the task of rebuilding a nation ravaged by war.

April 1948 President Manuel Roxas dies of a heart attack after delivering a speech at Clark Air Base. Vice President Quirino assumes the Presidency and serves the unexpired portion of Roxas' term.

1949 Incumbent President Elpidio Quirino defeats Jose P. Laurel, Sr., the wartime President of the Japanese-sponsored Republic. Quirino is faced with the specter of rebellion as the communist-led *Hukbong Mapagpalaya ng Bayan* (HMB) [National Liberation Army] launches an uprising.

1953 Quirino's Secretary of National Defense, Ramon Magsaysay, defeats his former boss, by running under the *Nacionalista* banner and bringing the party back to power. Relying on the strength of his success in quelling the Huk insurgency, the charismatic appeal of his barrio-to-barrio campaigns, and the alleged support of the Central Intelligence Agency (CIA), Magsaysay wins the election handily and opens the gates of Malacañang to the ordinary Filipino.

March 1957 Magsaysay dies in a plane crash. Vice President Carlos Garcia completes the remaining eight months of Magsaysay's term.

1957 Garcia wins the Presidency under the banner of the *Nacionalista* Party. For the first time in Philippine electoral history, the Vice President, Diosdado Macapagal, comes from the opposition party, the Liberals; thus, the two highest offices in the land shared by candidates of opposing parties.

1961 Macapagal puts the Liberal Party back in power by defeating the incumbent Garcia. Emmanuel Pelaez becomes the new Vice President. It is during Macapagal's term that Independence Day, which has been traditionally observed on July 4 every year, is changed to June 12, in recognition of the declaration of Philippine independence by General Emilio Aguinaldo in Kawit, Cavite, 1898.

1965 Senate President Ferdinand E. Marcos challenges his former partymate, Diosdado Macapagal, and wins the Presidency as a *Nacionalista*. In an agreement made in 1961, Macapagal is said to have promised Marcos that he will not run for re-election but will support the latter's candidacy as the Liberal Party's presidential candidate in 1965. But in that year, Macapagal decides to run for re-election, thus forcing Marcos to seek election by switching parties and running as a *Nacionalista*. He bests other *Nacionalista* stalwarts like Senators Arturo Tolentino, Gil Puyat, Fernando Lopez, and Emmanuel Pelaez, to win the nomination as the *Nacionalista's* presidential standard bearer.

1969 For the first time in Philippine electoral history, a President is re-elected for another four-year term. Ferdinand Marcos defeats the Liberal Party's candidate, Sergio Osmeña, Jr., son of the former President. Marcos defies tradition and becomes the first postwar President to serve two successive terms.

September 1972 President Marcos declares martial law. The 1935 Constitution is shelved and in its place, the 1973 Constitution, after having been allegedly ratified by citizen's assemblies, comes into effect. The 1935 Constitution would have barred the incumbent President from seeking a third term. But with constitutional guarantees temporarily suspended, Marcos is able to remain in office for 14 more years.

CORAZON COJUANGCO AQUINO
(1933-   )

Cory, as she is known, by Filipinos, is the seventh President of the Republic. In a country sharply divided between rich and poor, she was born into a landed family. She married a politician whose controversial career blurred her into the background, and whose long detention left her to raise the family. Her husband's assassination thrust Cory into the limelight, where her calm demeanor under pressure was appreciated by all. In the void for leadership of the opposition to a dictatorial regime, she began as a credible influence in choosing the opposition presidential candidate. In time, it became obvious that she herself was the best person to lead the people. It took a great deal of courage to run for President. Yet she saw it as a duty as well as a challenge, and took the mantle onto her shoulders.

January 25, 1933 Born to Jose Cojuangco, Sr., and Demetria Sumulong, an affluent couple from Tarlac.

1938-45 Goes to elementary school at Saint Scholastica's College.

1945 Spends a year at Assumption Convent as a high-school freshman.

1946-47 Leaves with her family for the United States and pursues her studies at Ravenhill Academy in Philadelphia.

1947-49 Finishes her junior and senior years at the Notre Dame Convent School in New York.

1949-53 Enters Mount Saint Vincent College in New York, where she graduates with a Bachelor of Arts, major in French and Mathematics.

1953-54 Returns to the Philippines to pursue Law at the Far Eastern University, but stays in school for only a semester.

October 11, 1954 Marries Benigno S. Aquino, Jr., a young colorful, and multi-awarded journalist and law student, at Our Lady of Sorrows Parish Church in Pasay.

1954-72 Becomes supportive but shy housewife, caring for their five children: Maria Elena (Ballsy), Aurora Corazon (Pinky), Benigno III (Noynoy), Victoria Elisa (Viel), and Kristina Bernadette (Kris).

September 1972 Becomes both father and mother to their children with Ninoy's incarceration. Constantly visits him during his confinement. Gives him moral support when he is forced to face a military court which later sentences him to death. First appears in public during the 1978 Interim *Batasang Pambansa* elections, when Ninoy runs for assemblyman while in his prison cell.

May 1980 - August 1983 Spends three years in Newton, Massachusetts, with her reunited family as Ninoy is allowed to leave for the United States for a heart bypass operation.

August 21, 1983 Loses Ninoy to an assassin. Returns to the Philippines for her husband's wake and funeral. Leads opposition supporters and sympathizers in the procession transferring Ninoy's body from their Times Street home to the Santo Domingo Church, where he lies in state until his funeral.

August 31, 1983 Leads the nation in the eleven-hour march to Ninoy's grave in Parañaque. Becomes the symbol and unifying force of the opposition to Marcos' regime. Joins the struggle for the restoration of liberty in the Philippines.

1983-85 Leads rallies in Liwasang Bonifacio, Santo Domingo Church, and Luneta Grandstand on the days commemorating important events: August 21 (Ninoy's death anniversary), September 21 (anniversary of the declaration of martial law, considered a "National Day of Sorrow" by the opposition), and November 27 (Ninoy's birthday). Becomes widely admired for grace under pressure.

In 1984, awarded an honorary doctorate by her alma mater, Mount Saint Vincent College, in New York. Given honorary distinctions by other schools as well as civic, religious, and professional associations.

May 1984 Urges the citizenry to take part in the parliamentary elections and supports the opposition candidates, signalling her first direct political involvement. Refuses to take part in the government investigation of her husband's assassination.

December 1984 Forms the Convenor Group with former Senator Lorenzo Tañada and businessman Jaime Ongpin. The

Group devises a system to select the opposition candidate in case of snap presidential elections. Urged by friends to be a nominee, she replies: "I have no political ambitions."

October 1985 Former publisher Joaquin (Chino) Roces leads the Cory Aquino for President Movement (CAPM), which begins a nationwide campaign for signatures to ask her to run. Agrees to consider running on two conditions: that Marcos call for snap presidential elections, and that she be presented with one million signatures endorsing her candidacy.

November 1985 Presented with more than one million signatures after Marcos announces the holding of snap presidential elections set for early 1986.

December 3, 1985 Files her candidacy for the Presidency. Several days later, announces Salvador Laurel as her running mate.

December 15, 1985 Proclaimed the presidential candidate of the UNIDO, the dominant opposition party, in a big rally at Liwasang Bonifacio.

December 16, 1985 Begins the nationwide campaign that will take her all over the country, working 16 hours a day, giving several speeches in a single day, promising hope to millions of well-wishers and supporters who patiently wait along highways and in plazas just to see or hear her. Covers much more territory than her opponent can manage. Her promise: "If elected I will not live in Malacañang. I will open it up to the people." Her rebuttal to the argument that she lacks experience: "They say I have no experience. It is true: I have no experience in lying, cheating, stealing, and killing. I offer you honesty and sincerity in leadership." Presents her major programs before business and civic organizations. Feels the pulse of the people through marathon dialogues over nationwide radio broadcasts.

February 4, 1986 Holds the UNIDO election eve rally at Luneta Park and speaks to a crowd of more than one million from a makeshift stage.

February 9, 1986 With the initial poll tallies showing her in the lead, joins the people in Thanksgiving Masses at the Santo Domingo and Baclaran churches.

February 16, 1986 Leads a rally of over two million people at the Luneta, proclaiming the victory of the people despite the *Batasang Pambansa* declaration of Marcos as winner of the fraudulent polls. Launches a seven-point civil disobedience program aimed at boycotting establishments owned by Marcos and his associates to force him to concede defeat. Vows to lead nonviolent protests throughout the country.

February 22, 1986 Continues the nationwide protest in Cebu City as a military rebellion breaks out in Quezon City.

February 25, 1986 Proclaimed the seventh President of the Republic in simple ceremonies at Club Filipino in Metro Manila. Takes the oath of office, invoking a people's resolution to justify her taking over the reins of government.

INTERVIEWS

By Monina A. Mercado:
- PRESIDENT CORAZON C. AQUINO
- JAIME CARDINAL SIN • RICARDO CARDINAL VIDAL • AURORA A. AQUINO • CECILIA MUÑOZ PALMA • JUNE KEITHLEY • EUGENIA D. APOSTOL • TEODORO BENIGNO • GEMINO ABAD • LOURDES T. CASTAÑEDA • VICTOR SISON • JOHN CHUA • MANUEL ESCASA • VIC OLAGUERA • VICTOR AND NANNETTE PUYAT • POY PANTALEON • SR. SARAH MANAPOL • PATRICIA TRINIDAD • MICHAEL TRINIDAD • LT. GRACIANO VICTOR

By Monina A. Mercado and Rofel G. Brion: PRECIOSA LOTILLA JAVIER

By Rofel G. Brion, Ancilla Maria A. Mercado and Mario S. Nery: FREDDIE AGUILAR

By Rofel G. Brion and Raul Rodrigo: FRANCISCO RODRIGO (SOC)

By Rofel G. Brion and Mario S. Nery: VICENTE T. PATERNO

By Ancilla Maria A. Mercado and Mario S. Nery: RENE OCAMPO, S.J.

By Mario S. Nery and John Cabato: LT. COL. GREGORIO CAGURANGAN LT. COL. ED PURIFICACION

SOURCES

CHAPTER I:

For the quotation from:
Luis Beltran: *Veritas*, 3 December 1983

CHAPTER II:

For the quotations from:
Agapito Aquino: *Mr. & Ms. Special Edition*, 3 February 1984

Margarita Cojuangco: *Mr. & Ms. Special Edition*, 12-18 October 1984

CHAPTER III:

For the quotations from:
Margarita Cojuangco: *Woman Today*, 13 March 1986

Neni Sta. Romana Cruz: *Mr. & Ms. Special Edition*, 13-19 December 1985

CHAPTER IV:

For the quotations from:
Corazon C. Aquino: *Asiaweek*, 23 February 1986

Carolyn O. Arguillas: *Veritas Extra*, 10 February 1986

Fr. Francisco Araneta: *Mr. & Ms. Special Edition*

James Donelan, S.J.: *Veritas Special*, 12 March 1986

Linda Kapunan: *Philippine Daily Inquirer*, 15-17 February 1986

Jaime V. Ongpin: *Veritas*, 23 February 1986

Neni Sta. Romana Cruz: *Philippine Daily Inquirer*

CHAPTER V:

For the quotations from:
Fr. Francisco Araneta: *Mr. & Ms. Special Edition*, 13 March 1986

Gus Miclat: *Sunday Magazine of Pahayagang Malaya*, 23 March 1986

Nino Nuñez: *Philippine Daily Inquirer*, 28 February 1986

Cristina Ponce-Enrile: *Mr. & Ms. Special Edition*

Armida Siguion-Reyna: *Veritas*, 9 March 1986

Maximo Soliven: *Philippine Daily Inquirer*

Col. Antonio Sotelo: *Philippine Daily Inquirer*, 13 March 1986

Jimmy Vicente: *Veritas*, 2 March 1986

Fe Zamora: *Mr. & Ms. Special Edition*

PHOTO CREDITS

Jacket cover (Stopping a tank in a Quezon City residential area, 25 February 1986) LINGLONG ORTIZ

Endpaper (Presidential candidate Corazon C. Aquino campaigns in Cebu City, January 1986) JOEY DE VERA

Chapter I The Assassination of Benigno Aquino, Jr., 1983
MANUEL FERRER — p. 19
JOHN CHUA — pp. 20, 21, 22, 23, 24, 25, 26 (upper), 26 (lower), 27, 30
RAFAEL GOZUM, JR. — pp. 28-29

Chapter II Rallies, marches and demonstrations, 1983 to 1985
ERWIN ELLOSO — pp. 37, 40
ROBERTO IGNACIO — p. 38
RAMSEY HORMILLO — p. 39
VICTORIA PANGILINAN — p. 41
JOHN CHUA — p. 42

Chapter III The Election Campaign, 1986
JOE GALVEZ, Jr. — pp. 57, 58
ALAN FAJARDO — pp. 59, 63
ROBERTO IGNACIO — pp. 60-61, 64
JOEY DE VERA — p. 62
WILLIE VICOY — p. 65
ALAIN COUDERT — p. 66

Chapter IV The Election and Ballot Watch, 1986
NOLI YAMSUAN — pp. 83, 87 (lower)
CAROL ARGUILLAS — p. 84 (upper)
LINGLONG ORTIZ — pp. 84 (lower), 96, 97
VERO PALOMA — p. 85
BEN AVESTRUZ — pp. 86 (upper), 86 (lower)
JOE GALVEZ, Jr. — pp. 87 (upper), 88 (upper), 90 (upper), 95 (lower)
ERWIN ELLOSO — p. 88 (lower)
BONG TIRADOR — p. 89
LUIS LIWANAG — p. 90 (lower)
CHRIS BAYANI — p. 91
ALAIN COUDERT — p. 92
ALY REYES — p. 93
PETE REYES — p. 94
JOEY MANALANG — p. 95 (upper)
SONNY CAMARILLO — p. 98
EMMANUEL MERCADO — p. 99 (upper)
ROBERTO IGNACIO — p. 99 (lower)
ROGER DE LARA — p. 100

Chapter V The People's Uprising, February 22 to 25, 1986
PETE REYES — pp. 111, 115, 117, 153 (lower), 160-161, 176 (lower), 178, 179 (upper right), 185 (lower), 222, 259, 272, 273, 299
LINGLONG ORTIZ — pp. 112-113, 130, 145 (upper), 220, 266, 267, 268-269
FRANZ LOPEZ — pp. 114, 177, 214 (lower), 223
EDGARDO CLEMENTE — pp. 116 (upper), 193, 260 (upper)
ISMAIL CAJOLO — p. 116 (lower)
BOBBY SACRO — p. 120
JOE GALVEZ, Jr. — pp. 129, 137 145 (lower), 147 (upper), 149, 159 (upper), 159 (lower right), 164, (upper), 167, 176 (upper), 184 (lower), 185 (lower), 235
ROMEO VITUG — pp. 140 (upper), 140 (lower), 141, 162 (lower), 163 (upper), 170 (upper), 170 (middle), 170 (lower), 171, 274 (upper), 275, 276, 277, 278, 279
ADOR BONQUIN — pp. 142 (upper left), 142 (upper right), 142-143, 143
MANUEL FERRER — pp. 144, 210 (lower), 215, 221 (lower), 224, 225 (upper), 225 (lower)
JOEY CAMARA — pp. 135, 155 (lower)
ROBERTO IGNACIO — pp. 146 (upper), 298
HERNANDO DE LEON — pp. 146 (lower), 181 (upper)
SONNY CAMARILLO — pp. 147 (lower), 150 (lower), 151, 154 (upper), 154 (lower), 158, 159 (lower left), 168, 187 (upper), 187 (lower), 214 (upper), 221 (upper), 260 (lower), 282, 283, 285, 294, 296
NESTOR BARNIDO — p. 148 (upper)
TERRY DUCKHAM — pp. 148 (lower left), 250, 274 (lower), 286-287, 288, 289 (lower right)
PETE CRUZ — pp. 148 (lower right), 217, 219 (lower)
JOHN CHUA — pp. 150 (upper left), 164 (lower left), 164 (lower right), 166 (upper left), 169 (lower), 172, 174 (lower), 182, 247
JOEY MANALANG — pp. 126, 132, 150 (upper right), 232, 280
MANNY FERNANDEZ — pp. 152, 258 (upper), 262 (lower right), 281 (upper left)

BIEN BAUTISTA — pp. 153 (upper), 199, 244, 295, 297, 301, 302-303, 253
JOEY DE VERA — pp. 155 (upper), 262 (left), 263
ROD TANCHANCO — p. 156 (upper)
WILLIAM LIM — p. 156 (lower)
BJORN ERLANDSON — pp. 157, 289 (upper right), 289 (middle right)
ROGER DE LARA — p. 162 (upper)
PATRICK FONG — p. 163 (lower)
PATRICK UY — pp. 165, 190, 300 (upper left)
PAUL MAGALONA — pp. 166 (middle left), 166 (lower left), 175
RUDY SAKDALAN — p. 169 (upper)
ROGER BUENDIA — pp. 173 (upper), 184 (upper)
AURORA CAPARAS — pp. 173 (lower), 238
DELSA MORTOLA — p. 174 (upper)
DENNIS MAGDAMO — p. 179 (upper left)
JOE BAUTISTA — p. 179 (lower)
RAMSEY HORMILLO — pp. 180, 181 (lower), 183, 281 (lower)
BONG TIRADOR — p. 186
DANTE PERALTA — p. 196
CHRIS BAYANI — pp. 202, 300 (upper right)
BENNY DE LA VEGA — p. 205
NOLI YAMSUAN — pp. 210 (upper), 211, 212, 213 (upper), 213 (lower)
VICTOR PANLAQUI — p. 216
JAIME UNSON — p. 218
ERNIE ENRIQUE — pp. 219 (upper), 258 (lower), 261
ALEC CRUZ — p. 219 (middle)
MON SANTOS — p. 226 (upper)
ERWIN ELLOSO — p. 226 (lower)
ROBERTO YÑIGUEZ — pp. 228 (lower left), 229 (upper), 290-291
BANNY HERMANOS — p. 229 (upper right)
ALAIN COUDERT — pp. 228 (lower), 229 (lower right)
ELBERT ZOSA — pp. 241
CORAZON PASIONA — pp. 264, 265
VIVENCIO SANTOS — pp. 270 (upper), 270 (lower), 271
DIDITS GONZALEZ — p. 284
RUDOLFO TAN — p. 293 (left)
RENE LUMAWAG — pp. 292 (upper), 293 (upper right)
LOY JURADO — p. 292 (lower)
BILL LUZ — p. 300 (lower left)

ACKNOWLEDGEMENTS

The editor and the staff are deeply grateful to:

- Her Excellency President Corazon C. Aquino, for her time and insights and for the privilege of being entrusted with her memories, even those memories steeped in her personal pain as the widow of Benigno S. Aquino, Jr.

- Antonio H. Ozaeta, president of PCIBank, for his faith in this book, to which he committed full support, sight unseen, within the week that it was first conceptualized

- James B. Reuter, S.J., for speaking well of us and for agreeing to be one of the conduits for photographs and anecdotes, the best of which were stories personally addressed to him

- Kaa Byington, for believing that it can be done

- Raul J. Bonoan, S.J., and Arnie del Rosario, for the use of computers and office space

- the Ateneo Alumni Affairs office for the use of the Blue Room

- Jose V. Burgos, publisher, for being the first to support our effort to gather photographs and for throwing open to us the photo library of *Malaya* newspaper, from which we got some of our best photographs, including the photograph on the book jacket

- *Veritas* newspaper, for opening to us the photo library and editorial files

- Sister Sarah Manapol, SPC, for welcoming with care and concern the many letters and photographs which came to her office

- Celso Pagaspas and Lilia Panaguiton for constant and cheerful service